BRITISH AND AMERICAN PLAYWRIGHTS
1750-1920
General editors: Martin Banham and Peter Thomson

Augustin Daly

OTHER VOLUMES IN THIS SERIES

Already published:

TOM ROBERTSON edited by William Tydeman
W. S. GILBERT edited by George Rowell
HENRY ARTHUR JONES edited by Russell Jackson
DAVID GARRICK AND GEORGE COLMAN THE ELDER
    edited by E. R. Wood
WILLIAM HOOKER GILLETTE edited by Rosemary Cullen and Don
    Wilmeth
GEORGE COLMAN THE YOUNGER AND THOMAS MORTON
    edited by Barry Sutcliffe
DION BOUCICAULT edited by Peter Thomson
ARTHUR MURPHY AND SAMUEL FOOTE edited by George
    Taylor
H. J. BYRON edited by J. T. L. Davis

Further volumes will include:

J. R. PLANCHÉ edited by Don Roy
A. W. PINERO edited by Martin Banham
CHARLES READE edited by M. Hammet
TOM TAYLOR edited by Martin Banham

Plays by

Augustin Daly

A FLASH OF LIGHTNING
HORIZON
LOVE ON CRUTCHES

Edited with an Introduction and Notes by
Don B. Wilmeth and Rosemary Cullen

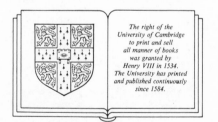

The right of the
University of Cambridge
to print and sell
all manner of books
was granted by
Henry VIII in 1534.
The University has printed
and published continuously
since 1584.

CAMBRIDGE UNIVERSITY PRESS

Cambridge

London   New York   New Rochelle

Melbourne   Sydney

Published by the Press Syndicate of the University of Cambridge
The Pitt Building, Trumpington Street, Cambridge CB2 1RP
32 East 57th Street, New York, NY 10022, USA
296 Beaconsfield Parade, Middle Park, Melbourne 3206, Australia

First published 1984

Printed in Great Britain
at the University Press, Cambridge

Library of Congress catalogue card number: 83-18929

British Library Cataloguing in Publication Data
Daly, Augustin
Plays. – (British and American playwrights. 1750–1920)
I. Title   II. Wilmeth, D. M. B.
III. Cullen, Rosemary   IV. Series
812′.4   PS1499.D85
ISBN 0 521 24090 5 hard covers
ISBN 0 521 28432 5 paperback

BB

GENERAL EDITORS' PREFACE

It is the primary aim of this series to make available to the British and American theatre plays which were effective in their own time, and which are good enough to be effective still.

Each volume assembles a number of plays, normally by a single author, scrupulously edited but sparingly annotated. Textual variations are recorded where individual editors have found them either essential or interesting. Introductions give an account of the theatrical context, and locate playwrights and plays within it. Biographical and chronological tables, brief bibliographies, and the complete listing of known plays provide information useful in itself, and which also offers guidance and incentive to further exploration.

Many of the plays published in this series have appeared in modern anthologies. Such representation is scarcely distinguishable from anonymity. We have relished the tendency of individual editors to make claims for the dramatists of whom they write. These are not plays best forgotten. They are plays best remembered. If the series is a contribution to theatre history, that is well and good. If it is a contribution to the continuing life of the theatre, that is well and better.

We have been lucky. The Cambridge University Press has supported the venture beyond our legitimate expectations. Acknowledgement is not, in this case, perfunctory. Sarah Stanton's contribution to the series has been substantial, and it has enhanced our work.

Martin Banham
Peter Thomson

CONTENTS

ILLUSTRATIONS

ACKNOWLEDGEMENTS

We would like to thank the following for assistance in our research: Dorothy L. Swerdlove, Richard M. Buck, and other staff members of the Billy Rose Theatre Collection of the New York Public Library at Lincoln Center; the staff of the Hoblitzelle Theatre Arts Library at the University of Texas at Austin; Martha Mahard, assistant curator, The Harvard Theatre Collection; and the staff of the Folger Shakespeare Library. We are also grateful for the assistance of Elizabeth Coogan of Brown University's interlibrary loan department.

We are especially appreciative of the support and encouragement given us by the general editors of the British and American Playwright series, in particular Peter Thomson, and for the advice and suggestions of Sarah Stanton and other members of the Cambridge University Press staff. Pamela Enos and Judy Wilmeth deserve recognition for their assistance in the typing of portions of the manuscript.

We would be remiss if we did not acknowledge the tremendous help that we received from the efforts of major Daly scholars, in particular Albert A. Asermely, Richard Harlan Andrew, Jean Cutler, Marvin Felheim, Marion Michalak, Ronald Reed, and David Schaal. We have attempted to give these experts specific credit in the notes to the introduction and the bibliography of sources.

Finally, Professor Wilmeth wishes to express a special word of thanks to the trustees of the John Simon Guggenheim Memorial Foundation for his appointment as a Fellow during the period of the preparation of this volume, thus providing the release time necessary for its completion.

Don B. Wilmeth
Rosemary Cullen

I Augustin Daly. Cabinet photo by Bassano

INTRODUCTION

The theatrical career of John Augustin Daly spanned almost forty years, from his beginnings as a journalist/critic in 1859 to his sudden and unexpected death in Paris in 1899. By the abrupt end of his career his contemporaries agreed that his was the outstanding management in America, compared favorably with the Lyceum Theatre operation of Henry Irving in London. Although by 1899 his work had begun to exert less influence, in large measure because of the imitation of his methods by competing managements, and because his taste had turned rather conservative, Daly's lengthy presence in the theatre – in New York, in London, and on his numerous tours – had made a lasting impact.

In retrospect, Daly's methods undeniably credit him as the first American régisseur, a director in the modern sense and a producer concerned with all aspects of the staging of a play, from the selection of the script to the final product. His insatiable capacity for work, his energy and vitality, his unswerving brand of idealism and desire for excellence led to an immersion in his craft unknown before in the American Theatre and justifiably earned him the title of 'Autocrat of the Stage'. Shortly after his death, the New York *Clipper* (June 1899) noted that Daly 'stood a unique figure in the tumult of management in which cupidity would replace artistic impulse and notoriety is thought to be more important than all else. He was, in short, a living protest against commercialism and an encouragement to all that commercialism instinctively opposes.' Even Bernard Shaw, a severe critic of Daly's taste in drama during the 1890s and one of those most distressed at his avoidance of European moderns such as Ibsen, Hauptmann or Maeterlinck, recognized that Daly was 'in his prime an advanced man relatively to his own time and place, and was a real manager, with definite artistic aims which he trained his company to accomplish'.[1]

Even if today Augustin Daly is remembered primarily by historians as the first modern American director and, to some degree, as a great teacher of actors, Daly's contributions cover the entire range of the theatre arts, and despite justifiable criticism of much of his work as a playwright and manager, most notably that he was too concerned with pleasing the public and making money (the latter a somewhat bogus attack), he deserves a prominent place in the history of the nineteenth-century theatre as a theatre manager, director, original playwright, adapter of foreign plays, producer and adapter of Shakespeare (and other writers of established fare), and a manager of an ensemble of actors that successfully carried Shakespeare and other drama to Europe and all parts of the United States.

From the outset it should be understood that in the area of playwriting and play production Daly was not a major innovator. He did encourage native American dramatists, although ultimately only if they filled his mold and serviced his company of actors. Many of his contemporaries thought of him as a scholar, an intellectual, and a man of high principles. But Daly did little to promote true realism, to

1

foster the literary taste of his audience, or to stimulate his patrons with drama of ideas. In 1899 one writer, cognizant of this shortcoming, rationalized, 'it was natural that after a lifetime spent in expounding and illustrating the best of the traditional arts of the theatre he should adhere to those arts, as he adhered to all his principles, rather than adopt the realisms of the new school'. In truth, as this writer recognized, Daly's productions were done so admirably, with such definite purpose, that his public applauded it, and, indeed, 'he had a public whose loyalty perhaps was the greatest of tributes to his artistic integrity'.[2] The illusion created on his stage was adequately summarized by Hillary Bell, an old friend and professional critic, who wrote that as a stage manager 'he painted pictures whose mimic splendour seemed real'. Ultimately, although he made major contributions to two of the most important trends in late nineteenth-century American drama, the Rise of Realism and the development of social comedy, as Walter Meserve points out, 'he did not continue in the development of American drama, and both in theory and practice became a negative influence'.[3]

I

An understanding and appreciation of Daly's accomplishments is impossible without a sense of the American theatre as it was prior to his involvement in full-time management beginning in 1869. His career spanned the most important transitional period in the history of the American theatre, from the dominance of the romantic style in acting, writing, and production techniques at the beginning of his managerial career to the emergence of realism by the end of the century, from the dominant structure of the stock company established well before the American Civil War to the breakdown of the permanent company by the end of the century and the emergence of the so-called combination system (the formation of a temporary company to tour a successful production), from frequent changes of bills to the long run, and, finally, from the power of independent managements to the rise of power in the late 1890s of the 'Syndicate' or theatrical trust.

Augustin Daly was born on 20 July 1838, at Plymouth, North Carolina. His father, Captain Denis Daly, an Irish-born retired officer of the British navy, had settled in the Carolinas and was engaged in the business of exporting lumber. His mother, Elizabeth Therese Duffey, a native of Montego Bay, Jamaica, was a daughter of an English army officer.[4] In 1841 Captain Daly died and the family moved to Norfolk, Virginia, where Augustin witnessed his first theatre at the local Avon Theatre. In 1849 the Dalys moved to New York City, at the insistence of Elizabeth's sister. Daly attended public school for a short time but soon entered a firm of house furnishers in Maiden Lane; his mother's sights were set on his becoming a merchant.

During this period Daly attended the theatre frequently and, between clerking for various concerns and studying in night school, joined several amateur dramatic societies. In 1856 he undertook his first managerial challenge by renting a theatre in Brooklyn and presenting, for one night, 'The Melville Troupe of Juvenile Comedians' in the farce *Poor Pillicody*, the second act of *Macbeth*, a comic song, and a two-act drama entitled *Toodles*. Daly played the porter in *Macbeth*, and this was virtually the end of his acting career.[5]

The New York theatre of the 1850s, Daly's initial period of exposure to established managements, was dominated by a small handful of theatres: the first Wallack's Theatre at Broadway and Broome Street; the Broadway Theatre, near Anthony Street; Burton's, first in Chambers Street and later in Broadway, near Bleecker; Laura Keene's and Niblo's, then at their height; the National in Chatham Street; the Bowery; and the 'lecture room' of Barnum's American Museum at Ann Street. The theatres of William E. Burton and James W. Wallack, both English-born actor-managers, were the major forces in Daly's theatrical training, according to his brother. E. A. Dithmar wrote in the *New York Times* (18 June 1899) that Daly told him that 'he felt more strongly the influence of Burton than that of any predecessor' and considered Burton's productions 'less formal and more life-like than those at Wallack's'.

W. E. Burton (1804–1860) opened the Chambers Street Theatre in 1848, where, for eight years, he attempted to resist the prevailing star system. While he remained in this small playhouse, with a capacity of only 800, he was successful. In 1856, when his operation was transferred to the Metropolitan Theatre, Burton was unable to fill this 5,000-seat theatre without stars and, failing to make this transition successfully, he retired in 1858. At Burton's Chambers Street Theatre Daly witnessed a fare peculiar to Burton's theatre. Burton's plays, classic or contemporary, were noted for their satirical or extravagant qualities, frequently topical and sprinkled with native humor. Burton, like most managers of the time, was actually his own star, and his performances were marked by strong elements of realism in his burlesque characters.

Burton's major competitor, beginning in 1852 at the Lyceum Theatre, was James W. Wallack (1795–1864), who also attempted to circumvent the star system. As Daly would be in only a few years, Wallack was more concerned with details both in front of and behind the curtain than were his competitors. After Wallack's son, Lester, assumed the reins of the theatre in 1863 and continued with his father's policies, Daly continued to be influenced by the Wallack touch. Of the remaining stock companies during Daly's formative period, he was most affected by that of Laura Keene (1820–1873), who was brought to New York from England by Wallack and was the manager of her own theatre from 1855 to 1863. Keene, known as the 'Duchess', was noted for the strict discipline of her rehearsals and the avoidance of 'lines of business' in an attempt to cast actors in a variety of parts.

It is significant that two of Daly's non-extant earliest plays, though rejected, were written for two of these actor–managers; a third was written for Mrs. John Wood, seen by Daly during the elder Wallack's management. Daly's first youthful effort, a one-act farce called *A Bachelor's Wardrobe*, was written in 1856 for Burton; his next play, a farce titled *Master and Man*, was sent to Mrs. Wood; his fourth play, *Napoleon III*, included the role of Empress Eugénie written especially for Keene. Daly's third play, *Joe's Wife*, was written for Joseph Jefferson III, the actor whose fame would rest almost entirely on the role of Rip Van Winkle. Daly was clearly attracted at this early date by Jefferson's tendency toward a kind of romantic realism. Each of these early Daly plays was rejected.

Up to 1859 Daly was simply flirting with the theatre; but, most important, he and his brother Joseph were witnessing a vigorous period in American theatre. Daly observed a long line of star performers: Burton, John Brougham, the Wallacks, Charles Mathews, E. L. Davenport, John Sleeper Clarke, E. A. Sothern, Laura Keene, Matilda Heron, Lucille Western, Kate Bateman, Maggie Mitchell, Dion Boucicault, Agnes Robertson, and many others. He saw the standard plays of the English repertory; probably he saw Rachel in French tragedy and heard Brignoli, Piccolomini, La Grange, Gazzaniga, and Carl Formes in Italian and German opera. He witnessed the advent of the young Edwin Booth when Edwin Forrest was still in his prime (indeed, one of his first critical pieces as a journalist was a comparison of the two). Comedies of the day included Tom Taylor's *Still Waters Run Deep* and *The Serious Family*; melodrama was represented by Boucicault's *The Poor of New York, Janet Pride,* and *Jessie Brown; or, the Relief of Lucknow.* At Wallack's Daly most likely saw Lester Wallack's *The Veteran, Central Park,* and *Pauline*; at Laura Keene's he would have seen Tom Taylor's *Our American Cousin*. Impressions were undoubtedly made by Burton's Cap'n Cuttle and Timothy Toodle, Lester Wallack's Charles Surface, the elder Wallack's Shylock and Benedick, Brougham's Irish roles, Davidge's clowns and comic old men, and on and on.

The position of the individual star was firmly entrenched in the American theatre. In the 1850s this usually meant that a performer travelled from one company to another or formed his own company to focus attention on his own starring roles. What impressed Daly most about the companies of Burton, Wallack, and Keene, however, is that attention was paid to all elements of production, and, though he was greatly impressed by these stars as individuals, Daly was aware that in these companies there was a difference. These stars were part of an ensemble company and as leaders of their profession they were attempting to alter the course of the prevailing star system by creating strong resident stock companies.

Daly's major involvement in the theatre began in the 1860s and ended just before the turn of the century. This was a period of major changes not only in the theatre but in the country itself. Urban centers were on the upswing; in 1870 only one-fifth of the nation's population was located in cities – by 1900 it had swelled to one-half. The population of New York alone grew from 1,478,103 in 1870 to almost three times that number by 1900. The American Industrial Revolution was well under way, as was the rapid expansion of railroads. These social and economic forces helped to change radically the nature of the American theatre in less than three decades.

Despite the position of the star in the nineteenth-century American theatre, the dominant organizational system was the stock company, in full force up to the

1860s. The system, as practiced in America, meant that permanent companies, each operating as an independent producing organ and each attached to a specific theatre which it controlled, played at their home-bases for most of the season. Like Wallack and Burton, the manager would hire a group of actors for the season with the intention of performing a large number of plays. In order to assure the casting of a large reportory, a manager would select actors on the basis of 'lines of business', that is the actor's suitability to play certain kinds of roles, such as leading man, light comedian, first old man, first old woman, and so forth. Ideally this meant that a manager would be assured that a company of actors already knew roles within their range: thus with minimal rehearsal and effort a great number of plays could be presented each season. Before the 1860s a typical stock company produced about 130 plays a year – or more. This number, of course, included both full-length plays and shorter afterpieces. It also made it possible for a star, frequently a previously disgruntled member of a stock company, to tour the country supported by an established company, an uneasy alliance at best and a practice that would undermine the very fibre of the stock system. In 1850 there were approximately thirty-five stock companies in the U.S.; in 1871 that number had grown to fifty.[6]

By the middle of the century stock companies began to change drastically as commercialism increased and urban centers grew. Two specific factors most directly affected the stock system: the growth of the combination system and the establishment of the long run. The introduction of the combination company has been credited to Dion Boucicault, who, in 1860, sent an autonomous company of *The Colleen Bawn* to the English provinces. By the mid-1860s the system was in vogue in America. By the 1870s the new system was clearly challenging stock throughout the country, including in New York City. The *New York Herald* reported on 12 August 1877 that not fewer 'than sixty troupes had been organized for the "road"' that season. Bernheim estimates that by the 1876–77 season the number of combinations was as high as 100, while the number of stock companies had dwindled to twenty.[7] New York theatre managers during the same period quickly realized that economic necessity would bring larger profits by increasing the run of each production and that their coffers could grow even fatter if they had one or more companies on the road while the home company continued the initial production.

Long runs in New York during the 1850s and 60s were not new, but did tend to be the exception: in 1853-54 *Uncle Tom's Cabin* ran for more than 200 performances; Keene's production of Tom Taylor's *Our American Cousin* ran most of the 1858-59 season; his *Ticket of Leave Man* survived for 102 performances in 1863; Lester Wallack's *Rosedale* ran for 125 performances that same season; Edwin Booth's *Hamlet* opened on 26 November 1864 and continued for 100 performances; and the musical extravaganza *The Black Crook* ran for a phenomenal 475 performances in 1866. By the 1870s and 80s the policy of the long run was firmly established. A prime example is the Madison Square Theatre production of Steele Mackaye's *Hazel Kirke* in 1880, which ran 486 performances and at the same time had five or six combination companies touring the U.S.[8]

As combinations and long runs increased, the number of traditional stock companies decreased.[9] By 1886 there were approximately 282 combinations and only a handful of true stock companies. The combination system had quickly cut into the slim profits of the stock theatres or had simply taken over major parts of their seasons. Of major stock companies in the Eastern U.S. in 1880, the *New York Herald* (August 1880) reported that five were in New York (Wallack's, the Standard Theatre, the Madison Square Theatre, Palmer's Union Square, and Daly's) and two were in Boston (the Boston Museum and the Boston Theatre). By 1889 only Daly and Palmer remained in New York (Wallack's company disbanded in 1888). The Boston Museum became a combination house in 1893 and Palmer closed his theatre in 1896. Daly, therefore, was the only major manager left to uphold the stock system; when he died in 1899 a significant era faded completely. Seen against this background and the changing nature of the American theatre, Daly would deserve a unique position in its history for his endurance as the manager of the leading stock company in the U.S., if for nothing else. A year before Daly's death, J. Ranken Towse assessed Daly's contributions, focusing specifically on his stock operation, and noted that Daly was the last 'surviving representative here of the type of managers who have formed, developed, and preserved the best traditions of the stage, and justified the claim of the theater to be numbered among the arts'. He stated further that

> The significance and honor of this distinction will be apparent to all those who recognize in the abandonment of the old system of stock companies the chief, if not the only cause of modern theatrical decadence, and who discern in the apparent tendency of some of his younger and more intelligent competitors to follow his example ground for hope of an ultimate restoration of the old sound and only progressive policy.

Referring no doubt to the pernicious commercialism of the theatrical trust and the decline in quality production, Towse concludes that Daly 'has set up a bulwark against the tide of frivolity and corruption which threatened to overwhelm the whole profession'.[10]

II

It is tempting to assume that the progression of Daly's career was one of happenstance and expediency, and this was quite naturally the case to a great extent until he was in a position to put his principles and policies into practice. His early plays were written for specific actors and actresses, instead of for an ensemble; roles were created that adhered to the principle of 'lines of business'; the initial management of stars represented the only way Daly could gain hands-on experience and recognition, since he was not an actor as were most contemporary managers. And, most tellingly, his nine years as a critic and journalist, during which time he made a number of theatrical excursions, provided for a concentrated period of thought and comment on the American theatre as it was and as he envisioned it.

In December 1859 Daly began to write for the *Sunday Courier*, turning out a weekly feuilleton signed Le Pelerin (The Pilgrim), in which, among other subjects, he dealt with stage affairs like a veteran. In 1864 he followed James Otis as dramatic critic of the *Evening Express* and began writing criticism in 1866 for Beach's *Sun*. In 1867 he was appointed dramatic critic of the *New York Times* for a brief time and later that year for the *Citizen*. For a time Daly held positions on all five papers simultaneously. During the same period he wrote stories for *The Chimney Corner*. In late 1867, after some success with his plays *Leah the Forsaken* (1862), *Taming a Butterfly*, *Lorlie's Wedding*, *Judith*, *The Sorceress* (all 1864), *Griffith Gaunt* (1866), *Under the Gaslight*, and *Norwood* (both 1867), Daly resigned from all but the *Times* to devote himself to playwriting and management. In 1869 he ceased writing for all newspapers and, shortly after his marriage that same year to Mary Duff, daughter of the theatre manager John Duff, he began his first term as a full-time manager.

His experiences as a journalist–critic were far more important in his maturation as a theatre artist than most writers have acknowledged. Here one can ascertain the formulation of his ideas and principles, later carried out as fully as was practicable in his own theatres. In general, his essays reflect his strong reactions against the standard practices of his time. He damned the brief rehearsal and preparation period for most productions, decried the practice of 'lines of business' and casting on the basis of stock roles, and criticized the lack of realism in actors of the day. Daly wrote quite literally thousands of essays, many on the theatre, for the five papers on which he worked. Although much of what emerges is idealistic and impractical, the essays do establish the presence of a man who is giving serious thought to the plight of the theatre and is beginning to formulate ideas for his own 'ideal' theatre.

In addition to his criticism and theatre pieces, Daly tried his hand at writing fiction, including a number of novels, short stories and philosophical essays.[11] These experiments led Daly to distrust the effectiveness of words and to rely on structure and action, a major characteristic of his later dramas. Significantly, one of Daly's early assignments on the *Courier* was to write a series of articles on the working girls of New York, finally broadened to the working classes in general. At the end of his first year he wrote a series on criminals, 'Shackles and Chains; or, Revelations of the Cells'. His treatment of criminals was quite sympathetic. This attitude and his research into New York's underworld clearly affected the writing of his spectacular melodramas, in particular *Under the Gaslight*, *A Flash of Lightning*, and *The Dark City*. At this early period, Daly's brother Joseph began the collaboration that was to continue throughout Augustin's career (see Section V).

Daly's essays underscore his admiration for the management of Burton, Laura Keene, and the Wallacks, as well as the acting of Joseph Jefferson III, Edwin Booth, Rose Eytinge, and Edwin Forrest, while at the same time attacking the star system. 'It was the star system itself he blamed as the primary cause for the decadence

that allowed such neglect of ensemble acting and scenery while it stifled imagination by its dependence on traditional or rather hackneyed methods of acting.'[12]
While expressing his ideas in the press, Daly was attempting to get a foot in the
theatre door and, in doing so, was seemingly contradicting his own principles.
The plays Daly wrote in 1862 and 1864 were typical of most nineteenth-century
romantic plays, both in setting and content. They were each based on either French
or German originals with no attempt to alter locales or update them. The plays,
written for specific stars (Kate Bateman, Mrs. John Wood, Marie Methua-Scheller,
and Avonia Jones), required large emotional display and exaggerations. Despite the
addition of a few touches of realism and awkward moments of humor, these early
efforts reflect little of the discontent with the contemporary modes articulated in
his essays. But it should be remembered that, when he failed to gain acceptance
from the stock companies he approached earlier, he had little recourse but to cater
to star performers. In addition, he had no control over any of these productions, a
situation that was most stifling to his creative impulses. It was, in fact, not until
1864–65 that Daly gained his first actual management experience, touring the
South with the actress Avonia Jones. After this five-month trek through the Union-
held areas of the South, Daly had a new perspective on reality and much of the
romanticism that taints his early work begins to diminish.

Daly's major criticism was written between the productions of *Griffith Gaunt* in
1866 and *Under the Gaslight*, his first original drama, in 1867. A dominant belief
expressed in this brief period, which colors his own work for the rest of his career,
was the need for a code of ethics in the drama. As Albert Asermely explains, Daly
'could serve up controversial subjects but he seldom was more than a half-step
ahead of the morality of his times'.[13] He found a great dearth of ethical values in
many of the plays that came under the scrutiny of his pen. He also found most
plays verbose and lacking in comic relief. Of the many actors he reviewed, he most
admired Joseph Jefferson III and Rose Eytinge, and found in them qualities he
would integrate into his own company. In Jefferson he admired 'a combination of
humor and sadness or a totality of life rather than one shaded aspect of it', and in
Eytinge 'intensity, intelligence and . . . sensual excitement'.[14] Even before his introduction to management, Daly expressed the belief in his reviews that nothing is too
good for the public and that the manager must be responsible for all aspects of production – acting, scenery, lighting, costumes, makeup, and so forth, a credo he
adhered to religiously throughout his career. Similarly, he stated his belief in the
loftiness of all art that resembles nature, his conviction that presenting what seems
actual is more artistic and successful than the reality itself. Drama should both
amuse and present a moral view of life, through deeds and action. Melodrama can
be raised to the level of tragedy, and comedy should expose to censure and ridicule
mankind's vices and follies. The public deserves the best, both in the theatrical
offering and in the atmosphere of the theatre itself. The actor should concentrate
on the scene at hand and not the audience. These tenets did, in fact, become
motivating principles behind his own management.

Historians are quite correct when they conclude that Daly was not a true realist. He did, however, even in the flimsiest of his products, give the audience the best he was capable of producing; he immersed himself in all aspects of production, directed his actors always with the ensemble in mind, even after members of his company had risen to star status in everything but billing, and attempted to integrate all production elements, including the sensational moments for which he is most often remembered. Perhaps most significantly, he used 'art', as he understood it, rather than literal duplication to create his illusion of reality.

III

The turning point of Daly's career occurred in 1869, two years after the production of his sensational melodrama *Under the Gaslight*, presented first on 12 August 1867 at the New York Theatre with an initial run to 1 October. The play was revived at the same theatre less than two months later (4 December 1867 to 29 January 1868). For the first time Daly had some control over all production elements. In addition, with over a hundred performances in its first season, *Under the Gaslight* brought Daly the recognition he needed to move successfully into the next phase of his career.

On 16 August 1869 Daly rented the Fifth Avenue Theatre from James Fisk, Jr., for the then staggering sum of $25,000 a year. He clearly stated that his theatre would be guided by the 'production of whatever is novel, original, entertaining, and unobjectionable, and the revival of whatever is rare and worthy in legitimate drama'.[15] This began a management career that lasted, despite numerous ups and downs, for almost thirty years. The details of Daly's management are too numerous to discuss in a brief introduction; only a broad outline will be presented here.

During Daly's first season at the Fifth Avenue Theatre on 24th Street, adjoining the Fifth Avenue Hotel, his management, as the New York *Evening Post* (8 June 1899) suggests, was 'marked by lavish liberality, admirable taste, great boldness, and a general ardor for progress'. That first season, competing with the two leading New York theatres, Wallack's and the new Booth's Theatre, Daly presented an amazing repertoire of twenty-one plays in six months until his first major success, an adaptation of Meilhac and Halévy's sentimental drama *Frou-Frou*, which ran for 103 consecutive performances. This season included an eclectic group of plays: *As You Like It, Twelfth Night, Much Ado About Nothing, The Good-Natured Man, A New Way to Pay Old Debts,* and *She Would and She Would Not,* representative of the classic repertoire and standard 'old English' comedies; modern comedies by his two favorite playwrights, T. W. Robertson and Dion Boucicault; romances, *The Duke's Motto* and *Don Caesar de Bazan*; and French social drama, *Frou-Frou* and *Fernande,* the latter adapted from Sardou. Also, he assembled the first of the outstanding companies that would be one of his major trademarks: E. L. Davenport, George Holland, William Davidge, Clara Jennings, Mrs. G. H. Gilbert, Mrs. Chanfrau,

II Interior view of the Fifth Avenue Theatre on 28th Street, New York

Agnes Ethel, James Lewis, Mrs. Scott-Siddons, D. H. Harkins, George Clarke, J. B. Polk, and Fanny Davenport.[16] The first season closed on 9 July 1870; 337 performances of twenty-five plays had been presented.

During the second season Daly presented Clara Morris as Anne Sylvester in *Man and Wife*, his own dramatization of Wilkie Collins's novel. Morris, under the tutelage of Daly, would quickly become a star (she was a replacement for Agnes Ethel, who found the role of Anne too immoral). Still, Daly continued to manage his theatre as a traditional stock company with none of his stock company receiving star billing and only an occasional visiting star engagement, and sustained such a system with minor changes and refinements for the next thirty years, fusing traditional methods with expedient innovations. During this second season Daly also introduced Bronson Howard's *Saratoga*. Howard, who would become the 'Dean of American Playwrights', owed much of his success to the encouragement of Daly.

The hit of the third season was *Divorce*, Daly's adaptation of Anthony Trollope's novel *He Knew He Was Right*. By the end of this season Daly had begun to establish a clear policy. He was gradually moving away from a standardized repertory by emphasizing comedies of 'contemporaneous interest', giving the audience the 'impression' of reality about which he had written frequently in his criticism. *Divorce*, the logical culmination of the first two seasons, ran uninterrupted from 5 September 1871 to 18 March 1872. On 6 September 1871, the New York *Herald* provided a notice indicative of the kind of experience that a Daly audience grew to expect, even when the critic found the play lacking in substance:

> In this theatre the prevailing feature is a naturalness in dialogue and action, and a finish which invests even the most commonplace scenes with interest, and takes away much of the stereotyped character of acting of the present day. Whether the scene be in a drawing room, a garden, the country, the illusion is perfect, and the skill of the scenic artist, the stage manager, the very upholsterer and costumer, seems to transport the audience from the theatre to the scene of action. Such perfection of *ensemble*, even down to the minutest detail, is the main secret of the success of the Fifth Avenue.

By 1872 Daly had established his working habits, characterized by relentless self-confidence, boundless energy and complete absorption. His day at the theatre often began as early as 7:30 in the morning, usually preceded by early mass, and frequently ended at midnight or later. On many occasions he would work all night with the scene painter and stage carpenters until seven in the morning, breakfast, and begin on the business of another day. Otis Skinner, a later member of his company, relates the following impression:

> No martinet was ever more strict in discipline and cast-iron rule. While he had able lieutenants, he left little but the veriest drudgery to them. He ran the entire establishment from ticket office to stage door. He was ubiquitous. At one moment he was on the paint frame, criticizing the work of the scenic artist, then in the property-room issuing orders for furniture, draperies, and bric-a-brac, and his trail could be followed into the

costume workshop, the carpenter shop, to the business office whose windows over-looked Broadway, and then plunging back again into his own
private den in the rear to labors of play-writing, work with his translator,
and the thousand and one things that were crammed into each of his
twenty-four hours. His capacity for work was limitless.[17]

During the fall of 1872, competition for Daly increased, most notably from the
management of A. M. Palmer at the Union Square Theatre. Daly was to lose a number of his company to Palmer, beginning, prior to the opening of the season, with
Agnes Ethel, D. H. Harkins, and George Parkes, and the major loss of Clara Morris
in 1873, and, later in the same season, Kate Claxton. Until 1873, however, Daly
prospered, even surviving the financial panic of 1873, which ruined Booth's management. On 1 January 1873 Daly experienced a temporary check to his energy – the
destruction by fire of the uninsured Fifth Avenue Theatre, with a loss of at least
$100,000. Undaunted, he leased the old New York Theatre, illustrating his reputa-
tion for making swift decisions and for resilience, renovated it to a semblance of
the burned Fifth Avenue Theatre, and reestablished his company there within three
weeks, opening with Clara Morris in *Alixe.* By the end of that year he found himself
the manager of three theatres: the old New York Theatre at 728–30 Broadway,
renamed the Broadway, a new Fifth Avenue Theatre on 28th Street near Broadway,
and the enormous Grand Opera House.[18] A cartoon published in *The Daily Graphic*
on 11 November showed Daly, bending beneath the burden of the Opera House,
supported only by a small staff labeled 'Fifth Avenue Theatre' with the caption 'An
Atlas of Theatres'.

By 1873, though localized, 'contemporaneous' productions were beginning to
dominate, Daly's theatres offered the New York audience a varied repertoire
including Shakespeare, old English comedies, his own plays (both 'originals' and
dramatizations or adaptations), and the best of contemporary English and American drama. With financial problems always on the horizon, Daly frequently offered
plays that had a good chance of success, appealing to the respectable audiences that
flocked to his theatres. Daly also began to take his company on tour, usually a
financial boon. Unlike the usual combination system, Daly always sent out the
same or an equal company and production that had been seen at his theatre, and,
as important, he went with his company himself, overseeing each tour stop as carefully as he did at his home base. In 1874 (17 February) Daly discovered a new
source for adaptation, German comedy, with Gustav von Moser's *Ultimo*, which
he renamed *The Big Bonanza* and transposed to New York, localizing all action and
references to America. This was the first of many German 'society Plays' translated
and adapted by Augustin and Joseph Daly.

In 1877 the second major period of Daly's career ended because of the sheer
financial burden of operating three theatres.[19] On 10 September he posted closing
notices, finding himself over $45,000 in debt, largely as a result of the failure of
The Dark City, a melodrama in the tradition of *Under the Gaslight* written by the

Daly brothers. During the next year Daly tried touring the Southern and South-western circuit with an inferior part of his original company and, for a brief time, managed Booth's Theatre where he presented Joseph Jefferson in *Rip Van Winkle*. Finally, he decided to spend the better part of a year in England, trying to peddle his plays while at the same time studying English theatre methods. Disappointed, he returned to America having discovered that the theatre in England was in much the same condition as the theatre in America. He did learn that money and popularity were going to producers of amusing musical pieces; in time he would venture into this new field as well.

On his return Daly obtained financial backing from his father-in-law, John Duff, and on 17 September 1879 opened the renovated Wood's Museum on the west side of Broadway between 29th and 30th Streets as Daly's Theatre, thus beginning the final and most successful phase of his long career. Daly's policies and methods were firmly established by the beginning of the 1880s; a new order was beginning to offer fresh competition for Daly and his contemporaries. By the mid-eighties Wallack was forced to offer sensational melodrama in hopes of enticing more audience, but his company foundered and disbanded by 1888, as did Palmer's (Palmer left the theatre in 1883). By 1885 the stock company at the Union Square had given way to the combination system. Only Daly of the old guard lasted into the 90s. The last quarter of the century saw the emergence of director–managers very much in the mold of Daly – Steele Mackaye, David Belasco, and the Frohman brothers, Daniel and Charles. Unlike Daly, however, these new competitors favored the long run and generally avoided the traditional stock company system.

In his new management Daly, supported once more by his father-in-law (Duff withdrew support at the beginning of the second season owing to policy disagreements), was faced with the dilemma of finding a way to deal with the movement toward long runs and combinations while at the same time retaining a strong stock company. Slowly Daly's grew in strength and became for the next two decades America's foremost theatre. In the early 1880s Daly, with encouragement from his brother Joseph, pointed the direction for his company. Comedy, whether contemporary, musical, or classical, was to become Daly's forte. A prologue delivered on opening night 1880, and cited in the New York *Herald* (22 September), concluded:

> For truth to tell, our art alone would please
> By mirthful methods, nor depart from these,
> We bid farewell to melodrama's wiles . . .
> To ceaseless fun we dedicate our stage
> Through every utterance, though we speak or sing,
> The allegros of glad comedy shall ring.

Daly's had become in the 1880s the 'polite and refined' theatre that Daly had dreamed of as early as the 1860s. George C. D. Odell, who characterized the Daly audience as 'the best in the city in the realms of fashion, literature, and art!', recalled especially first nights as special occasions in which 'one was proud to be in so distinguished an assembly'. Furthermore, in his own inimitable style, Odell describes the theatre which he 'entirely remodeled, redecorated, and refurbished, until it became really a drawing-room home of the drama':

> Many remember fondly the long and richly refurbished entrance (once the exhibition room of freaks and museum-pieces) which by broad steps led to the luxurious lounges which Daly ultimately made an art-gallery of things pertaining to the stage. Daly encouraged his patrons to arrive early, in order to inspect the treasures of art therein exhibited. How charming it all was! And do you remember the Chinese boy in Oriental dress who, in later years of the theatre, used to hand you your programme, as you went up the richly carpeted steps? Ah, Daly's, love of our hearts, when comes there such another theatre.[20]

After an experiment with musical comedies, Daly turned to comedy in 1881–82 to the exclusion of all other forms of drama. Such a decision was stimulated in 1880 by the production of *Needles and Pins*, featuring Ada Rehan, John Drew, Mrs. G. H. Gilbert, and James Lewis, who soon became known as the 'Big Four'. Such a discovery for success, based on a formula of comedies built around these four actors, led Daly to devote the remainder of his career in a large measure to adapted German farces, Shakespearean comedy, and the traditional 'old English' comedy that had always been a part of his theatre.

In 1884, A. C. Wheeler (Nym Crinkle) of the New York *Sun* singled out what he considered prime ingredients of Daly's Theatre:

1. the pursuit of art for its own sake, not merely to make money
2. the encouragement of native talent
3. the creation of a new order of drama, e.g., *Frou-Frou, Divorce, Pique*
4. the introduction of elaborate stage settings
5. the creation of a thoroughly adequate stock comedy company

Wheeler might have added, as the *Herald* pointed out on 20 November 1881, that whatever was produced at Daly's was done 'without taint of vulgarity'. And this included all productions of Shakespeare, pruned and cleansed as Daly (and his advisers) felt prudent. William Winter, critic of the New York *Tribune*, and one of his major advisers on such judgements, clearly approved. In 1887, when Daly presented his best-known Shakespearean production, *The Taming of the Shrew*, Winter made a comment typical of those who supported Daly's position (which, it should be added, was not unusual in the 1880s). Winter wrote in the *Tribune* (19 January 1887):

> many lines of the original, indeed, were not spoken. No one of Shakespeare's plays ever is given upon the stage, or ever should be given there, word for word, as Shakespeare wrote it. A judicious excision rejects both the language that is coarse, and the language written to supply the place of scenic illustration, and in this way insures refinement and reasonable expedition.

Apparently, few members of the audience found Daly's liberties bothersome, for

contemporary reviews report constant laughter reverberating through Daly's at virtually all productions. Little concern was given for content, probability, or the
'trifles' or 'tissue of transparent triviality' that some critics found quite disturbing.
Even the *Herald* (25 February 1886) simply concluded, for example, that *Nancy
and Company*, produced that year, 'was absurd, artificial, and very cleverly acted'.

In 1884 Daly felt that his company could help establish the legitimacy of American theatre abroad, reversing the normal pattern of European companies playing in
the United States. The initial reception was lukewarm but Daly had nonetheless
made the first foray into Europe of a complete American company. Ultimately,
Daly made a total of nine European trips, playing, in addition to England, in France
and Germany, where Daly's was the first English-speaking company in nearly three
hundred years to be seen on a German stage. With each visit, Daly's company
received more cordial treatment. In 1893 (27 June) Daly opened his own theatre
in London, Daly's, in Cranbourn Street, off Leicester Square. During the winter
season of 1893–94 the entire company remained in London to perform at the first
theatre named after an American. Despite difficulties in the operation of his London theatre, ostensibly under the management of the English producer George
Edwardes, Daly's trips abroad were profitable in a number of respects, most notably
in the contacts he made with British playwrights. Daly's was the first theatre in the
U.S. to present some of the major works of W. S. Gilbert, T. W. Robertson, Frank
Marshall, James Albery, H. J. Byron, Jerome K. Jerome, A. W. Pinero, and Alfred
Tennyson, the latter choosing Daly to produce in 1892 his last dramatic work, *The
Foresters*, a pastoral comedy based on the legend of Robin Hood and Marian.

On 14 May 1899 Daly sailed for England with his wife and Ada Rehan with the
intention of facing legal action brought by Edwardes over the control of Daly's
London Theatre[21] and then spending part of the summer at Rehan's bungalow in
the county of Cumberland. On 7 June, while on a shopping trip in Paris, Daly
collapsed from heart failure, after a severe bout of pneumonia on the ship to
England, and died suddenly. Daly's death, which brought eulogies from virtually
every publication in every city where Daly's company had ever played, ended an
era in the American theatre.

IV

For thirty years Daly and his theatre exerted considerable influence in establishing
theatrical standards in New York and elsewhere. During this lengthy period Daly
affected no artist more than the actor. The actors under his tutelage numbered in
the hundreds. A few, such as George Clarke, Richard Dorney, Ada Rehan, Mrs.
G. H. Gilbert, and James Lewis, remained with Daly for twenty years or longer. He
worked with both neophytes and established stars, such as Edwin Booth, E. L.
Davenport, Joseph Jefferson III, Mr. and Mrs. Charles Mathews, Charles Fisher,
John Brougham, George L. Fox, Adelaide Neilson, and E. A. Sothern. One of Daly's
outstanding assets was his ability to discern and develop talent, hiring actors with

III Daly reading a new play to his company in 1882. Daly is seated at right center with manuscript in lap; facing him on his right is John Drew; Ada Rehan sits below Drew; Mrs. Gilbert sits next to Drew; James Lewis sits in the chair on the left.

little or no experience for minor roles, and experienced actors, without star status, for leading roles. Fostered by Daly, many performers were brought into prominence or assisted notably in the perfection of their art. He established on the New York stage such actors as Clara Morris, Agnes Ethel, Catherine Lewis, Fanny Davenport, Sara Jewett, Edith Kingdon, and Ada Rehan. The New York *Dramatic Mirror* (17 June 1899) lists well over seventy-five prominent actors who owed their success to the Daly factory.

Although Daly has been credited with abolishing lines of business, in reality he simply modified the older practice. He did consistently cast actors in roles for which their personality and appearance suited them. Older actors certainly retained their accustomed roles, while younger, less well-known actors were cast in a greater variety of roles. What is most significant, and unique for the times, Daly did cast whomever he wanted for whatever role he believed best suited the actor, within the limitations imposed by a permanent company, and, most notably, he consistently strove for an ensemble effect. 'Mr. Daly was very exacting in his training of the subordinates,' wrote Mrs. Gilbert, 'and would not tolerate anyone standing about as if uninterested in the action of the piece.'[22] In return for training a young novice, Daly expected complete trust in his methods. Daly once confirmed to Clara Morris that he did not want 'individual successes' in his theatre and added, 'I want my company kept at a level, I put them all in a line, and then I watch, and if one head begins to bob up above the others, I give it a crack and send it down again.'[23]

Daly's insistence on ensemble acting and production details earned him the appellation of the 'Vestris of the American stage' from the critic for the *Dramatic Mirror* (18 December 1880), who compared his methods to those of Wallack and Palmer, to the detriment of the latter. Another critic, quoting George Augustus Sala, compared Daly's theatre to the 'Meiningers in their rare intelligence, artistic fitness and perfect discipline'.[24] And, although the material handed his actors was far from true realism, the impression on the audience was that of naturalness. Jean Cutler, in his detailed study of Daly's company, concludes: 'Particular emphasis was placed upon a life-like style of delivering lines and of comporting oneself on the stage. Actors lost their stilted habits because they were taught not to mouth their lines, rant, or pose or exaggerate. Inappropriate ad-libbing and talking between scenes were forbidden. The actors were instructed never to notice anyone on the other side of the footlights, for the audience had to be to them as if it did not exist. Whenever necessary Daly gave the actors a reason for their action.'[25] It is transparent in Daly's letters that he was aware as early as the 1870s that he was introducing a more natural style of acting into the theatre. Critics and audiences were likewise aware that in a Daly production the acting ensemble was unique. 'There is an ease, a confidence, a perfect mastery of their art, in all that they do,' stated the Philadelphia *Inquirer* (21 August 1885).

Daly's success, then, was inextricably bound up with his players, and in turn, their effectiveness was the result of a carefully considered method of preparation. In order to stay afloat financially, Daly was forced on rare occasions to compromise and book short star engagements, but these moments were the exceptions. All things considered, the fidelity to his stated aims was exceptional. In a speech to the New York Shakespeare Society, prepared for him by his brother Joseph and reported in the New York *Tribune* (23 April 1896), Daly left no question as to what he considered his purpose.

> And what a debt does the manager owe the actor? Managers have not the reputation of recognizing this obligation. It would be entirely unjust to complain of the want of it in the janitor manager, for he is not expected to know what an actor is. He deals with combinations only, and may know as little of their component parts as he does of the parts of his watch. It is sufficient for him that they go. I speak of the manager who has trained men and women to the higher walks of the drama, who has been more pleased to see the first dawn of promise in a beginner than to see growing houses, who has exulted in seeing his company play to great audiences, not because it means so much profit, but because it was the highest public appreciation of his creation, and the creation of the manager is the perfectly acted performance.

Despite obvious weaknesses in Daly's methods, and several significant quarrels with company members as temperamental as he was,[26] Daly managed consistently to keep a resident company from which all plays were cast. And, even though actors left his management to become stars, none became a star under his management until Ada Rehan received that privilege in 1894, although, as discussed below, a quartet of actors, known as the 'Big Four', were essentially promoted by Daly to star status much earlier.

In large measure, Daly succeeded because of his strong stock system at a time when actors had few other opportunities to learn their art. During a period in the American theatre when actors trained in stock were quickly disappearing, Daly provided virtually the only school for actors in America. 'Mr. Daly's Theatre has been the nearest approach to a national school of acting we have had in America,' stated William Dean Howells. 'His work in elevating the American Stage can scarcely be over-estimated.'[27] In 1898 J. Ranken Towse stated unequivocally that Daly's 'theater is now the richest repository of the best dramatic tradition, and the only true school of acting in the United States'.[28] During his second trip to England, the *Saturday Review* likewise acknowledged the excellence of his actors and their training, even though specific reviews of plays presented were frequently tepid. 'There is not now in London an English company as well chosen, as well trained, as brilliant in the abilities of its individual members, or as well harmonized as a whole as the admirable company which Mr. Daly directs,' wrote the critic. Furthermore, he added, 'They suggest the Comédie Française at its best.'[29]

Daly was not, however, without detractors, both within and outside his own organization. Daly's method was undoubtedly unconventional and he refused to alter his beliefs. In a letter from his brother Joseph, Augustin was encouraged in 1874 to stay with his backstage system, even though it might have been against all theatrical tradition for the 'little people of the stage to get the same respect from the Manager as the big people. It is against all reason that the leading actress should not trample on the lesser ones. Well, stick to your way. This is the theatre for ladies and gentlemen not for tyrants and slaves.'[30] To many performers, however, Daly did treat actors as slaves, or at least his disciplinarian ways did not sit well with those who truly wished to rise in the ranks to star status. As other managements held out the opportunity of stardom as an inducement, a number of major actors left Daly, including Agnes Ethel, Clara Morris, and, finally, John Drew. Unquestionably Daly, in his attempt to build a well-balanced and disciplined organization, treated his actors autocratically when the occasion demanded it. As one writer explains, Daly did not cover his hand of steel with a velvet glove. 'The sight of the steel acts at once as warning and corrective.' In Daly's theatre caprice had no place; his rules were meant to be obeyed. For some these rules were carrying autocratic control too far; to others, 'with brains and energy and a sense of the fitness of things', they were simple and easily observable.

Backstage at Daly's, a list of sixteen rules was printed, framed, and kept plainly visible for all to see. What irked some personnel was that Daly's regulations regarded personal as well as professional behavior, and frequently handwritten postings from Daly appeared on the notorious bulletin board reaffirming his intentions and the fines payable for infractions. 'He was relentless when disobeyed,' reported the New York *World* on 9 June 1899. 'No captain on a quarterdeck exercised greater authority than the manager did on the stage of Daly's Theatre.' Daly's rules were many – and some quite curious. For example, on 5 January 1890 Daly posted a warning, with a fifty-cent fine for infraction, stating that smoking in costume at the stage door was prohibited. Not only was this practice harmful to the costumes, but 'smoking in the hours of duty or business is a very bad habit, and I wish all who have hitherto indulged in it would stop it'. A fine of $5 was imposed for going into another's dressing-room; visits backstage were prohibited, for 'much mischief has been known to issue from the thoughtless remarks and gossips which are often interchanged in these "flying calls" . . .'[31]

Despite some extreme measures, Daly's methods accomplished his ends. Those willing to remain under his control, though these same individuals might have been loudest in their denunciations of his autocratic methods of training, became efficient in their art and often rose to prominence. That he was a truly great acting teacher is irrefutable. Dora Knowlton Ranous praised his abilities, stating, 'I believe he could teach a broomstick to act; he shows everyone just how to move, to speak, to look; he seems to know instinctively just how everything should go to get the best effect.'[32] In 1927, long after his triumphs at Daly's, the actor John Drew still acknowledged that Augustin Daly was his 'friend and preceptor', the one person responsible for his success.[33] Ultimately, having established a new mode of acting, Daly tended to standardize it, and what was once innovative became conventional; the actor's individuality had been minimized and he had been turned into an automaton. Lewis Strang concluded in 1902 that for years Daly was the acknowledged head of his profession and 'although for several seasons before his death his influence had been diminishing, the cause was not so much that Daly was in his decline as that the American stage had made tremendous progress along the Daly lines, a condition for which Daly himself was chiefly responsible'.[34]

In addition to the great care Daly gave every aspect of production, no matter what period or type of play presented, much of his success resulted from his rehearsal methods, unique in his day. Daly insisted on full preparation and sufficient rehearsal time. The amount of time depended upon the complexity of the play and whether or not it was a revival.[35] If the actor did not enjoy frequent, long, strenuous rehearsals, Daly's was not the place to work. Otis Skinner remembered that Daly drove himself and the company nearly to the limits of endurance. 'We felt horribly abused, but the chief never stopped his drive, and while for an hour or so we did get a chance to tumble into bed, for all anyone knew he never slept!'[36] Daly, according to Mrs. Gilbert, would begin rehearsals, after the compulsory reading of the play to the company by the 'Governor', sitting in a chair on the apron of the stage. 'But more often,' she says, 'he was in among us, telling us what to do, and showing us how to do it.'[37] The later rehearsals he conducted from the auditorium. 'Using one technique or another Daly guided his company through a series of long, carefully planned, rehearsals and brought them to opening night well prepared, though occasionally a little frazzled.'[38] George Parsons Lathrop explains that 'moving about rapidly and energetically to illustrate his meaning in the business and the gesture or the tone and the emphasis he desires, he develops that abundance of thought and suggestion, and definite, comprehensive play, which command the admiration of every one, and show how thoroughly he has matured the whole conception in advance ... His work, indeed, is not simple rehearsing, but *directing*; it is the work of a master.'[39] The ultimate result of his careful procedures, cited by many critics, was an acting style noted for its quiet, subdued, and apparently spontaneous manner, an acting method that 'dispelled any impression of theatricalism'.

Both the positive and negative aspects of Daly's methods are best illustrated during the last two decades or so of his career. His later productions became increasingly elaborate in scenic and lighting effects, with lavish, realistic mountings and details which frequently became obtrusive and distracting. His productions of plays dealing with contemporary life, represented in this collection by *Love on Crutches* (1884), appear to have achieved a modified kind of realism. Also, after 1880 Daly came to rely more and more on the attraction of his major performers, Ada Rehan, John Drew, James Lewis, and Mrs. G. H. Gilbert – the 'Big Four'. As Garff Wilson points out, the need to make money in the competitive and risky theatrical market led him to take to the extreme a practice that had been his from the very beginning of his career, that is, the tailoring of plays to fit and exploit the personalities of his most popular players, and in particular the 'Big Four', and, finally, Ada Rehan alone.[40] During this final period the success of the Daly company was in the directing and the acting, which made box-office hits of rather inconsequential plays, including his drastic alterations of Shakespeare, usually changed to exploit the charms of Ada Rehan.

The 'Big Four' demonstrated to perfection Daly's ensemble approach. At the same time, they became the stars of Daly's in everything but billing; it was the 'Big Four' the public came to see and their success led Daly to aim for the long run during the final phase of his career. Perhaps most damaging to any forward momentum on Daly's part was his insistence on staying with his (and his brother's) adaptations of contemporary German farces, which were Americanized and adapted to fit the 'Big Four' like kid gloves. Bernard Shaw acknowledged that in the 1880s these farces were 'natural, frank, amusing, and positively lifelike in comparison with the plays which were regarded as dramatic masterpieces' then (he mentions *Diplomacy, Our Boys,* and *Forget-Me-Not* as examples). In 1889, however, Ibsen 'smashed up the British drama of the eighties', and, although the public did not like Ibsen ('he was infinitely too good for that', says Shaw), they liked less H. J. Byron, Sardou, Boucicault, and Daly, pronounces Shaw.[41] Shaw's last assessment, of course, could easily be disproved on the basis of attendance, but what he does illustrate is that Daly was allowing himself to become old-fashioned and was hanging on to a fad losing its appeal in the 1890s.

To understand the attraction of these sentimental comedies in the 1880s and the possibilities of staging a farce like *Love on Crutches* today, it is necessary to explore briefly the formula Daly developed around these four actors. In all they appeared together in twenty-nine contemporary plays, but in only two Shakespearean comedies, *The Merry Wives of Windsor* and *The Taming of the Shrew,* and in only one old English comedy, *The School for Scandal.* Apparently they played Shakespeare and old comedy in much the same way they played German farces.[42] In most of their contemporary vehicles, the 'Big Four' changed their roles only with respect to the intricacies of slightly different situations; the plots of these plays are amazingly similar. As in many television comedy series today, these actors became more the attraction than the play.

When the 'Big Four' began their unique combination in 1880 with the production of *Needles and Pins,* Mrs. Gilbert had been acting professionally for almost thirty years, and James Lewis had been on the stage for twenty years; each had spent eight of those years under Daly at the Fifth Avenue Theatre. John Drew, a member of the famous Drew–Barrymore family, was a relative beginner, with only eight years under his belt, four of them with Daly. Ada Rehan, also with eight years' experience, had joined Daly in 1879 and played first at the Olympic Theatre in Daly's version of *L'Assommoir.*

Drew, Lewis, and Gilbert had first played the types of roles subsequently associated with them as part of the 'Big Four' in the 1875 production of *The Big Bonanza.* With the addition of Rehan in 1880, the quartet was complete. That there was a special chemistry when these four appeared together is an unassailable fact. And, under the guiding hand of Daly their ensemble work was truly exceptional, creating rather simplistic but believable characters adored by the audience. Drew, a young gentleman of good breeding and impeccable manners, stayed close to his own personality, playing the dashing young professional man who wins the hand of the vivacious young woman, played by Rehan. In *Love on Crutches* the role is that of a 'gentleman of Leisure, who has Written Something'. Like Drew, Rehan played roles capitalizing on her own personality, one of vivacity, high spirits, remarkable energy, and a coquettishness that proved an effective foil to Drew's ease of manner, suavity, and good looks. The character of Annis Austin, 'an Ideal of the Misunderstood', in *Love on Crutches* is fairly typical. Lewis and Gilbert offered a contrast to this youthful and lively couple by playing comic older roles. Mrs. Gilbert, who spent much of her career playing 'dear old ladies, foolish virgins and peppery viragos',[43] received much love and veneration from the public. Lewis, a short, thin, wiry man with an animated face and an eccentric, high voice, was frequently considered funny on stage in spite of poor material. Together, Lewis and Gilbert were irresistible. The London *Daily Telegraph* (1 August 1884) found them extremely natural and without noisy extravagance. To that critic they did not seem as stage types or even as if they were on stage but 'in the great theatre of the world'. In Daly's plays they usually played a hen-pecked husband and his wife, the parents of Rehan's role, or else Lewis would amuse the audience as an old bachelor pursued by the spinster of Mrs. Gilbert. In *Love on Crutches* they played the standard comic married couple.

In 1892 Drew left Daly to join Charles Frohman as a star. Daly attempted to replace him, first with the English actor Arthur Bourchier and in 1896 with Charles Richman, but with little success. Rehan and Richman appeared in a concoction devised by Daly for Rehan in 1896 called *The Countess Gucki*, which, although it did little to establish a Rehan–Richman duo, did make Rehan an individual star once and for all. Rehan continued in starring roles until Daly's death in 1899. It is revealing that Rehan ceased to act within half a dozen years of Daly's death. Lewis and Gilbert continued in their usual roles until Lewis's death in 1896. After Daly's death Mrs. Gilbert moved on to Frohman's and died in 1904.

Without the 'Big Four' Daly's reputation for ensemble work diminished and his position began to wane. Still, in the final analysis the following estimates of his accomplishments, though perhaps overstated, are appropriate conclusions to a long and fruitful theatrical career. 'His sense of harmony in color, proportion and motion amounted to a passion,' wrote the *Mail and Express* on 8 June 1899. 'He was a stickler for details. His aim was completeness – and to this, together with his capacity for organization and discipline, we owe the foundation of a distinct school of American acting which has won the delightful approval of the English-speaking world . . . His actors were invariably dominated by his conception of their allotted roles, while the sumptuous costuming, scenic accessories and other embellishments with which their performances were provided were bewildering revelations of good taste which marked the farthest advance of art and science in theatrical management.' And finally, a day later the New York *World* noted that Daly 'taught the

IV Typical pose of John Drew and Ada Rehan in a Daly production

men and women under him to step into and maintain dignified places among cultured people. Had there been more Augustin Dalys, the stage would now suffer
fewer stigmas.'

V

Any assessment of Augustin Daly the playwright and adapter must take into account
Daly the collaborator and the role of his brother Joseph. Ironically, throughout
Daly's theatrical career virtually no hint emerged that Daly relied heavily on Joseph
for advice in all matters theatrical and personal and, most tellingly, that Joseph was
in no small measure responsible for much of the writing of his plays, in particular
those adaptations from contemporary French and German dramas, a mainstay of
Daly's theatres.

The case for Joseph's contributions toward the writing of plays attributed solely
to Augustin was not made until 1956 by Marvin Felheim, although during Augustin's lifetime frequent mention was made of the counsel of Joseph and the closeness
of the brothers. Indeed, brotherly love has had few equals to their relationship.
Thousands of letters passed between them, indicating a closeness rare even within the
closest of families. On 19 April 1864, for example, Augustin wrote to Joseph, 'I
believe you are the only real brother anybody has in this living world . . . and you
are all mine.' Such expressions of endearment are common in the Daly correspondence, especially on Joseph's side, although as years pass there are infrequent disagreements and moments of personal reprimand.

To Augustin, Joseph was Joe, Buddy Joe, Josey, or Bubs; to Joseph, Augustin
was Brother, Buddy John, or Bubsey (never Augustin, although Augustin frequently
signs his letters as Gustin, and close friends, outside of the family, called him Gus).
Such a close relationship was fitting, especially for Augustin, who had few close
friends and was thought by many who did not know him well to be aloof, cold, and
distant.

His colleagues and employees knew him as the Governor; his lawyer, A. Oakley
Hall, called him the Commodore; and Augustin saw himself in his professional
capacity as the Commander. In a letter to the actor Richard Mansfield, dated 31
May 1892, Augustin wrote that he could not 'afford to be less than Commander in
Chief of all my forces from the highest officer under me to the humblest. Only in
this way can I lead you on to victory . . .'[44] Clearly, there was a marked disparity
between the public and private Daly.

That Joseph was Augustin's close collaborator, and on some occasions sole
author, on the majority of his literary efforts, including speeches, promotional
brochures, important letters, published essays, and even his personally published
biography of the English actress Peg Woffington is glaringly obvious from even a
cursory reading of their unpublished letters.[45] On 5 December 1882 Joseph wrote
to Augustin that it had been twenty years since their first play was staged, clearly
referring to *Leah the Forsaken* and thus dating the beginning of their collaboration

at least to the first produced adaptation attributed to Augustin Daly. Joseph's only
public admission of his service to Augustin appears in his biography of his brother,
published eighteen years after Augustin's death and well after Joseph had ceased
serving the public as a judge. In a brief sentence Joseph writes that during Augustin's absence while managing Avonia Jones's tour in 1864 'I substituted for him
upon his various newspapers.'[46]

That he did a great deal more than cover for Augustin during his brief absence
in 1864 is indisputable. And for many years Joseph's contributions resulted in no
compensation. On 14 December 1864 he wrote, 'I take a pleasure in Dramatic
Writing but apart from you I would not touch it for an instant, so if you desire to
use me you must find the incentive to action.' A number of letters indicate that
their best work occurred in discussion, frequently while strolling uptown from the
courthouse in the late afternoon. Nonetheless, Joseph did most of his work for
Augustin during the summer months, while vacationing in central New York State
at a location known as Worcester.[47] At such times Augustin missed Joseph's personal
presence in New York City. In August of 1877 he wrote to Joseph that he missed
his 'companionship, his cheery encouragement, his strong advice, and his happy
influences'. On 13 July 1878, during the one major lull in Augustin's managerial
career, Joseph writes of the melancholy in most of Augustin's letters and the gloom
that has required Joseph to rally round him even in his most prosperous days. He
writes:

> I suffer agonies at your heartrending despondencies, at your claims to be
> utterly helpless and weak and deserted. I am ready to say to you take all
> I've got - I'll live in a garret if you'll be happy. But the thought intrudes
> itself that you were just the same when you had a theatre and work to do.
> I never saw you suffer so much as in the fall of 1873 when you had three
> theatres . . . You know also brother that when you toiled, I toiled - that
> I have had *two* professions to follow.

Indeed, Joseph may have chosen to keep his contributions silent in large measure
because of his first occupation, that of lawyer and then elected judge. From 1855
to 1862 he read law with S. W. and R. B. Roosevelt; when admitted to the bar in
1865, he succeeded to the business of that firm. In May 1870 he was elected judge
to the Court of Common Pleas. In 1884, at the expiration of his term, he was re-
elected by a wide margin. In 1890 he became the Chief Justice of the Court, and
when that court was merged with the New York Supreme Court be became a Justice and served until he was defeated for reelection by Tammany forces in 1898.
Like his brother, Joseph was known for his constant and persistent hard work, and
for his patience and industry, traits frequently useful in dealing with brother Augustin. It is quite possible that Joseph found it more appropriate, given his public
office, not to acknowledge any part in Augustin's theatrical affairs, or to receive
any compensation. By the 1880s, however, this feeling was slightly altered and
Joseph began to receive payment for his work, usually $500 per play and a 2%
royalty per performance. On 24 January 1890, in response to a series of letters

between the brothers on this matter and Augustin's failure to meet his financial obligation, Joseph wrote:

> I am sorry that you think me ungenerous in any pecuniary matters. I thought that I had proved the contrary many times. It goes against me to say a word in reminder of the many years I worked for no hope of reward, only to help my brother in the dark period from 1873 to 1884. If I kept an account of author's fees for many of the plays then written how would our accounts stand? And as to these particular plays of 'Pique' [1875] and 'Divorce' [1871] was I not satisfied to give no thought of my joint interest in the plays, but to regard all the royalty as yours, to cover your indebtedness? What share has your ungenerous brother ever had for years of any sale of these plays? And it was only last summer that I received two per cent for the later pieces in your handling engagements. Yet in what principle of justice let alone generosity was I ever denied it?
>
> As to any question of what should be generous between us, what did I ever disclose as to my feeling when the question of payment for 'International Match' [1888] came up and I asked the usual $500 and it was refused on the ground that you had so much trouble in deciphering the mss. because it was not written over or copied? I knew and recalled the effort I made to get it into your hands as soon as possible. Copying would have been delay. But I made no protest. I have accepted your fiat without question in every case. If I have been ungenerous say so and I will abide by it again. I have always shrunk from having any difference about money with you and what ever you decide after thinking the matter over shall be agreeable to me.

Augustin apparently did give Joseph's letter thought, for after Augustin's death, among the letters found in his desk, also dated 24 January 1890 and addressed to his wife Mary, was the following:

> If Brother is so inclined I would like to have him prepare a copyright edition of my favorite plays: those in which I had the benefit of his assistance. You and he may select what you deem most worthy - they should be prepared for readers. If any profits arise from this publication - divide it between you, & spend a few dollars for masses for the repose of my soul, & in atonement for any wrong I may have done any one through these plays.[48]

By 1899 the wrong to Joseph was unimportant and forgotten, and no volume of collected plays ever appeared. This is unfortunate, since, as even Felheim's close analysis discloses, we shall probably never know the total extent of Joseph's contributions to the Daly plays.

What is clear is the method of the Daly collaboration. The majority of the plays undertaken by the brothers were contemporary French and German plays. Felheim discusses at great length the fact that most of these were first translated literally by others, then put into the hands of the Daly brothers. In an 1886 article in *The*

North American Review, prepared by Augustin with the probable assistance of
Joseph, Daly publicly acknowledges his belief in collaboration and the importance
of pursuing a plan of collaboration, 'which alone assures success to beginners' (and,
he might have added, to the experienced). His plan in this essay, it should be under-
scored, is graphically corroborated in the letters. He explains:

> By this plan or system the writer of clever dialogue assists the inventor of
> interesting plot and of striking incident and character; or writers of equal
> invention and wit assist each other in that fuller development of the possi-
> bilities of plot or situation which one mind alone is commonly unable to
> accomplish; or, and this is most important, if not indispensable, dramatists
> of unquestioned experience help to shape for the stage the productions of
> playwriters of little or no experience.[49]

In the system followed by Augustin and Joseph, Augustin would normally supply,
in addition to a literal translation, a synopsis of scenes, devices or effects that he
wished incorporated, and a list of characters; Joseph's job was to deal with structure and dialogue following Augustin's plan. Frequently then the draft would pass
back and forth between the brothers, or conferences would be held to suggest additional changes in character, structure, or dialogue. Quite frequently specific characters (the names of which Augustin most frequently devised) would be altered to fit
one of Daly's major actors. Their work was, in the best sense, a collaboration with
little jealousy or ego as a hindrance to compromise and adjustment.

VI

Daly has been severely castigated by critics and historians for bringing little to the
American stage that was original or indigenous; moreover, his place in the development of American drama has been lessened because of the accusation that he made
no effort as a producer to encourage American playwrights or to foster modern
drama. Admittedly, Daly was offered plays by Ibsen and Shaw which he turned
down as inappropriate for his theatre or audience, and was thus condemned by such
critics as Archer, Huneker, and Shaw. It is also true that his own plays, both originals and adaptations, offered little that was new or especially good by our standards. They have been thought of as significant only because of Daly's use of
realistic scenes, and because Daly 'possessed a keen sense of what the public en-
joyed and a flair for creating episodes, characters, and staging which were novel,
appealing, and exciting'.[50] In reality, although he was not a playwright of real
stature, he was an exceptional contriver of effects and theatrical moments, and certainly during his heyday in the 1870s and 80s his offerings were far superior to the
melodramas and comedies offered by his competitors. As flimsy, contrived, and
predictable as his German adaptations were, for example, they contain a sophisti-
cation and polish not to be found in other comedies of the day.

Not to be overlooked is the atmosphere he created through his plays and productions which helped prepare both the theatre establishment and the audience for

the true realism to come. His taste was revealed early in his career, when, as a critic, he indicated his favorites: Douglas Jerrold, T. W. Robertson, and the young Dion Boucicault, certainly among the best playwrights of the English language at mid-century; Daly demonstrated his favoritism by presenting two Robertson plays (*Play* and *Dreams*) as the initial offerings of his first season at the Fifth Avenue Theatre in 1869.

Daly was obviously concerned about the quality of American drama and on several occasions made strong pleas to American writers to turn their attention to the stage and criticized those journalists who, on the one hand, bemoaned the lack of native material and, on the other, attacked viciously those indigenous efforts that did appear. Most important were his efforts either to produce other American playwrights or to entice some of the most important writers of the day to try their hands at playwriting. He produced three of the first four plays of Bronson Howard, as well as plays by Olive Logan, Edgar Fawcett, W. D. Eaton, and James Herne. He corresponded with and sought plays from Bret Harte (he did produce Harte and Mark Twain's *Ah Sin* in 1877), William Dean Howells, Henry James, and others, and produced plays by Boucicault, John Brougham, Richard Penn Smith, all considered American writers, and stage adaptations by such American writers as Fred Williams, Logan, M. F. Egan, Brougham, T. D. de Walden, Henry Paulton, Joseph Hatton, and Sidney Rosenfeld. He expressed a sincere interest in the work of Clyde Fitch. Numerous writers sent him plays and in most cases Daly read them and sent back suggestions.

Certainly one cannot dismiss out of hand the ninety or more plays that reached the stage that Daly (and frequently his brother Joseph) had a hand in creating. Though it is tempting to disregard most of these because they are adaptations of French or German originals, or dramatizations of novels, such a judgement is unfair, since Daly adaptations, especially those from the German, were tailored to his company and localized and Americanized in terms of character and incident so that they had little resemblance to their originals and had become truly 'American'. Otis Skinner pointed out that 'the original German characters under his hand became credible Americans', and Odell stated that 'the characters . . . were made to appear entirely American. Personally I never thought of them as anything but native to our soil.'[51] The use of French and German plays for adaptation furthermore was so common during Daly's lifetime, and long before, that it was quite natural for him to do what most producers had done before him.[52] Personally, he found most French plays morally distasteful and thus preferred the romantic sensationalism of Victorien Sardou and Alexandre Dumas; German plays were too dull for his liking but could be easily enlivened. Thus, although Daly is credited with only ten more or less original dramas, his adaptations, especially those from the German, and his dramatizations from novels, of which there were ten, deserve recognition for their originality and imaginative recasting.

Of his more obviously original plays, Felheim has identified three distinctive types, two of which are represented in this collection. First, there are the plays on which Daly's reputation as a playwright largely rests, sensational melodramas such as *Under the Gaslight* (1867), *A Flash of Lightning* (1868), *The Red Scarf* (1868), and *The Undercurrent* (1888). Daly truly believed that native tragedy could grow out of melodrama, and, although he obviously knew what would also appeal to an audience as well, he had no appreciation for critics or artists who looked with disdain on melodrama as a valid theatrical form. *Horizon* (1871), also included in this volume, is both a spectacular melodrama and an historically important frontier drama. The last category is the panoramic spectacle that depicts 'low or unusual life in great metropolitan areas': *Round the Clock; or, New York by Dark* (1871), *Roughing It!* (1873), and *The Dark City and Its Bright Side* (1877). Felheim concludes that 'These spectacular plays, featuring melodramatic scenes strung together on the thinnest of plots, add nothing to Daly's stature as a playwright, and of course he probably wrote only the scenarios anyhow . . .'[53]

The success of *Under the Gaslight; or, Life and Love in These Times*, produced first on 12 August 1867 at the New York Theatre, led Daly to compose two more sensational melodramas the following year. *A Flash of Lightning; or, City Hearthsides and City Heartaches*, Daly's second original play, was produced at the Broadway Theatre on 10 June 1868. Based in part on Sardou's *La Perle Noire*, it received generally favorable reviews and even though playing in the summer ran for seven weeks. *The Red Scarf; or, Scenes in Aroostock* followed on 12 October at Conway's Theatre.

In each of these sensational melodramas, Daly created one consummate climactic moment, which, though seeming realistic to the audience, was truly sheer spectacle. In *Under the Gaslight* it was the famous railroad scene in the final scene of Act IV in which Snorkey, a thoroughly likeable character who suffers without self-pity, is tied to the tracks at the Shrewsbury Railroad Station. Laura, the heroine, is nearby in a shed, locked up intentionally for her safety while she waits for the 10:30 p.m. down express train. Frantically she attempts to escape in order to free Snorkey while the sounds of the train get progressively closer. Although not the first to put railroad tracks on stage, nor the last, Daly managed to create a sensation through the psychological use of the sounds of the approaching train.[54]

In *A Flash of Lightning* the climactic incident features the burning of a North River steamboat and the rescue of the heroine, Bessie, locked in her stateroom by the nominal villain Skiffley. Such a gimmick was certainly not original with Daly, for Boucicault had already shown burning buildings in *The Poor of New York*, burning ships in *The Octoroon*, and a water spectacle in *The Coleen Bawn*. Nonetheless, the effect, heightened by the last-minute rescue, was an enormous success, and even, according to Joseph, 'disclosed a source of danger from steamboat furnaces that was commonly overlooked'.[55]

The Red Scarf, no longer extant, featured a sawmill scene in which the hero, Gail Barston, is trapped by his rival, Harvey Thatcher, bound to a log about to be sawed in two, followed by the last-minute rescue. To add more tension to the moment, Daly had Thatcher set fire to the mill in order to destroy all traces of

Barston. A later but unsuccessful sensational melodrama, *The Dark City*, added one last gimmick to Daly's bag of tricks, a scene in which the hero descends from a roof by a rope that the villain cuts from its anchorage.

Daly's melodramas, in particular *Under the Gaslight* and *A Flash of Lightning*, were severely criticized, and continue to be, for their improbable and overly complicated plots. If one accepts the very premise of melodrama, however, such shortcomings are predictable and easily overlooked. In fact, such criticisms have caused most contemporary historians to ignore the virtues of Daly's original works. Although the characters might be considered stock, they also represented recognizable types to Daly's audience, in the case of *Lightning*, according to an unidentified critic, 'a homely set of characters encountered daily, such as engineers, firemen, and clerks of steamboats, Greenwich St. aristocrats, policemen, postmen, minstrels, school girls, and others equally familiar and commonplace'.[56] The scenes depicted in all of his melodramas are clearly localized for the audience. In *Lightning* the audience sees a Greenwich Street house, a scene on Fifth Avenue, an all-night's lodging cellar called 'Jacob's Ladder', and a Hudson River steamer. Certainly Daly's early melodramas reflect very clearly his concern with urban society during the Reconstruction period following the Civil War. Both *Gaslight* and *Lightning*, as slight as their plots surely are, suggest Daly's concern that a new American society should be created based on industry rather than inherited wealth and family.[57]

Daly's early experiences as a journalist and his investigation into the low life of New York ring loud and clear in *Gaslight* and *Lightning*. He shows in both character and dialogue his concern for ethnic groups in New York (and attempts to individualize them through dialect) and the effects of class division. The same contemporary critic cited above suggested that Daly 'causes us to "sup full" with the vices, eccentricities, vicissitudes, dangers, miseries, and underground horrors of metropolitan life', and indeed the characters that people *Lightning* are 'too human not to enlist our sympathies' and 'help to fill and sustain a rather thinly concatenated plot'. Although some of Daly's character additions are quite irrelevant to the central plot, they invariably add to the sense of realism in *Lightning*. One such instance is recounted by his brother: 'Going home one night, Mr. Daly heard a boyish voice of wonderful power flooding the night air with "Garibaldi's Hymn" and "Santa Lucia". Tracing the music to a back street, he came upon two little Italian wandering minstrels. With his usual enterprise he added them and their parents to his collection of human documents for his forthcoming play.'[58]

Under the Gaslight is still considered one of the most extraordinary American plays of the 1860s, drawing on every innovation of the Western theatre of its time and blending them into a coherent whole. *A Flash of Lightning* is in fact just as credible a melodrama as *Gaslight* and was even considered superior by several critics who found its plot more compact, its incidents better arranged, and the dialogue more carefully and pithily written. With *Lightning* Daly 'brought the sensational drama up to its present high standard of popularity'. There is no question but that Daly considered both plays serious efforts, commentaries on the quality of life in the 1860s, as well as entertaining, sensationalized dramas. With our modern sensibilities, both plays seem overpowered by tears and sensations and partly justify Felheim's conclusion that *Lightning* is a 'melodramatic melange that is improbable, frequently to the point of sheer stupidity'.[59]

Daly's major weakness as a dramatist was undoubtedly his inability to structure a plot that was not contrived, improbable, complicated, or overly theatrical. He was far more successful in his handling of effects, the creation of characters with crude individualization and strength (especially his heroines), identifiable localized settings, and non-stop, bristling action, frequently more important than motivation. The plot line of *Lightning*, though excessively complicated, is really quite simple. The play centers upon two sisters, Rose and her older sister Bessie. Their father, Garry Fallon, an Irish immigrant made good, has spoiled Rose, the beautiful, snobbish and selfish daughter, and virtually ignored Bessie because of her lack of his kind of driving ambition, demonstrating his preference for Rose with a gift of a necklace and his dislike for Bessie by accusing her of the theft of the same necklace when it disappears during a violent storm and turning her over to the police represented by the obnoxious but clever Skiffley. Bessie accepts her fate and in so doing tries to shield the man she loves, Jack Ryver, whom she believes guilty. The remainder of the play centers on Skiffley's attempt to gain control of Bessie, while Jack attempts to save her and prove to her his innocence. Somehow, they all miraculously end up on a steamboat which blows up and catches on fire while racing with its competitor. It is this setting that provides Daly's most heroic and spectacular incident. After Bessie is saved from a fiery death, she is locked up in her room by her cruel father awaiting the outcome of a formal investigation of the theft. Fallon has complicated matters by dreaming up the notion that the coal in his home is rife with gold. Enter Jack Ryver, trained as a civil engineer, who, much to Skiffley's chagrin, explains the truth of the situation, and Fallon's crazed notion of a rich deposit in the coal, by showing in Holmesian fashion how the necklace had been destroyed by the real villain of the piece, a flash of lightning, and the gold melted into hunks of coal by the fireplace. Before the explanation is completed, Bessie attempts to kill herself in anticipation of a jail sentence, but she lives to see another day.

For all its obvious weaknesses, *A Flash of Lightning* is an intriguing and frequently entertaining but shallow play. It is easily on a par with the better-known *Under the Gaslight*, and holds up today as well or better. Its initial run from 10 June to 1 August 1868 was quite a healthy one for the 1860s. In fact, its run was actually continued by Mrs. Conway at her Park Theatre in Brooklyn in September. Other New York productions followed in 1873, 1875, and 1877. A burlesque version, *A Flask of Jersey Lightning*, by Bryant's Minstrels, was performed concurrently with the original production. It was twice produced in England: at the Leeds Amphitheatre on 11 August 1870, and at the Grecian Theatre, London, 21 November 1870.

Though it is not his most successful original play, *Horizon* is historically the most significant of the plays in this collection. It was first seen on 21 March 1871 at the Olympic Theatre under the management of Daly's father-in-law John Duff. Joseph

Daly says his brother 'wrote, rehearsed, and produced' the play.[60] Daly, then in active management of his first Fifth Avenue Theatre, made this gesture to Duff to assist the fading fortunes of the Olympic and loaned Agnes Ethel to him for the role of the heroine, Meddie. Also featured in the original cast were George L. Fox (best remembered for his earlier successes as Humpty Dumpty in his American pantomime), J. K. Mortimer, Charles Wheatleigh, Hart Conway, Mrs Prior and her daughter Lulu, and Mrs Yeamans and her daughter Jennie. The initial run lasted for seven weeks.

Daly's play belongs to the tradition of American Western drama which dates from James Kirke Paulding's *The Lion of the West* with its hero Colonel Nimrod Wildfire and includes such dramas as Robert Bird's *Nick of the Woods* (1838), Mordecai Noah's *The Frontier Maid* (1840), and W. R. Derr's *Kit Carson, The Hero of the Prairie* (1850). In frontier dramas of the 1830s the West was Kentucky and inspiration tended to be James Fenimore Cooper's Leatherstocking series. By the 1850s the frontier had moved toward California and the 'noble savage' had become a 'varmint Redskin'. By the 1870s the American public hungered once more for Western spectacle, Western customs and Western characters, as Meserve suggests.[61] Such a stir of interest in the West no doubt was stimulated by the appearance in 1868 of Bret Harte's short story 'The Luck of Roaring Camp' in *The Overland Monthly*, which suggested characters, situations, humor and sentimentality, and actions rife with local color. Daly, who knew little of the real West, was the first to write a successful sensational melodrama based on such a setting, and it was the most important frontier drama thus far written.

A. H. Quinn suggests that the scene in which Loder renounced his claim upon Med's affections in favor of her Eastern lover, a scene noted for 'simplicity of language and restraint of passion', supports the claim that Daly was the first of the modern realists in American playwriting.[62] However, as in all of Daly's plays the atmosphere throughout is very moral and romantic. Indeed, at the moment of the Rowse party's arrival at Rogue's Rest the 'wooden city' is experiencing a 'change of moral atmosphere', described so frequently in the work of Bret Harte.

Felheim has questioned much of the originality of *Horizon*. He sees in Med's situation a similarity to that of the actress Lotta Crabtree and cites evidence in Constance Rourke's *Troupers of the Golden West* in which Lotta's starring vehicle, *Heartsease*, produced in May 1870, seems to anticipate some of the effects and characteristics of *Horizon*. The opening of Act II sounds a definite similarity to the opening of Harte's 'The Outcasts of Poker Flat', and John Loder is a striking parallel to Harte's gambler, John Oakhurst. Furthermore, Felheim illustrates Daly's dependence upon current events of the Indian wars for many details of his plot. Despite such possible influences, Daly created his own plot construction and gave his characters individualized touches, never more so than in his handling of the Indian Wannemucka. Through the words of his Eastern characters Daly provides us with the conventional notion of the redskin - from the noble savage of Cooper, the murdering savage who kills women and children with no qualms, to the simple-minded uncivilized Indian easily duped. In reality, Daly presents us with an Indian tainted with cynicism, although our final view of Wannemucka is somewhat poeticized. Ultimately, this untrustworthy, lazy Indian, though also capable of great courage and strength, is like all good Indians better off dead, soundly defeated by the American cavalry.[63]

The first act of *Horizon*, set in a fashionable parlor in a New York city house, offered few surprises for the New York audiences. However, with the rise of the second-act curtain the patrons were shown an unusually realistic picture of a scene in 'one of the wooden cities of the West' called Rogue's Rest, sixty miles from Fort Jackson, in the Far West somewhere 'just this side of the Horizon'. This opening scene of Act II, though not the most spectacular in terms of effect, was full of local color and was an effective way to introduce the audience to 'a play of contemporaneous events upon the borders of civilization', the description used for Daly's copyright. The place names alluded to in the plot, with its focus on Indians, politicians and politics, vigilante lynching committees, Indian attacks at night and on a stockade, mysterious letters, and last-minute rescue by American troops, are given such unusual and colorful local names as the Big Run River, Dog's Ears, All Gone, and Hollo Bill. The story line built around these atmospheric locales, though minus the traditional frontier hero, is simple and predictable: Sundown Rowse, a prominent man with influential Washington connections, a crooked politician, and the prototype of many subsequent stage lobbyists, goes West to take charge of lands given him by a Congressional grant. With him goes Captain Van Dorp, a West Point graduate and the adopted son of the wealthy, socially prominent Mrs Van Dorp, whose husband (known out West as Whiskey Wolf) left his wife and ran away to the West years earlier with his daughter Med, 'White Flower of the Plains'. With the attraction of Captain Van Dorp for Med complications come quickly, and the remainder of the play deals with the unwinding of these entanglements, largely through the efforts and self-sacrifice of the noble gambler, John 'White Panther' Loder, who protects Med against the Indian Wannemucka and clears a path for the marriage of young Van Dorp and Med.

Daly's play, despite its romantic and moral touches, was a major departure from the then popular and sentimental glorification of the West. Daly chose instead to portray a more realistic picture. Herron has pointed out that Daly's technique 'takes the form of humorously satiric commentary on social problems connected with enterprising Rogue's Rest and the vast plains surrounding it'. She elucidates as follows:

> The currents of his thoughts about the Far West touch upon the typical frontiersman's independence of traditional legal authority and his tendency to rely on expedience rather than law. The citizens of Rogue's Rest, boisterous and freedom-loving, scoff at Congressional law and disregard local decree as they wish. Their mayor or 'boss', one Rocks of Tennessee, recognizes the power of a newly formed Vigilance Committee . . . Rocks admits ruefully that the 'civil authority wasn't able to control' all of the

'blacklegs, horse-thieves and other alibis and aliases' which had overrun the settlement. He, therefore, is 'much obliged' to the 'hard-fisted hard-working men' of the Vigilance Committee who unite to clean up the town themselves. The spirit of frontier lawlessness is highlighted further by the admission by . . . Rowse . . . that he knew 'one town where every inhabitant's got another name'. They take ranks there according to the amount of debts they ran away from. The worst insolvent is elected Sheriff.[64]

For all its obvious shortcomings, *Horizon* was praised by such competent critics as Brander Matthews and Laurence Hutton, and Daly's rival manager at the Union Square, A. M. Palmer, admitted to Joseph Daly years later that *Horizon* was 'the best American play I have ever seen; more than that, it was the best play your brother ever wrote; and it was the least appreciated by the public'.[65] Finally, *Horizon* initiated a succession of plays recreating frontier life and brought to the stage the traditions of a raw but rapidly growing border town on the plains.

Before examining briefly Daly's various adaptations and dramatizations, and the play from this category selected for this volume, it is significant to note that Daly was unique among adapters in that as a man of honor he usually acknowledged the original author and paid royalties at a time when copyright laws were wholly inadequate to protect playwrights.

Daly staged sixty-five productions of French plays over a thirty-five-year period; forty-four were adapted in whole or part by him (and his brother), the remainder by others. Daly discovered early that French plays were easy to adapt, settling often for quite literal translations. They proved to be excellent 'star' vehicles and American audiences, who still believed that anything French had to be civilized, were drawn to them, thus assisting him in developing the cultured and socially elite audience that he sought. His first French adaptation was *Taming a Butterfly* (1864) from Sardou's *La Papillonne*, written with a fellow-journalist, Frank Wood, and his last, also a Sardou original, was *Madame Sans-Gêne*, which ran for only two weeks in 1899. Only two French adaptations, *Frou-Frou* (1870) and *The Lottery of Love* (1888–89), achieved initial runs of at least a hundred performances. Indeed, he was never as successful with French adaptations as he was with German, which could more easily be localized. Only three French plays were Americanized: *Love in Harness* (1886), *The Lottery of Love*, and *Love in Tandem* (1892).[66] Daly also attempted two French pantomimes, *The Prodigal Son* (1891) and *Miss Pygmalion* (1885), with limited success. After 1875 most French adaptations were one-act curtain-raisers designed to show off Drew and Rehan or Gilbert and Lewis.

Daly's German adaptations began in 1862 with *Leah the Forsaken*, based on Dr. S. H. Mosenthal's *Deborah*, and concluded with *The Countess Gucki* in 1896, one of the more inane of the lot. In all Daly adapted some thirty-five to forty German plays and produced on his stages forty-two, six of which lasted for at least a hundred performances during their initial run. Daly, no doubt riding the wave of a long-popular tradition bolstered by the emigration of 400,000 Germans to the U.S. in the 1880s, literally struck 'the gold mine of German farce' in the 1880s, as Odell puts it, which consistently provided Daly with plays 'of money, love and haste, in which there is endless confusion and at last speedy deliverance from lover's woes'.[67] As we have seen, Daly found German farces that bore marked resemblances to each other and tailored them to fit his 'Big Four'. Admittedly, these plays were trifles, but they provided the income necessary for Daly during the same period to produce plays of more literary and historical value; 'he could recoup by means of a German farce the enormous expenditure involved in staging Shakespeare and the old comedies in lavish style', says Felheim.[68]

Representative of Daly's German adaptations, and superior to most, is *Love on Crutches*, not unlike the vast majority of German situation farces which appealed to Daly and his audiences so thoroughly. It belongs to a group of 'love' plays produced by Daly in the 80s, along with *The Lottery of Love, The Railroad of Love, Love in Tandem,* and *Love in Harness.* Marion Michalak provides an excellent summary of these and other 'Big Four' plays:

> Each gains its comic effect by placing a group of characters in an intricate plot development. The compounding and unraveling of the plot provides an abundance of broad farcical situations which are presented in rapid fire sequence. Disagreements between married couples and lovers abound. Secret correspondences, which are on the verge of being intercepted, can provide the main action of an entire act. The men in their struggle with their wives or sweethearts can add to the complexity of a play by their extravagant plans to attend a forbidden play or opera. A fabulously successful novel or play written anonymously turns out, after an intricate process of discovery, to be the product of a lover or a husband. And, finally, the inevitable stuff of farce appears: a mass of misunderstanding among a group of characters is brought to a hilarious climax when the participants, without each other's knowledge, are all led to the same room or house. The denouement is held in abeyance as a rapid fire game of hide and seek ensues. Amid the split second opening and closing of doors near discoveries are made, while other characters are almost caught as they hide behind drapes, under blankets, or behind furniture. Incidents like these are presented in a spirit of great fun. In the end all lovers are reconciled . . .[69]

Little more need be said to prepare the reader for *Love on Crutches*. Each of the 'Big Four' took one of their accustomed roles. The plot revolves around a novel written by Sidney Austin (Drew) under the assumed name of Marius; the novel has passed into its tenth edition and has surpassed the success of Stowe's *Uncle Tom's Cabin*. Austin's wife, Annis (Rehan), has married him through an arrangement of convenience. Although she is indifferent toward her husband, she is totally enchanted by Marius's novel *Tinsel* and has begun a correspondence with Marius, with predictable consequences. Neither Sidney nor Annis realizes the true identity of the other, since Annis signs her letters 'Diana'. Sidney's confidant is Dr. Quattles (Lewis); Mrs. Gilbert played his wife, Eudoxia. From this point on Michalak's description applies; one coincidence or misunderstanding leads to further complications, culminating in the final reconciliation in Act III, in which Quattles affirms 'those two lovers had to swim through a sea of ink to get to each other'.

There is no eternal message in this lightweight comedy, but it does sparkle and intrigue; it is, as one reviewer commented, 'as delicate as gossamer, as light and fragile as the soap-bubbles which are blown about the stage in the last act'.[70] Without question, the success of this play depended largely on its casting. The *Dramatic Mirror* critic (6 December 1884), who found it superior in plot construction and language to the average humorous pieces of the day and closer to high comedy than most of Daly's adaptations, also noted that 'the actors appear more familiar to you; you recognize that you are at home with them again'. Indeed, such a sentiment was expressed out of town as well. In Philadelphia a critic for the *Inquirer* (21 August 1885) found it to be one of the most brilliant of all the many that Daly had undertaken, and commented, 'Mr. Daly is doing more for our stage, for its elevation and purification than all the other helpful influences combined.' This critic, echoing the *Dramatic Mirror*, singled out the effect of the company on the audience: 'There is a fellowship and friendliness between the stage and the front. We shake hands with them across the footlights.'

Love on Crutches, based on Heinrich Stobitzer's *Ihre Ideale*, opened on 25 November 1884, following unsuccessful productions of *A Wooden Spoon*, adapted from von Schonthan's *Roderick Heller*, and Pinero's *Lords and Commons*. Joseph Daly says that the failure of Pinero's play 'hastened the appearance of one of the most delightful comedies connected with the memories of the theatre' and that it 'had lain upon Mr. Daly's desk for nearly two years'.[71] The success of *Love on Crutches* provided Daly with a popular vehicle to see him through one of the most traumatic periods of his life, for in January 1885 his two beloved sons, Austin and Leonard, aged eleven and fourteen, developed diphtheria and died within a few days of each other. In February Daly's, now on firm financial footing, withdrew *Love* and offered three old comedies in quick succession: *She Would and She Would Not, The Country Girl,* and *The Recruiting Officer.*

Joseph Daly felt *Love on Crutches* could almost play itself and be more than merely effective in lesser hands than the Daly company. The success of Edith Kingdon as Mrs. Margery Gwynn, loyal friend to Rehan's character, however, was clearly a factor in its success, as were the usual triumphs of the 'Big Four'. It is our opinion that in the hands of good actors, well directed and with an understanding of the ensemble approach that spelled success for Daly, *Love on Crutches* would still make an entertaining evening of theatre. Daly continued to use the play in his repertory for some time. In August 1886 it opened his German season in Hamburg; it was played in Berlin, and later in Paris and London. In 1893–94 it was revived in a season featuring eight other revivals of previous favorites, along with five new pieces. It was also revived in 1896 in London at the Comedy Theatre.

In addition to Daly's German and French adaptations, some comment should be made regarding his novel dramatizations, and his stagings of Shakespeare and old English comedies (usually meaning eighteenth-century comedy).

Ten novels were adapted by Daly. This, like the use of French and German plays, was a common, acceptable practice in the nineteenth century. Boucicault, for example, frequently pilfered plots and characters from novels; numerous versions of Harriet Beecher Stowe's *Uncle Tom's Cabin* appeared in play form; and Joe Jefferson's most famous role was adapted from the Washington Irving short story with the character of Rip Van Winkle. Most dramatizations of novels were far less successful than either Boucicault's or Daly's efforts. And the Dalys, as noted in numerous letters between the brothers, considered their dramatizations as 'original' plays and commented frequently on the difficulties involved, stating that such plays and novels are 'essentially and radically different literary achievements'. For material to dramatize, Daly turned to Charles Reade, Henry Ward Beecher, Charles Dickens, Wilkie Collins, Anthony Trollope, Edmond About, Florence Marryat Lean, and Emile Zola. The most successful was *Pique* (1875), based in part on Lean's *Her Lord and Master*, which, along with *Divorce* (1871), represent a rare glimpse in the Daly canon of significant social commentary and a striking contemporaneousness. *Pique* went about as far as stage realism could, and in fact antedates both the scenic realism of David Belasco and the first production of a Zola play in America by several years. It ran initially for 238 performances, was frequently revived, and was presented in England at the Brighton Theatre Royal in 1882 as *Only A Woman*.

Daly was a true lover of Shakespeare, and, although one would undoubtedly conclude that his acting versions frequently butchered the original, expurgated passages for tenuous reasons, and rearranged scenes and passages to focus on specific actors, in particular Ada Rehan, he nonetheless sustained an interest in Shakespeare on the American stage and offered lavish and effective productions for his audience. In all, Daly staged sixteen Shakespearean plays, beginning with *Twelfth Night* in 1869 and concluding with *The Merchant of Venice* in 1898–99, the latter with magnificently spectacular results. His productions also included *The Merry Wives of Windsor, A Midsummer Night's Dream, As You Like it, Love's Labour's Lost* (never before seen in New York), *The Two Gentlemen of Verona, Romeo and Juliet, Much Ado About Nothing, The Tempest,* and his most famous Shakespearean production, *The Taming of the Shrew*. Daly's *Shrew*, presented first on 18 January 1887, is still considered one of the truly great productions of the play.[72] It played initially for 121 consecutive performances, creating a furor over Rehan's Kate, and was seen a year later at the Lyceum Theatre during Daly's third European tour and on 3 August 1888 at Stratford-upon-Avon for the benefit of the Library Fund of the Shakespeare Memorial, supposedly the first performance of the play given there. In addition to his own arranged texts (most done with the help of the critic William Winter) and productions, in 1875 Daly presented Edwin Booth in six Shakespearean plays and in 1877 Adelaide Neilson in three.

Daly also had a special fondness for English comedies, most frequently those of the eighteenth century. Most, like those by Sheridan, Goldsmith, or Farquhar, were tried and true classics. Others, however, were plays rarely seen on the American stage, for many of which Daly's revival was also to be their final professional New York production. As in his Shakespearean productions, Daly rearranged and adapted these standard plays at will. The list includes, in addition to predictable titles such as *The School for Scandal*, *She Stoops to Conquer*, and *The Recruiting Officer*, comedies such as Colley Cibber's *She Would and She Would Not*, Mrs. Centlivre's *The Busybody*, Mrs. Cowley's *A Bold Stroke for a Husband*, Elizabeth Inchbald's *Wives As They Were, Maids As They Are*, and, his final revival in 1897, Centlivre's *The Wonder*.

Notes

1   George Bernard Shaw, *Our Theatres in the Nineties* (London: Constable, 1932), III, 208.
2   New York *Clipper*, June 1899.
3   Walter J. Meserve, *An Outline History of American Drama* (Totowa, New Jersey: Littlefield, Adams, 1965), p. 137.
4   The most complete biography of Daly was written by his brother, Joseph Francis, two years his junior. See Joseph Francis Daly, *The Life of Augustin Daly* (New York: Macmillan, 1917).
5   Joseph Daly (p. 12) says that 'He was absolutely without ambition to act', and recalled only two occasions when he did act – in the *Macbeth* appearance mentioned here and 'one in a small literary society when he took the part of Julius Caesar'.
6   Edward William Mammen, *The Old Stock Company School of Acting* (Boston: Boston Public Library, 1945), pp. 10–11.
7   Alfred L. Bernheim, *The Business of the Theatre*, reissue (New York: Benjamin Blom, 1964), p. 30.
8   Material in this section has been drawn largely from Marion Victor Michalak, 'The Management of Augustin Daly's Stock Company, 1869–1899' (unpublished Ph.D. dissertation, Indiana University, 1961).
9   The combination system was stimulated in some measure by the enormous increase in railroad mileage, from 9,000 to 30,000 in the 1850s alone.
10 J. Ranken Towse, 'An American School of Dramatic Art. A Critical Review of Daly's Theatre', *Century Magazine*, 56 (1898), 261–64.
11 Daly never acknowledged these other writings after he became a successful playwright and manager; indeed, he ceased such writing after 1867 and only ventured into non-theatrical writing late in his career with his biography of Peg Woffington.
12 Albert A. Asermely, 'Daly's Initial Decade in the American Theatre, 1860–1869' (unpublished Ph.D. dissertation, The City University of New York, 1973), p. 62. Asermely provides a superb discussion of Daly's critical principles.
13 Ibid., p. 161.
14 Ibid., pp. 166–67.
15 William Winter, *Vagrant Memories* (New York: George H. Doran, 1915), p. 273.
16 Daly's first season established a pattern of actor training continued for the

next three decades. Agnes Ethel, for instance, began the season an unknown and ended the first year as the leading performer not only in *Frou-
Frou* but also in *Fernande*.

17   Otis Skinner, *Footlights and Spotlights* (Indianapolis: Bobbs-Merrill,
         1924), p. 135.

18   The Grand Opera House had never been a successful theatre. Daly leased it
         with a separate company and staff, for the production of entertainments
         advertised as spectacles, musical extravaganzas, and sketches with music.
         He opened with *Le Roi Carotte* with book by Sardou and music by Offen-
         bach. Among other offerings Daly presented his own musical extravagan-
         zas *Round the Clock* and *Roughing It!*

19   The Broadway Theatre closed in December 1873 and the Grand Opera
         House in March 1874. Losses had been so great that the next three years at
         the new Fifth Avenue did little to help restore stability.

20   George C. D. Odell, *Annals of the New York Stage*, 15 vols. (New York:
         Columbia University Press, 1927–49), XII, 421; XI, 13.

21   Edwardes was the owner of the theatre, Daly the lessee; the dispute was
         over the division of profits.

22   Charlotte M. Martin, ed., *The Stage Reminiscences of Mrs. Gilbert* (New
         York: Charles Scribner's Sons, 1901), p. 210.

23   Clara Morris, *Life on the Stage* (New York: McClure, Phillips, 1901), p.
         319.

24   Boston *Herald*, 9 October 1888.

25   Jean Valjean Cutler, 'Realism in Augustin Daly's Productions of Contem-
         porary Plays' (unpublished Ph.D. dissertation, University of Illinois, 1962),
         pp. 109–10. See also Dora Knowlton Ranous, *Diary of a Daly Debutante*
         (New York: Duffield, 1910), p. 53, and Ronald Michael Reed, 'The
         Nature of the Scenic Practices in Augustin Daly's New York Productions:
         1869–1899' (unpublished Ph.D. dissertation, University of Oregon, 1968).

26   Otis Skinner, who spent five years in Daly's company, wrote in *Footlights
         and Spotlights* (p. 136): 'His hobby was the perfect running of the
         machinery of his organization. Suspicious of the loyalty of those about
         him, he was absolutely blind to the virtue or merit of a contrary view of
         his own. There could be but one method of accomplishing anything; that
         was the method of Augustin Daly.' When Clara Morris left Daly, his brother
         wrote on 12 September 1873 that such talents are 'small-minded, whimsi-
         cal, and trying, because they are over fretted socially and have every reason
         to be happy but want some excuse for being miserable and finding fault'.

27   Quoted in Marvin Felheim, *The Theater of Augustin Daly* (Cambridge,
         Mass.: Harvard University Press, 1956), p. 18.

28   Towse, 'A Critical Review of Daly's Theater', p. 264.

29   Quoted in Felheim, p. 287.

30   15 September 1874. The letters cited in this introduction between Joseph
         and Augustin are from 10 vols. of correspondence, 1858–99, in the Billy
         Rose Theatre Collection, New York Public Library of the Performing
         Arts, Lincoln Center, New York.

31   Daly holograph notes, The Folger Shakespeare Library, Washington, D.C.;
         the latter two dated 23 February 1899 and 31 August 1898.

32   Ranous, *Diary of a Daly Debutante*, p. 30.

33   'John Drew', *The Nation* (2 July 1927), p. 52.

34   Lewis C. Strang, *Players and Plays of the Last Quarter Century*, 2 vols.
         (Boston: L. C. Page, 1902–03), II, 125.

35 See David George Schaal, 'Rehearsal-Direction Practices and Actor–Director Relationships in the American Theatre from the Hallams to Actor's Equity' (unpublished Ph.D. dissertation, University of Illinois, 1956), and Schaal, 'The Rehearsal Situation at Daly's Theatre', *Educational Theatre Journal*, 14 (March 1962), 1–14.
36 Skinner, *Footlights and Spotlights*, p. 147.
37 Martin, p. 211.
38 Schaal, 'Rehearsal-Direction Practices', p. 277.
39 George Parsons Lathrop, 'An American School of Dramatic Art. The Inside Working of the Theatre', *Century*, 56 (June 1898), 268.
40 Garff B. Wilson, *Three Hundred Years of American Drama and Theatre*, 1st ed. (Englewood Cliffs, New Jersey: Prentice-Hall, 1973), p. 248.
41 Shaw, *Our Theatres in the Nineties*, I, 164.
42 For a thorough discussion of the 'Big Four' and their individual careers see Richard Harlan Andrew, 'Augustin Daly's Big Four' (unpublished Ph.D. dissertation, University of Illinois, 1971).
43 Skinner, p. 139.
44 Daly Correspondence, 1861–99, Folger Shakespeare Library. Also see note 30.
45 The Woffington biography (1888) apparently was researched and written by Augustin. Joseph, however, did write the preface to the second edition (1889), signed by Augustin when published.
46 Joseph Daly, p. 59.
47 Felheim assumes this to be Worcester, Massachusetts, but a reference in the Daly correspondence to Ostego County places it in New York State. There is no such place name today in New York.
48 Daly was a devout Roman Catholic; in 1894 he was awarded the Laetare Medal by Notre Dame University.
49 Augustin Daly, 'The American Dramatist', *The North American Review*, 142 (May 1886), 485–92.
50 Wilson, p. 217.
51 Skinner, p. 138; Odell, V, 420.
52 Daly adapted only one other non-English play, a Spanish play by Manuel Tamayo y Baus (Estabanez) entitled *Un Drama Nuevo* (1867), which Daly presented unsuccessfully as *Yorick: A New Play* in 1874.
53 Felheim, p. 79.
54 A similar effect was first seen in an unsuccessful English play, *The Engineer*, at the Victoria Theatre in 1863. Daly's scene was so effective that he patented it and obtained a court injunction when Boucicault's *After Dark* opened in New York on 11 November 1868 with a similar scene.
55 Joseph Daly, p. 80.
56 Unidentified cutting from Vol. 1 of Daly correspondence and documents, Lincoln Center.
57 Asermely develops this idea thoroughly for *Gaslight*, in which he suggests that the train symbolizes the old society crashing in on the new (p. 145).
58 Joseph Daly, p. 80.
59 Felheim, p. 59.
60 Joseph Daly, p. 106.
61 Travis Bogard, Richard Moody, and Walter J. Meserve, *The Revels History of Drama in English. Vol. VIII: American Drama* (London: Methuen, 1977), p. 186.
62 Arthur Hobson Quinn, *A History of the American Drama, from the Civil*

War to the Present Day (New York: Appleton-Century-Crofts, 1936), p. 14.

63 Felheim, pp. 67–74.

64 Ima Honaker Herron, *The Small Town in American Drama* (Dallas: Southern Methodist University Press, 1969), pp. 136–37.

65 Joseph Daly, p. 106.

66 Major adaptations of foreign plays and dramatization of novels are listed on pp. 200–4, with authors of originals.

67 Odell, XII, 218; New York *Herald*, 2 November 1887.

68 Felheim, p. 185.

69 Michalak, p. 157.

70 Philadelphia *Sunday Press*, 26 August 1885.

71 Joseph Daly, p. 377.

72 For a complete analysis of Daly's version of the play and its production, see Tori Haring-Smith, '*The Taming of the Shrew*: A Stage History 1594–1978' (unpublished Ph.D. dissertation, University of Illinois, 1980).

BIOGRAPHICAL RECORD

20 July 1838	John Augustin Daly born at Plymouth, North Carolina.
1849	Daly family moved to New York City, where AD became active in amateur theatrical organizations.
6 April 1856	Rented a theatre in Brooklyn, New York, and presented 'The Melville Troupe of Juvenile Comedians'.
December 1859	Hired by *The Sunday Courier* as a 'general writer'.
8 December 1862	*Leah the Forsaken*, adapted by AD, opened at the Howard Athenaeum in Boston with Kate Bateman.
1863	Sent *The Red Ribbon* to L. Keene; rejected.
19 January – 21 February 1863	*Leah* at Niblo's Garden in New York.
Spring 1863	AD in Philadelphia as manager for the Batemans.
1 October 1863	*Leah*, with Bateman, opened in London at the Adelphi Theatre.
25 February – 19 March 1864	*Taming a Butterfly*, adapted from Sardou by AD and Frank Wood, produced at the Olympic Theatre in New York.
June 1864	Became drama critic on *The Evening Express.*
September 1864 – January 1865	Toured parts of the South as stage manager for Avonia Jones.
1866	Became drama critic of *The Sun.*
7 November 1866	AD's adaptation of *Griffith Gaunt; or, Jealousy,* from novel by Charles Reade, opened at the New York Theatre. Daly's first major success (six-week run).
1867	Became drama critic of the *New York Times*, and, later in the year, of the *New York Citizen.*
12 August – 1 October 1867	*Under the Gaslight*, original melodrama by AD, presented at the New York Theatre. Daly rented his first theatre from the Worrell sisters.
11 November – 4 December 1867	*A Legend of 'Norwood'*, adapted by AD and Joseph W. Howard from the novel by Henry Ward Beecher, presented at the New York Theatre.
Late 1867	AD resigned as critic from all newspapers but the *New York Times.*
22 January – 3 February 1868	AD's adaptation of Charles Dickens's *The Pickwick Papers* at Worrell Sisters' Theatre.
20 April 1868	First British production of *Under the Gaslight* at the Tyne Theatre, Newcastle.

42

10 June – 1 August 1868	AD's second original melodrama, *A Flash of Lightning*, performed at the Broadway Theatre.
20 July 1868	*Gaslight* opened at the Pavilion Theatre, London.
12 October 1868	*The Red Scarf; or, Scenes in Aroostock*, melodrama by AD, performed at Conway's Theatre, Brooklyn.
30 November – 5 December 1868	*Red Scarf* at the Bowery Theatre, New York.
9 January 1869	AD married Mary Duff, daughter of theatrical entrepreneur John Duff.
16 August 1869	AD opened his first theatre, the Fifth Avenue Theatre, with Robertson's *Play*.
4 October 1869	AD's first Shakespeare, *Twelfth Night*, with Mrs. Scott-Siddons.
1870	AD's son Leonard born.
15 February 1870	AD's first major success, *Frou-Frou*, adapted from play by Meilhac and Halévy, opened.
1 August 1870	*A Flash of Lightning* produced in England at the Amphitheatre, Leeds.
13 September – 19 November 1870	Second season opened with AD's *Man and Wife*, adapted from Wilkie Collins's novel.
21 November 1870	First London performance of *Lightning* at the Grecian Theatre.
21 December 1870	Presented Bronson Howard's *Saratoga* at Fifth Avenue Theatre.
21 March 1871	AD's *Horizon* produced at the New York Olympic Theatre.
5 September 1871 – 18 March 1872	Opening of third season with AD's *Divorce*, from Trollope's novel *He Knew He Was Right*.
2 April 1872	AD's *Article 47* produced with Clara Morris. Based on play by Adolphe Belot.
26 August 1872	AD's musical spectacle *Le Roi Carotte*, from French operetta of Sardou and Offenbach, produced at Grand Opera House.
3 September 1872	Fourth season opened with Howard's *Diamonds*.
25 November 1872 – 30 January 1873	AD's city spectacle *Round the Clock; or, New York by Dark*, partially based on French vaudeville by Henri Cremieux and Henri Bocage, at the Grand Opera House.
1 January 1873	Daly's uninsured Fifth Avenue Theatre destroyed by fire; immediately leased New York Theatre for two years.
21 January 1873	Temporary Fifth Avenue Theatre opened with AD's *Alixe*, adapted from contemporary French comedy.
18 February 1873	AD's spectacle *Roughing It!* opened at Grand Opera House.
19 August 1873	*A Midsummer Night's Dream* opened the second Grand Opera House season.

Autumn 1873	Financial panic of 1873; AD was building the New Fifth Avenue Theatre and managing the Grand Opera House and Daly's Broadway Theatre. Company went on tour. During this period AD's second son, Francis Augustin (called Austin), was born.
3 December 1873	Opened fifth season at the new Fifth Avenue Theatre at 28th St. and Broadway with *Fortune* by James Albery.
13 December 1873	Gave up Broadway Theatre management.
Early 1874	Withdrew from Grand Opera House management.
21 February – 2 March 1874	Produced *Love's Labour's Lost*, first time ever in New York.
12 September – 10 October 1874	AD's adaptation of *The School for Scandal* staged.
11 January 1875	*The Merchant of Venice* first produced by AD; shortened version with E. L. Davenport.
17 February – 28 June 1875	AD's *The Big Bonanza; or Riches and Matches*, based on *Ultimo* by G. von Moser, first seen. First of numerous German adaptations.
25 October – 10 November 1875	AD engagement of Edwin Booth; opened with *Hamlet*.
14 December 1875	AD's *Pique* opened, based partly on Lean's *Her Lord and Master*.
12 September 1876	Eighth season opened with Bulwer's *Money*, featuring Charles Coghlan.
5 December 1876	Elaborate revival of *School for Scandal*.
15 January 1877	AD's *Lemons; or, Wedlock for Seven*, from Rosen's *Citronen*, staged.
4 September 1877	Ninth season began with AD's *The Dark City*, based on Cogniard and Nicolaie's *Les Compagnons de la Truelle*. Financially unsuccessful and caused AD to give up management on 14 September.
Autumn and Winter 1878 – Spring 1879	AD went to England, France and Italy for a year.
30 April 1879	*L'Assommoir*, based on Zola's novel and the dramatization by Busnach and Gastineau, performed at the Olympic Theatre, New York, with Ada Rehan in small role. Daly may have been involved in adaptation.
17 September 1879	Daly's new theatre, formerly Wood's Museum and then the Broadway, opened as Daly's Theatre; financial support from John Duff.
10 April 1880	AD's *The Way We Live*, from L'Arronge play, staged with John Drew and Ada Rehan first seen in the comic parts for which they would become famous.

18 August 1880	John Duff withdrew support over policy dispute with AD.
4 November 1880 – 15 January 1881	*Needles and Pins* by AD, based on Rosen's *Starke Mitteln*, began the series featuring the 'Big Four': Drew, Rehan, Gilbert, and Lewis.
5 September 1882	Fourth season opened with AD's *Mankind*, adapted from original by Merritt and Conquest.
16 October 1882	British opening of *Pique*, renamed *Only a Woman*, at Theatre Royal, Brighton.
24 February 1883	*Seven-Twenty-Eight*, by AD, from play by F. Von Schoenthan.
2 October 1883	AD's *Dollars and Sense*, from L'Arronge original.
19 July 1884	Daly Company opened at Toole's Theatre, London, with *Seven-Twenty-Eight*.
7 October 1884	Sixth season at Daly's opened with AD's *A Wooden Spoon*, based on play by von Schoenthan.
25 November 1884	*Love on Crutches*, based on Stobitzer original, opened.
5 January 1885	Daly's sons, Austin and Leonard, died of diptheria.
4 March 1885	AD's *A Night Off*, from German play by F. and P. von Schoenthan, premiered.
21 April 1885	Clara Morris appeared in AD's *Denise*, adapted from a play by Dumas fils.
14 January 1886	AD's adaptation of *The Merry Wives of Windsor*, his first Shakespeare in six years; after this, one a year until 1899.
24 February 1886	AD's *Nancy and Company*, from Rosen original, produced.
Summer 1886	AD and company in England.
19 August 1886	First performance in Germany (Hamburg). Moved to Berlin and then to Paris.
September 1886	Company in Liverpool and Dublin.
5 October 1886	Eighth season at Daly's began with AD's *After Business Hours*, adapted from Blumenthal original.
16 November 1886	AD's *Love in Harness*, from French play by Valabrègue.
1 November 1887	AD's *The Railroad of Love*, adapted from German farce.
1888	Publication of AD's *Woffington, A Tribute to the Actress and the Woman* and of *A Portfolio of Players*.
31 January 1888	AD's adaptation of *A Midsummer Night's Dream* presented.
3 May 1888	London season began at the Gaiety with *Railroad of Love*.
29 May – 31 July 1888	AD's *Taming of the Shrew* first seen in London; in August taken to Stratford-upon-Avon.
Late Summer 1888	Company performed at the Vaudeville Theatre, Paris.
9 October 1888	AD's *The Lottery of Love*, from Bisson/Mars original, opened U.S. season.
13 November 1888	*The Undercurrent* by AD opened at Niblo's Garden.

5 February 1889	AD's *An International Match*, from von Schoenthan's *Cornelius Voss*, premiered.
17 December 1889	AD's adaptation of *As You Like It*, with Ada Rehan, presented.
10 June 1890	Company opened in London at the Lyceum with *Seven-Twenty-Eight*.
3 March 1891	AD's *The Prodigal Son*, pantomime from *L'Enfant Prodigue* by M. Carré fils, music by A. Wormser, presented.
31 August 1891	Daly Company's third appearance in Paris.
9 September 1891	Company at the Lyceum, London.
9 February 1892	AD's *Love in Tandem*, from Bocage and de Courcy farce, at Daly's.
17 March 1892	AD's adaptation of Tennyson's *The Foresters*, with music by Sir Arthur Sullivan, presented.
27 June 1893	AD's company opened for a year in London at Daly's Theatre.
2–7 July 1895	Last appearance of the Daly Company at Daly's Theatre, London.
28 January 1896	AD's adaptation, *The Countess Gucki*, from original by F. von Schoenthan and F. Koppel-Ellfeld.
Early Spring 1896	Daly Company at the London Comedy Theatre for six weeks.
Summer 1897	Company toured England.
19 November 1898 – 2 January 1899	Production of AD's last Shakespeare adaptation, *The Merchant of Venice.*
9 February – 7 June 1899	*The Great Ruby*, a melodrama, was the last play presented under AD's management.
13 May 1899	The Dalys and Ada Rehan left for Europe; Daly taken ill on board ship.
7 June 1899	AD died in Paris.
18 June 1899	Daly's funeral at St. Patrick's Cathedral in New York attracted a crowd of 5,000.

A NOTE ON THE TEXTS

The texts in this volume are taken from the published versions privately printed for Augustin Daly. Stage directions have been shortened and standardized; those that seemed overly restrictive for a modern performance have been omitted, where the sense of the action could be retained without them. Descriptions of the stage settings indicate the placement of entrances, windows, furniture, etc., but references to 'flats' and 'backdrops' have been deleted.

Broadway Theatre

Business Manager..W. A. Moo
Stage Manager................Mr. J. Moore. | Conductor.................Mr. W. Withe
Treasurer.. ....H. M. Pray. | Scene Artist...........Mr. G. W. Dayto
Admission ··50 Cents.

Every Evening and Saturday Matinee

A

Flash of Lightning

A DRAMA OF

CITY HEARTH·SIDES AND CITY HEART-ACHES,¹

BY

Mr. AUGUSTIN DALY, Author of " Leah, the Forsaken," " Taming a Butter

fly." " Under the Gaslight." &c., &c.

The Cast of Characters composed of the Best Artists that could be Selected !

Jack Ryver, fresh from Julesbury, on the Pacific Railroad.......................Mr. J. K. MORTIME

Fred. Chauncey, the representative of one of our old families, with a strong disposition
    to raise up a new one—a young heart notwithstanding the antiquity of his blood...Mr. Mc KEE RANKI

Skiffley, of the Metropolitan Detective Police Force, an arm of the law...................Mr. J. CARDE

Mr. Garry Fallon, American by choice, Irish by birth, and the master of his own house.
                                                            Mr. J. H. JAC

Sam Pidge, the gentlemanly and obliging clerk of the Steamer "Daniel Doo," Mr. J. C. WILLIAMSO

Benedetto, the Keeper of an all-night cellar in th First Ward...........................Mr. G. F. BROWN

The Engineer of the Steamer "Daniel Doo".................................Mr. H. RYNA

Terry, from Castle Garden, with an original Song of "The Irish Boy's Return,"..............Mr. STUAR

Bob, one of Uncle Sam's Veterans, on Postal Service....................................Mr. G. JORDA

The Captain of the Steamer "Vonderbilt".......................................Mr. COWA

Patsey, a Savoyard Boy, performing on the First Violin......................Master WILLIE HEAR

Davy, another, performing on the Harp of Eleven strings.............................Master HENR

Ebriosus, a Fireman on a North River Steamer.............................Mr. G. JAME

Ned, a hand on the same..Mr. WILSO

Gammit, a sailor ashore..Mr. PEC

The Nervous Passenger, from the Opposition Boat..............................Mr. EBEKMA

       (Officers of the Metropolitan Force, Passengers, All-Night Lodgers, Savoyard Boys.

Bessie Fallon, the Beauty without Ambition.................................Miss BLANCHE GRE

Rose Fallon, Graduate of the Spinster Institute for Young Ladies on Fifth Avenue. with
    an aim in Life... Miss KITTY BLANCHAR

Mrs. Fallon, the kind-hearted wife of the Greenwich Street Aristocrat...........Mrs. G. H. GILBER

Mrs. Dowderry, with credentials from the Commissioners of Emigration........Miss AMELIA HARRI

Ann, the domestic, whose back was continually broke............................Miss ELLA TURNE

Annie Kemp, one of the spinsters of the Institute.................................Miss CAV

                      Lady Passengers, School Girls, &c., &c.

V   *A Flash of Lightning* program. Broadway Theatre, 10 July 1868

A FLASH OF LIGHTNING

A drama of life in our day, in five acts

First produced at the Broadway Theatre (Late Wallack's), under the management of Mr. Barney Williams, June, 1868.

Dramatis personae and original cast:

MR. GARRY FALLON, American by Choice, Irish by birth, and the master in his own house.	Mr. John Jack
JACK RYVER, Fresh from Julesburg on the Pacific Railroad.	Mr. J. K. Mortimer
FRED. CHAUNCEY, Descendant of an old family – resolved to raise up a new one: a young heart, notwithstanding the antiquity of his blood.	Mr. McKee Rankin
SKIFFLEY, of the Metropolitan Detective Police Force – an arm of the Law.	Mr. Carden
SAM PIDGE, The gentlemanly and obliging clerk of the Steamer Daniel Doo.	Mr. J. C. Williamson
BOB, One of Uncle Sam's Postmen – not to be caught.*	Mr. Geo. C. Jordan
BENEDETTO, The Keeper of an 'All Night' Cellar in the First Ward.	Mr. Geo. F. Brown
TERRY.	Mr. Frank H. Murdock
The ENGINEER of the Steamer Daniel Doo.	Mr. H. C. Tyner
The CAPTAIN of the Steamer Vonderbilt.‡	Mr. Jordan
The NERVOUS PASSENGER from the opposition boat.	Mr. W. H. Beekman
PATSY, a Savoyard boy performing on the First violin.	Master Hearne
DAVY, Another – performing on the Harp of Eleven strings.	———
EBROSIUS, A Fireman on the North River Steamer.‡	Mr. J. Moore
NED, Another.	Mr. Peck

Officers of the Force; Sailors at Benedetto's; Steamboat hands; Passengers; Savoyard boys; Newsboys on the dock; Crowd in final scene; Ned Dowderry.

BESSIE FALLON, The Beauty without Ambition.	Miss Blanche Grey
ROSE FALLON, Graduate of the Spinster Institute for Young Ladies, on Fifth Ave. With an aim in Life.	Miss Kitty Blanchard
MRS. FALLON, The humble wife of the Greenwich St. Aristocrat.	Mrs. G. H. Gilbert

---

five acts: the play is actually in four acts.

* Unnamed in text.   ‡ Does not appear in text.

ANN, The Domestic – whose back was 'contin'ally
    broke'.   Miss Ann Turner
MRS. DOWDERRY, From Castle Garden.   Miss Amelia Harris
SUE EARLIE, One of the Spinsters of the Institute. §   ——
ANNIE KEMP, Another.   ——

Girls at the Institute; Nell Dowderry; Baby Dowderry.

---

§ Called 'Sis Sewell' in text.

ACT I

Scene 1. *The house of* MR. GARRY FALLON, *in Greenwich Street, New York. An apartment on the ground floor. A fire-place with grate and mantle above it at right. On mantle a picture, a clock, and cheap ornaments. At left of scene an enclosed staircase leads to an upper story. An open door at center. Fanlights and sidelights to door; also bolts and lock. A rack at each side of this passage; hats on one, an old coat and shawl hanging on the other. Old-fashioned lamp hanging from the hall ceiling. An opening at right of this passage leads to an apartment in which there is a window looking out upon the street. On window-sill are flower-pots. Old-fashioned furniture about. A low door at left; another door at right.*

At rising of curtain a group of immigrants is discovered partly in the hall-way, and partly in the room. This consists of MRS. DOWDERRY, *an old woman, sitting on a chair;* TERRY, *her son, a young fellow, who is at the back;* TED, *a boy, who carries a* BABY *in his arms, and* NELL, *a small girl. These latter are huddled together, standing; beside them are some boxes and bundles.* ANN, *a raw servant-maid, is crossing stage from the door at left to the fire, which she fills with coal from a scuttle that she has brought in.*

ANN: (*Stops and turns toward immigrants.*) An' th' Missis told ye to come here herself?

MRS. D: She did, herself.

ANN: Where did she find ye's?

MRS. D: We were standing at the street-corner, for all the world like a flock ov geese on a road turnin' – not knowin' whether to go on, go back, sit down or stand still, and the very legs droppin' off us, we were that tired.

ANN: (*Brushes the hearth and rakes fire.*) Ah, poor craythurs! (*Stops.*) Sure, ye're not long over?

MRS. D: We came from shipboard only yesterday.

ANN: Look at that now! But it's green ye are. (*Goes on working.*)

MRS. D: An' how long must we be in Ameriky till we wear th' green off?

ANN: That depinds. Some wear it on a mortal time. Some drop it aisy, aisy like, till ye'd niver know. There's Missis now! Mrs. Fallon!

MRS. D: The Lord be good to her; she's got a kind heart.

ANN: She has the green in it, though her two eyes niver saw the land it grows in. She does be always bringin' in th' poor immigrants, and giving thim a bite and a sup, although my master, Misther Garry Fallon –

MRS. D: (*with effusion*) Ah! The saints make his bed in glory!

ANN: Do ye know him, now?

MRS. D: No, sure.

ANN: Thin don't ye trouble yerself to make his bed, till ye know where he's going to lie.

> (*The hall door opens and* MRS. FALLON *enters. She is dressed very neatly and has a basket on her arm, as if just from market; also an umbrella.* MRS. D. *goes towards her, and all curtsey.*)

By the Civil War there were 1,700,000 Irish immigrants in the U.S.

MRS. F: Well, good folks, you *did* come! I'm right glad. Here, Ann, take the basket. And there's the baby! Bright as a new pin! Stop, Ann! (*Takes apple from basket and gives it to child.*) Have you given them something to eat. (*Takes off bonnet and shawl.*)

ANN: Yes'm. (*Takes basket to table in apartment at right.*)

MRS. F: Has Mr. Fallon gone out yet?

ANN: No'm.

MRS. F: Oh, well! Go up very quietly and bring down that bundle of clothes, those old trowsers and things, in my room. But be careful he doesn't see you.

ANN: (*Takes scuttle of coal and goes toward staircase.*) All right'm! But you know, he's a deep 'un. (*Exits up staircase.*)

TERRY: Sure, ma'am, it's an angel ye are, and I hope I may yet be able to repay you for your kindness to my old mother and the children.

MRS. D: Ah! But this Ameriky is heaven's own spot, ma'am, and there's no denyin' it. An' sure there's a place made ready in Albany state for Terry, and sure he'll arn enough to kape us all, and wid the blessin' of heaven he'll be an alderman yet.

MRS. F: Industry will do everything here. My husband was very poor once, but he set his face to making money, and has succeeded. And yet, don't let that be your only aim in life. In the race for riches, happiness is the first thing we leave behind.

        (ANN *comes down precipitately, but triumphantly, with a bundle.*)

ANN: (*out of breath*) Here they are, ma'am, and he never saw me once.

MRS. F: (*Gives the bundle to* MRS. D.) Take these and fix them to suit your wants. You'll find something even for the baby, for dear little baby. (*Takes its face in her hands.*) It is so much like my Bessie was a little while ago, and now she's as big as me.

MRS. D: Bessie, ma'am? That's your youngest?

MRS. F: Yes.

MRS. D: And you love her best, ov coorse. What mother of us doesn't? and the reason is because the *youngest* reminds us so much of the first.

        (FALLON *appears at stairs, slowly and suspiciously. He pauses, puts on glasses and looks at group.*)

ANN: Whist, ma'am!

FALLON: (*quietly but sharply*) What's this?

MRS. F: Only a family just landed, Garry. I found them homeless in the street.

FAL: (*to immigrants*) Hem! you've been fed, I suppose. You look it. Well, if my wife thinks our money ought to go and support strangers, I suppose it can't be helped.

MRS. F: Surely we have plenty, Garry; and you know *we* were poor once.

FAL: Exactly; and having had enough of poverty for a lifetime, I don't choose to be beggared again. What's that they've got tied up in your apron there?

MRS. F: Some old clothes which I have given away.

FAL: Given away! and there's Moriarty round the corner stands ready to pay cash down for them. You *are* a blessed fool, and no mistake.

MRS. D: (*blustering up*) An' it would be a chape bargain for you if you could be blessed yoursel' at th' price of being' a fool, Misther Fallon.

FAL: What's that?

> (MRS. F. *motions for* MRS. D. *to be quiet.* TERRY *and the children pluck at her gown to restrain her. She advances a step, highly inflamed.*)

MRS. D: Mebbe you're proud bekase you come over before us and had the first pickings of the counthry, Misther Fallon. Sure that's always the way. The Merrykins axes us to come over, and it's our own that tries to walk over us when we get here.

FAL: Your own? You don't call me your own, I hope?

MRS. D: Don't I! Isn't it a Fallon of Kerry you are? Sure I know it, for the Fallons of Kerry – bad luck to 'em! – would scrape a shilling on both sides before they paid it out for one an' sixpence worth ov mate any day.

FAL: Well, are you going to stay here all day?

MRS. D: Faith, now we've seen you we're willing to go.

MRS. F: Garry, do be gentle with the poor creature.

FAL: Gentle! and they insulting me in my own house, on the strength of my own bread and mate!

MRS. D: (*ironically*) Mate! Ha! ha! Look at the rich Amerykin, wid his tell-tale brogue! *Mate!* Sure I'd be ashamed, though I've just landed, to say *mate* when I meant *mate!*

FAL: (*flaming*) Ann!

> (*Enter* ANN *from right.*)

FAL: Open that street door! (ANN *flies to obey.*) Now you get out! and if you meet any of your friends don't advise them to come here. (*All edge their way along the passage.*) I mean to keep a dog that hates Irish, to bite 'em.

MRS. D: (*bitterly*) A dog that hates Irish! th' best ye can get is one that was born Irish but has got fat on Amerykin scraps, he'll bite 'em.

FAL.: (*passionately*) Will you get out! or I'll –

> (SKIFFLEY *appears at hall door. He looks at group, and then comes forward impudently. Dressed flashily; red side whiskers and goatee.*)

SKIF: Hallo, Fallon! what's the trouble? Who are these? Some of your relations from the old country – heard you got rich – come to share!

FAL: (*to immigrants*) Here's an officer, if you don't get out he'll arrest you.

MRS. D: (*quietly*) I'm going, sir! Come, childer! The blessin' ov heaven on you, ma'am! (*Exit group, center door.* MRS. F. *takes basket from table and exits right.*)

SKIF: Irish relations rather troublesome, eh?

FAL: I have no Irish relations.

SKIF: Oh, come now! Where were you born?

FAL: That was accidental. My wife's American, my daughters are American, and my *dollars* are American.

SKIF: O, blow nationality when you talk of money and pretty girls; they are of no country; they are gifts from the other world, falling to every clime, like the dew (*relapsing*), only not so plentifully, I'm sorry to say.

FAL: (*grimly*) I think not. You're not over flush yourself, young fellow. How does your new profession suit you? Let's see! you're on the police, ain't you? I think that when I told you last month I'd sooner see my Bessie blind, lame and ugly, than your wife, you said you had an opening in the force, or something.

SKIF: Yes, I'm on the Detective force.

FAL: What do they pay you?

SKIF: Oh, the salary's nothing. That wouldn't wash my shirts. It's the *chances* that foot up. You see, I am detailed to work up a case. I do it – slowly. The anxious party, who is interested, quickens me with a little present: I work like a horse. By and bye – dead stop – stand still: insurmountable obstacle. Anxious party comes down again, and I surmount the *in*surmountable, discover wonders. Just at the climax of discovery, I report an impassable difficulty; he comes down again, and I pass the impassable.

FAL: But suppose the anxious party don't come down?

SKIF: Then I treat him as a mean-spirited hunks. I sell out to the party I'm detailed to watch; he does the handsome, and I report that I can't surmount the insurmountable, nor pass the impassable, so the game goes up.

FAL: I congratulate you – you'll make your fortune.

SKIF: And when I do, I'll come back to a certain kind parent that I know, tell him I've got a snug little sum, and – ha! ha! – and ask him for his daughter again.
(MRS. F. *appears in the room from the right.*)

FAL: And he'll tell you, he'll see you and your fortune in – !

SKIF: That'll do! Don't say it out!

FAL: The fact is, I don't sell anything in my house. I wouldn't sell you the old cat in the kitchen.

SKIF: But why? What puzzles me is – why you refuse me when I ask for Bessie – when it's common gossip that you don't care a cent for the girl, and that Rose is your favorite.

FAL: Does that puzzle you? Well, I'm rich enough to indulge in puzzles.

MRS. F: (*Comes forward.*) Why not tell him your reason, Garry, and not let Mr. Skiffley suppose you have none. (*to* SKIF.) Bessie has been promised long ago.

FAL: (*quickly*) No, she hasn't – if you mean young Ryver!

MRS. F: I *do* mean young Ryver.

FAL: I never promised him.

MRS. F: He understood it so. You said that night, no man should have your daughter 'till he earned her, and Jack started the next day with all he had in the world – the clothes on his back – to try his fortune at the West. You know he wrote us he had been employed on the railroad, and that every mile of it was so much in his pocket. Don't act like a monster, and break his heart when he comes back.

FAL: A man that works on the railroad gets too precious tough, to break anything about him easily. You believe Jack Ryver will come back rich? *I* don't. In the first place, he loves company too much, then he loves liquor too much.

MRS. F: Now, Garry, don't say another word! It was you that first asked him to drink, and then laughed at him, because his head was too light to stand it.

hunks: foreign laborer.

FAL: (*as if relishing the recollection*) Ha! Ha! Ha! You should have seen him, Skiffley! A perfect infant in liquor.

SKIF: Where is he now?

MRS. F: When we last heard of him, he was at Julesburg, on the Pacific Railroad.

SKIF: Julesburg is a good place for a young man who is fond of company. But where is Miss Bessie, and how is Miss Rose?

FAL: Rose! Aha! She's coming home to-day. She's done with schooling. She's learned all they can teach her: French on the tip of her tongue, pianner at the ends of her fingers, arithmetic in her head, and her eyes a geography where you can see worlds mapped out! I've spent a power o' money on that gal, but she's worth every cent of it as she stands. I love her like – like a man will love, that's saved up his affections for twenty years, to lay it out in one investment. (*Looks at clock.*) Why, Mary! Look at the time! She ought to be here now.

SKIF: Well, she'd better get under cover soon, if you don't want your favorite drenched. There's a big storm brewing.

FAL: (*to* MRS. F.) Has she got an umbrella?

MRS. F: (*Goes to door to look out.*) You know, she never will carry one.

FAL: I recollect! She told me that everything about a young lady should be in harmony; her hat, her boots, her gloves – but an umbrella never harmonizes. Why the devil can't they invent harmonious umbrellas! Mary, get me my coat.
(MRS. F. *takes it off hook and comes toward him.*)

SKIF: Well, I'll be off. Going my way?

FAL: Which way is that?

SKIF: Up.

FAL: No!

SKIF: By the way, I've an errand down too.

FAL: (*abruptly*) I'm going across.

SKIF: Oh, very well; good morning! (*Goes to door and opens it; it is immediately slammed by the wind. Wind is heard.*) Phew! it's blowing up! (*Exits center door.*)

FAL: (*Gets his coat on, assisted by* MRS. F.) That girl will get wet.

MRS. F: Perhaps some one will see her home. You know Mr. Chauncey has come with her two or three times.

FAL: (*Stops short.*) Did he ever come in?

MRS. F: Oh yes; he's been quite friendly; once or twice he came in and had a chat with us.

FAL: With whom?

MRS. F: Bessie, Rose and me.

FAL: He's a rich fellow – very rich, and one of the old sort – aristocratic! So he comes home with old Fallon's daughter, eh? to Greenwich street! He's smitten with her, damned if he ain't! Warn't I right to send her to the aristocratic school where she'd get in with that kind? He's smitten – he's a gone aristocrat! damn him! he's a sensible fellow! 'None of your high blood for me!' that's

---

Julesburg: small Colorado town near the Nebraska border.

what he says. I like him already. (*suddenly*) You never told him I was one of his father's porters once, did you?

MRS. F: (*brushing coat*) I told him nothing.

FAL: That's right! not that I'm ashamed of it, but he might be. Come, hurry with that brushing. I'm going for that gold chain I ordered for Rose. Wait till *he* sees that! Solid gold! I told the jeweller to have the weight stamped on it.

MRS. F: You never buy anything for Bessie.

FAL: Why should I? she never asks for anything – spiritless, vulgar little toad; she'd never bring a rich man's son home after her.

MRS. F: She'd be frightened at the thought of any one speaking to her, unless she met him at her own home.

FAL: How's Rose to get into society if she don't scrape into it herself! I don't know any, you don't know any, and I want her to rise – she's made for it. (*going, then stops*) You bring up Bessie your way – your vulgar, grubbing way; but I tell you one thing, you don't bring any vulgar grubs here to court her. Rose shan't have to be ashamed of any brother-in-law, that's flat! (*Exits center door; slams; wind heard.*)

MRS. F: Oh, dear, dear! who would be a mother? Where's Bessie?

(BESSIE *appears above on stairs.*)

BESSIE: Here, mother! (*She comes down; has her dress tucked up behind, hand- kerchief tied on head, broom in hand.*) I've been sweeping Rose's room, and fixing it just as papa would like to see it on her birthday. (*Kisses her mother.*)

MRS. F: Then make haste and fix yourself; you know he hates to see you that way.

BESSIE: It plagues him, and I rather like that. He insists that it is very low and vul- gar, not a bit like Rosie's style.

MRS. F: I declare, I don't blame your father!

BESSIE: Now, mother! I didn't expect that of *you*. (*trying to kiss her*)

MRS. F: Don't be foolish. You don't please your father, and you ought to. Look at the presents he gives Rose, and you might have just as good, if you liked.

BESSIE: But I don't want them.

MRS. F: That's the very thing that angers him. You ought to try and make believe you do.

BESSIE: Well, ma, you may think it right to trick father out of his affection, but it's not needed.

MRS. F: Ah! I'm afraid you are building too many hopes on Jack's return – that's the trouble.

BESSIE: No, I'm not. I never think of Jack (*turning aside*) at least, not in the way you suppose.

MRS. F: Why do you change color, Bessie? You are not forgetting the poor fellow, are you?

BESSIE: Please don't ask me anything, mamma. Don't speak to me of Jack any more.

MRS. F: Why? you haven't found another you love better?

BESSIE: (*pleadingly placing her hand on her mother's arm*) Don't ask me.

MRS. F: Daughter! it's not doing the right thing to let the lad go off full of hopes, to risk life and limb in gaining a few dollars to marry with, and then turn your back on him when he comes to claim you.

BESSIE: When Jack comes to claim me, I shall satisfy him, mamma! I will speak
    to him, and tell him –

MRS. F: Tell him what?

BESSIE: What I have to tell him, and what he must hear.

MRS. F: (*solemnly*) Bessie, child! pause before you trifle with a good man's heart.

BESSIE: O, mother, promise me one thing – promise that you will not forsake me!
    Don't ask me to marry at all. Let me live with you, that is all; let us two live
    one life together! (*Throws herself on her mother's shoulder.*)

        (*Rumbling of wheels heard outside. The scene grows gradually
        darker from this time. ANN runs in from right.*)

ANN: There they are, ma'am. Miss Rose an' the illigent gintleman. He's brought
    her home in a grand coach.

MRS. F: Quick! let them in! (ANN *opens the door; a carriage is seen in the street.*)
    Bessie, dry your eyes – go to the fire!

        (BESSIE *goes to mantle.* FRED CHAUNCEY *assists* ROSE *from
        carriage, and both enter. Wind strong; door slams, pulling* ANN
        with it.*)

MRS. F: I hope you did not get wet?

FRED: (*at fire*) Oh, it don't rain yet, but we'll have a storm presently. (MRS. F.
    offers him a chair.)

ROSE: Somebody do take off my things! (ANN *comes forward.*) Go away, you
    dirty thing! Bessie, why don't you help me? I'm sure it's the least you can
    do. (*Her mother offers.*) Oh, ma! you are so clumsy! (BESSIE *comes for-
    ward.*)

FRED: (*Rises.*) Sister Bessie looks sad to-day. (*He puts out his hand;* BESSIE *takes
    it after hesitation, her face averted.*)

ROSE: Bessie, something's caught my hat, do unfasten it. (BESSIE *assists* ROSE.)

MRS. F: Dinner is waitin' for you, dear.

ROSE: Don't say *waitin'*, ma! Waiting, mind your *G's*. I don't want any dinner.

MRS. F: Don't want any dinner! why, my dear, your papa –

ROSE: Where is pa? Oh yes, out, I suppose. I'm so sorry, Mr. Chauncey, you'd like
    papa.

MRS. F: Oh, yes, for Mr. Fallon likes you, Mr. Chauncey, very much.

FRED: (*coolly*) Does he, really? What a good sort of soul he must be.

BESSIE: Oh, no; he isn't that sort of soul at all. He don't like every one.

FRED: Better and better! Then I'm an exceptional favorite, I declare! I regret his
    absence exceedingly. How long is he likely to be gone?

MRS. F: Only a little while. He's went to get a surprise for Rose.

ROSE: (*aside to* MRS. F.) He's *went*!! Do, for goodness sake, speak correctly, ma!
    Don't say, he's *went* – say he has *gone*. (*aloud*) What is the surprise, ma?

MRS. F: Oh, I wouldn't dare to tell you. Wait till your father reveals it himself. But
    I must go and look after dinner. Excuse me, Mr. Chauncey. Perhaps you'll
    stay and dine with us.

FRED: You are very kind. But I fear, I will intrude.

ANN: Oh, no, you won't intrude. Sure, we've sot an extra plate for ye, Sir. (*Great
    embarrassment;* FRED *eyes* ANN *with glass.*)

MRS. F: Ann, go to the kitchen, this instant! (*Exits right, driving* ANN.)

ROSE: (*Rises, petulantly.*) Oh, pshaw! What's the use of waiting? Pa isn't here. Besides, I have to go to Sis Sewell's, and invite her to come to my party to-morrow. Do you want to go? You can, if you promise to be good. Just wait 'till I get my black jockey. I don't want to ruin this hat. (*Goes left.*)

BESSIE: I'll get the hat for you, Rose. (*Takes bonnet from* ROSE *and exits up stair-case.* FRED *looks after her with admiration. She glances back as she is dis-appearing.*)

ROSE: Don't look too hard at the room, Mr. Chauncey. I've begged pa 'till I'm tired, to move to one of his up-town houses, but he *will* live here.

FRED: (*still looking off*) I can't suffer you to decry the casket that contains such a jewel.

ROSE: I declare, that's the first pretty compliment I ever heard in this house.

FRED: What an unimpressible set of visitors you must have had then.

ROSE: We haven't had any.

FRED: No beaux?

ROSE: No.

FRED: And your father's friends?

ROSE: Bless you, he hasn't any. When he does invite any gentlemen here, the next thing we know, he puts them in jail.

FRED: That's the most remarkable instance of close friendship I ever heard of.

ROSE: It's not friendship, it's debt. (FRED *laughs.*) Funny, isn't it? But he took a fancy once to a young man who saved our house, when there was a fire next door.

FRED: A fireman, eh? That's the stuff for a hero.

ROSE: Oh, Jack wasn't a bit of a hero; he used to get his hair singed off regularly once a month, going into blazing buildings after babies and other things that people forgot to throw out of the windows. And you know, heroes never have their hair singed off.

FRED: No, their fiery dispositions don't often affect them that way.

ROSE: Well, Jack used to come here and be funny for us by the hour. At last they began to put out fires with horses instead of men, and he went out West to seek his fortune; and now he's doing something to the Pacific Ocean.

FRED: Bless me! that's bad for the Ocean.

ROSE: No! no! not the Ocean – the Pacific Railroad. He's fireman on the railroad. I wonder what they want a fireman for on a railroad! Is there anything to put out on a railroad?

FRED: Nothing but the passengers, I suppose. Perhaps he has to rush in and save the sleepers on the road.

ROSE: Oh, you tease! So you see, having no friends here, pa sent me to the Insti-tute.

FRED: An admirable resort – for there a girl acquires the art of adding to her acquaintances, subtracting from her timidity, multiplying her accomplish-ments, and dividing her time between dress, deportment and love.

ROSE: You torment.

FRED: I'd like to get an idea of the rudiments of love.

ROSE: Nothing easier. As to the geography of love – it is bounded by marriage; has two capitals – a house in town and a country seat; its principal productions: jealousies, elopements, and the Divorce Court!

FRED: You'd make an excellent master. What will you charge for a course of lessons?

ROSE: Terms cash, payable at the commencement of the course – in *gold*! (*Holds up ring-finger, then laughs heartily. BESSIE comes down stairs with hat.*) Here's my hat. Where's the glass? Of course, I ought to know better than look for any conveniences here! I suppose, I must go up-stairs to see myself. I'll be down in a minute, Fred. (*She takes the hat and runs up stair-case. BESSIE has arranged her own dress.*)

FRED: Why, how charming you look.

BESSIE: Rose is the belle, Mr. Chauncey, and has a right to all the flattery.

FRED: Exactly, and that which is not flattery belongs to Bessie. Admiration, sincere, and true, this belongs to Bessie.

BESSIE: Ah, sir, I don't seek them, indeed. They are making Rose for praise and admiration. I'm to be contented here. I fear it is because I seem so confused and ignorant that you take pity on me.

FRED: Why, human nature is like a harp: touch it with a bold and hardy finger, and it answers boldly; but press it with a timid hand, and it is gentle too. (*Takes her hand.*) This is the timid hand evokes the kindness you wonder at.

ROSE: (*above*) I shan't be long.

FRED: (*Starts.*) Rose! (*quickly, to* BESSIE) Can you keep a secret if I tell you one?

BESSIE: O, I fear –

FRED: There's no time now; but when you are alone you'll find it here. (*Gives her letter enclosing a pair of jewelled ear-rings.*) Quick, hide it!

BESSIE: Hide it, why?

FRED: What! a secret, and not hidden?

> (FRED *goes quickly to fire-place and assumes an indifferent air.*
> BESSIE *hides the letter, as* ROSE *comes down.*)

ROSE: Now we're ready. Bessie, tell pa I'll be back soon.

> (*She goes to front door;* FRED *follows her, turns, presses his fingers upon his lips to* BESSIE. ROSE *opens the door; as she does so a flash of lightning almost dazzles her. She starts back with a scream.*)

FRED: Had you not better defer the call?

ROSE: No, I'm not afraid of a little rain.

> (ANN *enters from right as the door is opened again; wind heard loud, and* ROSE *and* FRED *exit, shutting the door.* ANN *takes off shoe and flings it at door. The carriage is heard to drive off.*)

ANN: Good luck go wid yee's both!

BESSIE: O, Ann, how you startled me!

ANN: They'll meet wid some kind of luck in such a storm as is comin' up. Faith, the sky is like a great cloud ov smoke on all sides. (BESSIE *goes to fire-place.*) Sure there's something the matter wid you, Miss Bessie! (*a flash*)

BESSIE: No! go away, Ann, leave me!

> (*Thunder heard.* MRS. F. *enters from right.*)

MRS. F: Ann, come up stairs and close the windows, the rain is falling now. It will be a fearful storm. (ANN *exits up stairs.*) I wish your father were home. Hurry, Ann!

> (*The thunder rumbles low. MRS. F. exits up stairs. A furious ring at the bell heard, and BESSIE is running to open the door. FALLON flings it open, and dashes in, shutting it quickly; his umbrella is torn, and he has lost his hat. BESSIE closes the door.*)

FAL: (*Comes forward.*) Phew! curse the wind. Spoiled me an umbrella I've had for nine years, and lost me a hat.

BESSIE: Father, the door won't catch, what's the matter?

FAL: I suppose I've spoiled the lock in my cursed rage. I broke the key; put a chair against it. (*He kicks one towards her.*) War'nt that Rose went away in a carriage?

BESSIE: Yes, sir.

FAL: (*angrily*) What the devil did you let her go for?

BESSIE: (*surprised*) Why, father –

FAL: Don't answer me! You envious little wretch. Look at this! (*Takes case from pocket, and displays an enormous gold chain.*) Feast your eyes on it, you jealous little devil. It's hers. You shan't put me out of conceit with her by your sly dodges. Did that young fellow come with her?

BESSIE: Yes, sir.

FAL: Grind your teeth at that, too! She'll have a rich young spark, while you'll content yourself with a devilish poor mechanic. Where's your mother?

BESSIE: (*Turns slowly away.*) Up stairs, sir, in Rosie's room.

FAL: Then I'll go up and put this on her table, so it shall be the first thing she sets her eyes on when she enters. Ha, ha! my little queen! but there's gold enough here (*kissing the chain*) to make a crown for you! (*Calls at foot of stair-case.*) Mary!

> (MRS. F. *appears at the head.*)

MRS. F: Well?

FAL: Come down and get dinner. I won't wait any longer.

> (MRS. F. *descends;* FALLON *goes up and exits.*)

MRS. F: (*crossing stage*) Ain't you coming to dinner, Bessie?

BESSIE: No, father doesn't want to see me.

MRS. F: You'll wear my life out with this constant worry. (BESSIE *sits by the fire, her head resting on one hand.*) Moping there like a child. (*Exits right.*)

BESSIE: Oh! if I hadn't this! (*Takes letter from her pocket and presses it to her bosom.*) It weighs so heavy!

FAL: (*above*) There, just the thing! (*Appears, pushing ANN before him. She comes down and crosses stage, he after her.*) Go to the kitchen! I don't trust anybody that's poor; it's expecting too much of 'm. (ANN *exits right.*) There's too much money in that chain, and it's easy carried off. (*Stops a moment to look at* BESSIE, *then exits right.*)

> (*The lightning flashes, and there is a louder roll of thunder. The wind and rain heard.*)

BESSIE: His face changed, when he gave me this. Why, there's something in it.

What can it be? (*Opens and takes out pair of ear-rings.*) Jewels! (*disappointedly*) A birthday present for Rose. Everything is for Rose, and I – (*Wind heard. She reads letter by light of fire.*) 'Dear Bessie: Keep these little jewels; I chose them for you.' For me! (*delighted*) 'If you do not dare to wear them openly, put them on when alone, and say to yourself, they are the offering of a sincere and loving friend.' (*Rises.*) They are for me, and not for Rose! I, too, have my gifts, my jewels, my friends. All are not harsh to me. One, at least, thinks of me. (*Kisses the jewels.*) Oh, you darlings! They sparkle like his glance. Yes, I will wear you. (*Looks around.*) I am alone.

> (*As she puts the ear-rings on, the chair is pushed away from the door and it opens. JACK RYVER enters quietly. Sees BESSIE. Starts. Replaces the chair; comes forward and watches her as she fastens in the jewels.*)

JACK: Bessie!

BESSIE: (*Turns.*) Jack! (*She seems overcome with emotion and surprise.*)

JACK: (*cheerily*) Why, Bessie, darling! you never expected me, did you? Here I am, come nine hundred miles on a run to surprise you. (*Holds out his hands. She goes to him constrainedly. He does not seem to notice it, and draws her to him, then holds her off.*) Handsomer than ever. Fatter, too, and just the sort of angel to meet on entering that paradise – a home!

BESSIE: You, Jack – returned! I thought –

JACK: (*gaily, standing by fire and shaking hat*) You thought I was on the wilds of the West with the snorting locomotives, didn't you? Bless your heart, I've slept with 'em, ate with 'em, and played with 'em, until I'm sort of locomotive myself. Don't I act as if I had a full head of steam on? Phew! what a storm. (*Loosens a wrapper from his neck.*) It's gathering again, and we'll have some damage done, or I'm no prophet. How are the old folks?

BESSIE: Father and mother are well.

JACK: Don't call them! I shan't show myself *now*! The old boy would laugh at me! 'This your riches?' he'd say. By Jingo! I'd have to come back in a coach to make *him* glad to see me. I know him. No, I only came to see you; to tell you that I'm fighting for money, and I'm bound to win!

BESSIE: Poor Jack! poor Jack!

JACK: Not a bit of it. Why, Bessie, I would have been a rich man now, if it wasn't for – what do you suppose? – if it wasn't for you.

BESSIE: For me, Jack?

JACK: Just listen. You know out West where I've been, on the borders of the world, *I* think the people are not the sort of people you see here. I don't believe there's a decent fellow among 'em. No homes, no love, no women! – and where there's not a woman, men are no more than brutes. Cheating, swindling, murder! I've had ten thousand dollars offered me just to look out one door in the mail train, while a few honest fellows were busy at the other.

BESSIE: Oh, Jack, and you?

JACK: I thought of you, darling, and kicked 'em out. Then they bullied me. Ha! ha! that wouldn't do with a New Yorker, would it? But they *did* get a pop at me after all. I was stretched out by a revolver slug, but I thought of you and got over *that*! Give me a kiss, Bessie! only one – just to make up for it. (BES-SIE *averts her head.*) Why, Bessie! Look at me, Bessie! Have I come back too soon – or have I come back *too late*?

BESSIE: Jack!

JACK: Have you had time to forget me?

BESSIE: (*trying to smile*) Why, you saw I had not forgotten you.

JACK: Your eyes remembered me – that's true. But I fear your heart is strange.

BESSIE: (*head down*) No, my heart is not strange.

JACK: (*Takes her hand.*) But you don't look at me.

BESSIE: (*Looks up.*) I'm not afraid to do so.

JACK: (*Drops her hand.*) Who spoke of fear? Bessie, don't be hard on me, because I'm poor still. I know I promised to come back rich, and fit to wed you; but that was a rash promise: *I* learned it soon enough. Those that have the dollars, keep them with a closed hand. I couldn't force them – that's dishonest. But I'll toil yet – and toil 'till the fingers loosen of themselves and drop the money into mine. Just say it's all right – say you haven't changed –

> (BESSIE *turns aside, and with both hands motions him away.* JACK *sees the jewels and points to them.*)

JACK: Who gave you those?

BESSIE: (*Covers her ears with hands.*) These?

JACK: I feared it. Your father gave you the choice between Jack Ryver and a hand-ful of jewels, and I went cheap. Oh, your father knew his own blood.

BESSIE: You wrong him – he did not give them – (*Checks herself.*)

JACK: No! Who did? (*She retreats.*) You shall answer me.

> (*Catches her arm. Lightning flashes and the thunder rumbles dis-tantly.* BESSIE *shrinks at* JACK*'s feet.*)

BESSIE: Oh, Jack, have pity; you frighten me!

JACK: You will not give his name?

BESSIE: You must not ask me!

JACK: Farewell! (*going*)

BESSIE: At least forgive me!

JACK: (*Lifts her up.*) I do forgive you! (*Presses her forehead and takes one of the jewels secretly from her ear.*) But not him. Good-bye! and if you wish to think of me, remember what I might have been – an honest man! What I shall be, is your work.

> (*Rushes to the door. Fearful flash of lightning and instantaneous peal of thunder.* BESSIE *falls on her knees.* JACK, *about to go to door, darts back and flies up staircase, dropping the jewel near door at center, as* ROSE *enters.* FALLON *and* MRS. F. *and* ANN *run in from right, all simultaneously; but no one sees* JACK.)

ROSE: (*Throws herself in* FALLON*'s arms.*) O, pa.

FAL: Rose, my pet!

MRS. F: (*Crosses to* BESSIE.) Bessie, dear!

ANN: Sure we'll all be murdered by the thunder.

FAL: Bah! it's all over in a second. What a precious flock of fools you are. (*ten-derly*) There! (*Places* ROSE *in chair by fire, then crossly to* BESSIE, *who is weeping in her mother's arms.*) Now look at that! one would suppose she never saw a storm before.

ROSE: (*Laughs.*) It's all over now; but I was scared; I would come home in the cars, and had to run from the corner. Well, pa! don't look so cross. Where's my present? I'm dying to see it!

FAL: Ah, you rogue! kiss me! Wait a moment! and I'll make your eyes dance. (*Goes up staircase.*)

MRS. F: Why, Bessie, darling, you are trembling and feverish. You have been crying.

(ANN *tries to shut door.*)

BESSIE: O, mother, I'm so miserable.

(FALLON *is heard to cry out* 'Damnation!' *All start, and look towards him as he comes down staircase with the empty jewelcase in hand.*)

FAL: I've been robbed – it's gone!

ALL: Robbed!

(SKIFFLEY *appears in center doorway, pushing* ANN *aside.*)

FAL: I placed it on the table up there! the case has been torn open; the chain is stolen.

MRS. F: Nonsense! who could have done it – who knew of it?

FAL: No one! I placed it there myself; yes, Bessie, you saw me. You have been here ever since.

(BESSIE *almost faints, as he advances toward her.*)

MRS. F: She is going to fall.

(*As* MRS. F. *is going to catch* BESSIE, FALLON *pushes her aside and clutches the girl's arm.*)

FAL: Stop! Answer me! You were here! Where is the chain?

BESSIE: (*aside, with deep emotion*) O, Jack! God forgive you!

FAL: Answer me! has any one been here?

BESSIE: No one.

FAL: It's a lie!

ROSE: (*Steps forward.*) O, father!

FAL: (*Waves her back.*) This is no business of yours; if no one was here, *you* must have the chain. Come, give it up!

MRS. F: You shall not speak to her in that way!

FAL: Silence! she is my child, and I have the right.

MRS. F: And she is *my* child, and I have some right. Bessie, darling!

SKIF: (*Advances.*) I beg pardon! take care how you step, or we shall have this pretty jewel crushed! (*Picks up the ear-ring, which* JACK *had dropped in his exit.*) I suppose it's yours, Miss Rose.

ROSE: I never saw it before.

SKIF: Ah, it is Miss Bessie's then. The mate is in her ear. (*Advances to give it.*)

FAL: (*to* BESSIE, *taking jewel from* SKIFFLEY) Where did you get these? You won't answer? (*Turns round heatedly.*) I hope you are satisfied. She is a thief. But we know how to deal with those people. Skiffley!

SKIF: (*briskly*) Enough said! you give her in my charge?

MRS. F: For heaven's sake, Garry, what are you about to do?

FAL: She has brought it on herself!

ROSE: Father have some mercy!

FAL: Well, I will have some mercy. Let her give me back the chain, or find a home there! (*Points to street.*)

CURTAIN

ACT II

Scene 1. *Fifth Avenue, near the Spinster Institute. On left is the Institute; on right is part of Reservoir railings, garden, and lamp-post with letter-box.* MRS. FALLON *and* ROSE *enter right.*

ROSE: There, don't come any farther, ma. You know, I don't want to have you seen by the girls at the school.

MRS. F: Yes, dear. But you will return home, won't you? You won't desert your sister and me at this cruel time?

ROSE: The fact is, ma, I'm disgusted. I don't mind the chain, but I hoped to have had such a nice birthday-party; and now I've got to make apologies to all the girls I've invited. It's too mean of pa. What shall I tell them? What can I tell them?

MRS. F: Tell them the truth, dear, it's easy.

ROSE: Tell them the truth! Excuse me, ma – but you must be crazy.

MRS. F: Why, you can tell them that somebody broke into the house and stole the chain.

ROSE: For them to laugh at me? Why, if those aristocratic girls had half their houses emptied by thieves, they'd never think of disappointing their friends. It looks so mean in pa – that's what troubles me. Why should he go on so?

MRS. F: You know, his rage is always ungovernable when opposed; and now he believes Bessie is defying him.

ROSE: Oh, it's always the way; just as I try to rise – to get on some sort of footing with better people – something happens; pa gets into a passion – down tumbles my plan, and I've got to go to work again to build another. It's hateful. I've got to tell fourteen girls that they needn't come to-night. Ugh! it looks so cheap.

MRS. F: Oh, Rose, dear, try and forget your own troubles in poor Bessie's. If she doesn't manage to have the chain back today, she sleeps to-night with strangers. Your father is merciless.

ROSE: Then why don't she and you do what any person of sense would – tell pa what she told you and me – that it must have been Jack, and then let the police ferret him out.

MRS. F: No. Bessie told us that under a solemn pledge of secrecy, and said, Jack must not be harmed. There is something that we do not understand. She accuses herself, too, as the cause of all the trouble.

ROSE: Well, ma, I'm going to stay in school all the week, 'till the trouble's over. I'm sorry Jack took the chain – I'm sorry for Bessie, if she caused him to take it. (*Takes letter from pocket and goes toward letter-box, and drops it in as she speaks. At the same moment* SKIFFLEY *appears, unseen by the others. He is wholly changed in appearance, being made up to represent a soldier-messenger.*) And I'm sorry that I should have had a birthday, so that pa should have got a chain for Jack to take. Ha! ha! it's so like the house that Jack built, that I must laugh, though I suppose I ought to cry.

MRS. F: For heaven's sake, Rose, don't be so heartless.

ROSE: Heartless! Who ever heard of one's heart existing for one's sister! I thought that was to be reserved for one's beaux.

MRS. F: I won't hear anything more of beaux. I knew, some judgement would come upon us for having you try to marry above your station. That young man shan't come to the house again, mind that!

ROSE: (*Suppresses anger.*) Very well, ma! try to make me as miserable as Bessie! *Do!* but you shan't! If Mr. Chauncey is not to come to our house, why then – (*Stops.*)

MRS. F: (*severely*) What then! Take care, daughter! Take care what you do! What letter was that you put in there?

ROSE: That's my affair. (*Looks at watch.*) It's time for me to go to school. Good-bye, ma. (*going off*)

MRS. F: (*Follows her and changes tone.*) Rosie, dear, don't go away and leave me so.

ROSE: Don't, pray, ma, don't come right up to the school door. You know, you're not dressed this morning, and the girls will wonder who you are. I don't like to say you're the cook, so please don't come. (MRS. F. *turns away sadly.*) There, don't take it so much to heart. (*Turns to assure herself that no one is watching.*) You know I love you and all that. But we must sacrifice our feelings, if we want to rise in the world. (*After ringing the bell and having the door opened for her, she exits into school.*)

MRS. F: Well, I suppose it is right for she must see how the others act. Oh, if Bessie could only feel as lightly, she might never have become so miserable.

SKIF: (*Advances.*) I beg pardon!

MRS. F: (*Looks up mechanically.*) Sir! Oh, Mr. Skiffley, I didn't know you in that dress.

SKIF: Disguise is a necessity of my profession. Do you know that there's the very mischief to pay down at your house?

MRS. F: O, Mr. Skiffley! can there be any deeper misery than that I now suffer?

SKIF: Why, Bessie has fled, and the old man is raving like a lunatic at her escape. Why, he has even applied for a warrant for her arrest, and I've got it here. How foolish of her to run away. Flight has convinced him, more than anything else, of her guilt.

MRS. F: But she is not guilty, Mr. Skiffley. (*Looks around cautiously and anxiously.*) O, if I thought I could rely on you, I –

SKIF: Now, if there's anything which pains me, it is want of confidence. Take away confidence, and I might as well shut up shop.

MRS. F: Bessie is suffering for the fault of another. (SKIF. *very attentive*) Now, why should she suffer, if she is not guilty? And if I *have* given her a pledge, as her mother, I'm to judge if her safety requires me to keep her secret.

SKIF: Exactly so. When people exchange their own silence for another's pledge, they must take the consequences of fluctuations in the new security. (*very mysteriously and knowingly*) She didn't take the chain, somebody else did! I suspected there was something like this. Now, who does she say took it?

MRS. F: Jack Ryver!

SKIF: (*aside, surprised*) Jack Ryver! (*aloud*) Ha, ha! Jack Ryver! come, that's good.

MRS. F: (*nervous and frightened*) Why, what do you mean?

SKIF: Don't it strike you, that this Jack Ryver must have a very long arm to reach from Colorado to New York?

MRS. F: But Jack returned yesterday, in the great storm: he has come back to New York.

SKIF: Did you see him?

MRS. F: No; but Bessie says he did, and she has never told me a falsehood from her cradle.

SKIF: My dear Mrs. Fallon, you know how deep my admiration for your daughter is; I would do everything to discover the real thief; but I must not be blinded. Now, I can't believe it was Ryver, for Ryver is not in New York. If he had returned, I would have known it.

MRS. F: (*tearfully*) What can I think? What shall I do? I am bewildered. Ah, who would be a mother!

SKIF: I don't think you need fear for Miss Bessie's safety. The warrant which her father has given me, couldn't be in kinder hands.

MRS. F: I don't fear for Bessie's safety, Mr. Skiffley, for I more than suspect she may try and go to my sister's in Albany, 'till her father relents.

SKIF: (*aside*) Ah! that's worth knowing. (*aloud*) As long as you believe her to be in no personal danger, go home peacefully, and leave the rest to me. It's not a matter of business, its a matter of friendship and affection now with me, to rescue her.

MRS. F: God bless you for your kindness, Mr. Skiffley – God bless you! (*Exits.*)

SKIF: The game's easy. I couldn't have got her out of the house without a warrant, and then she'd go to jail instead of coming to me. Last night I pretended to remonstrate with her father. He gives her four-and-twenty hours' grace, in which to find the chain, or reveal the thief. This morning *she* runs away, and *he* gets out the warrant. *I* do nothing. I simply avail myself of circumstances. Now I seek her; I arrest her; I imprison her! I'm judge, jury and jailor! and the term she serves out with me, shall be for life. (*As he is about to go off the* POSTMAN *enters and goes to letter-box, opens it and takes out letters.*) By jove! that letter from Rose! it has something to do with this Ryver business, or I'm a fool! Bessie must be lured to some den, in expectation of meeting the fellow; but it is I, that must manage the correspondence. (*Approaches* POSTMAN.) I say, my lightning express friend!

POST: (*busy with letters*) Well, my tulip.

SKIF: Could you oblige me with a look at the addresses of those letters?

POST: Not any.

SKIF: But there's one in the box I think is for me.

POST: (*Puts letters in bag.*) Quite a mistake! all the letters in that box are for *me*. All them as I have, are for the post office; after that office gets 'em, then *you* have your chance.

SKIF: Very well put! but really, (*showing official shield inside his coat*) matter of business, you know. Fact is, I'm on a trail, and want to see the address on a letter you have.

POST: (*Locks his bag.*) O, is that all?

SKIF: Yes, that's all.

POST: O, that's easy. You just write to the Postmaster-General at Washington, and ask his permission; when he gives it you, take it to the Secretary of State and get him to approve it; then you get it passed through both houses of Congress, and bring it to me, and I'll show you all you want to see. (*Goes off.*)

SKIF: Curse his smartness! The country's going to the devil, when a man can't get a favor even from a postman. What's the next move? she must be trapped; but which is the safest spot, let me see. (*Looks over mem. book.*) I can use Ryver's name as the bait!

　　　　　(PATSY *and* DAVY *enter from right and go to Institute. They are little brown Italian lads, of the kind usually seen in New York streets. They carry a small harp and violin. They look up at Institute, and commence to play and sing 'Not for Joseph.' At the first sound,* SKIF. *starts, endeavoring to proceed with his notes – then shuts up his book.*)

SKIF: Here, I say, cut that!

PATSY: No, we won't! Go on, Davy! (*They recommence.*)

SKIF: I've seen these little monkeys somewhere. O, yes! they belong to Benedetto's tribe – useful fellows, if occasion comes. (*Buttons up his coat and is going away, when he looks off the scene and starts back.*) Eh! luck! luck! and no mistake. The very runaway! but who's that with her! What is she doing up here? O, I remember (*looking up at Institute*), her sister's there. Here, you! (*to boys*)

PATSY: (*advancing with cap*) Give me penny!

SKIF: (*Fumbles in his pocket in order to lure boy on.* PATSY *approaches, when* SKIF. *suddenly seizes him.*) I've a mind to take you up for vagrants. (*Both boys commence to blubber.*)

PATSY: We ain't vagrants; wot we does is better nor stealing.

SKIF: I believe you, my infant. What boy is that – any relation of yours?

PATSY: Him! – yes, his mother married my father afore either of us was born: that's how I came to be intimate with him. Don't you cry, Davy. (*Gives* DAVY *a tap on the head with fiddle.*)

SKIF: Where's your kennel?

PATSY: Jacob's Ladder – with old Benedetto. Benedetto's the old fellow with only one eye; he wore the other one out trying to see wot was the matter in a row one night.

SKIF: Do you want to earn a ten cent stamp?

PATSY: How long will it take to do it?

SKIF: All the afternoon, perhaps.

PATSY: Can't be did. We's got to carry home a quarter a piece every night, or Benedetto wallops us. Shut up, Davy! (DAVY *stops crying.*)

'Not for Joseph': Comic song by Arthur Loyd, copyright 1868.

SKIF: Well, I'll make it a quarter for you.

PATSY: And one for Davy?

SKIF: O, I don't want him.

PATSY: Yes, but I do. Come now, make it half a dollar and it's a job. Dry up Davy!

SKIF: Well, say half a dollar.

PATSY: Don't *say* half a dollar – fork it over! (SKIF. *takes out money* – PATSY *holds out hand.*)

SKIF: Here.

PATSY: Now, what's the game?

SKIF: (*Points right.*) Do you see those two ladies there, just coming up? Mark the one on the inside.

PATSY: Yes.

SKIF: I want you to give her a message.

PATSY: From you!

SKIF: The deuce, no! Can you remember a name?

PATSY: Yes, if it ain't too long.

SKIF: It's Jack Ryver, try it – say Jack Ryver.

PATSY: Jack Ryver.

SKIF: Say it again!

PATSY: (*quickly*) Jack Ryver! Jack Ryver! Jack Ryver!

SKIF: That'll do. Now come with me, quick.

> (*All exit quickly right, as* BESSIE *and* ANN *enter without perceiving them.*)

ANN: Sure, Miss Bessie, don't be frightened! She's your sister, and she'll be glad to help you, for she has got plenty of pocket money.

BESSIE: O, Ann, I'm afraid to ask her. She will tell me that I must give up the search for Jack and return home, and I cannot do that!

ANN: But ye can't be walking the streets all day and at night – millia, murther! what'll ye do then?

BESSIE: I don't know. But heaven will not suffer me to come to harm, for at least I have not offended It.

ANN: Lord betune you and evil! But I'll go to Miss Rose, if *you* want. Just hide here a minute till I ax the schoolmarm to let me have a word of her.

> (ANN *goes to Institute; rings bell.* BESSIE *leans against letter-box. A file of girls enter from right and cross to Institute, the door of which is opened.*)

FIRST GIRL. (SIS SEWELL): (*looking at* BESSIE) What a pretty girl.

SECOND GIRL. (ANNE KEMP): Yes, but wretched taste. (SIS *slips letter in box.*) Oh, I saw you! Who's it to? (*All laugh.*)

> (ROSE *appears at door of Institute.*)

ANNE: Oh, Rose, when did you come back?

ROSE: Oh, just now. (*aside, after recognizing* BESSIE) I can't talk to her while all the girls are here. (ANN *advances and nudges* ROSE, *who pushes her aside.*) Do get out of the way, woman. (*All the girls exit into house with* ROSE.)

ANN: The mean – proud – stuck-up thing!

---

millia: a variant of the slang expression for a beating or thrashing.

BESSIE: No! no! don't scold her, Ann! Misfortune and Rose have nothing in common.

ANN: But what'll ye do, Miss?

BESSIE: Oh, I'll manage bravely enough. You go home, Ann. Mother is all alone – there – there! (ANN *cries*.) It'll be all right, when I find Jack. One word with him, and then I can return to father fearlessly. There, go. (*Pats* ANN *on shoulder, dries her eyes, and sends her off; bursting out afresh.*) Oh, if I could but see Jack! (*Leans against the post wearily.*) If I had not wronged him, I might be happy. What shall I say to him? Yesterday he would have fallen at my feet for a kind word: today he will laugh at me for casting off an honest man and seeking for a thief. But he is repentant, I know. I will show him the way of reparation – I will save him.

CURTAIN

Scene 2. *Street view. Along the Avenue. Enter* FRED, *reading* ROSE's *letter.*

FRED: 'Say papa sent for me, or anything else you please, invent any excuse – only rescue your Rose from pining to death.' (*Folds letter.*) What an extraordinary girl! I'm delighted with the idea of a holiday – in such excellent company. (*He turns and perceives* BESSIE *who enters slowly, looking back timidly.*) Why, that looks like her little sister. (*Puts letter in pocket.*) How pale she looks. That reminds me that I may be the cause. Pshaw! I wish I hadn't written that letter until after my tête-à-tête with Rose, during the storm. Hang it! I have been a fool.

BESSIE: (*Drying her eyes, is about to cross stage, and sees him. Delighted.*) Oh, Mr. Chauncey, is it you! Heaven has surely sent you here.

FRED: I don't exactly feel certain of that, Miss Bessie.

BESSIE: Oh, but I do, for I was so miserable, so sad; and when I saw you my heart gave a leap, as if it recognized a friend.

FRED: I'm afraid it was a case of mistaken identity, Bessie. It is I, that have caused you all your trouble, is it not?

BESSIE: Oh, no, indeed! All night long I have thought over your words, your dear kind words. And yet I have done wrong, and don't deserve you should ever think of me.

FRED: Done wrong! – impossible!

BESSIE: Yes, it was wrong, because it made me forget myself. Here – here. (*taking jewels and letter from her pocket hurriedly, and giving them to him*) Here is your letter and your present. Oh, do take them!

FRED: You scorn them?

BESSIE: Oh, no! no! (*Kisses them.*) for they – made me happy – but they are not for me – take them! See, I do not give back your present, you know, I only give you something in return. Think of it that way, and it will all be well – will it not?

FRED: (*aside; full of admiration*) By Jove! She's an angel worth winning. (*aloud*) Bessie, you shall not leave me in that way.

(SKIF. *appears in background with the boys – stooping down and pointing out* BESSIE *to them, then disappears.* PATSY *advances.*)

PATSY: (*in a low tone, pulling* BESSIE*'s dress*) I say, Miss!

BESSIE: (*starting*) What do you wish?

PATSY: (*mysteriously*) I've got a message for you.

BESSIE: (*amazed and shrinking towards* FRED) For me! From whom?

PATSY: (*after looking around cautiously*) From Jack Ryver.

BESSIE: (*joyfully*) From Jack! where is he? Quick, tell me!

PATSY: Follow me and I'll take you to him. He's hiding, you know.

BESSIE: At last! I knew it would be well at last.

FRED: Bessie, what is all this? What have you to do with these people?

BESSIE: It is hope – it is honor – it is life! (*Stops suddenly.*) But you do not know.
    You must not know. (*to* PATSY) Come!
                    (SKIF. *enters right.*)

FRED: Who is this Jack Ryver?

BESSIE: Oh, Mr. Chauncey, be merciful – don't ask me. (*to boys*) Come!

SKIF: You see, she don't explain. Perhaps you'd better ask me.

BESSIE: (*startled, to* FRED) No – no – no! ask *him* nothing!

SKIF: Why, sir, this young girl is the victim of a monstrous outrage: a low young
    fellow, whom she loved, has stolen –

BESSIE: (*Who has been pleading humbly with* SKIF., *at this point turns with a cry
    of agony and shame. To* FRED.) Oh, sir, don't listen to him – don't listen to
    him. (*Exit, with boys following, the latter exchanging significant glances with*
    SKIF.)

FRED: Now, sir, what is all this?

SKIF: Merely that this lover of Bessie Fallon's – this Jack Ryver – broke into her
    father's house, and robbed it. Suspected of being the thief, *she* was turned
    into the street. Now the girl's trying to find this Ryver – they'll vamose
    together. You'll perceive, sir, that's not the sort of person for you to be inti-
    mate with – not at all.

FRED: Enough! I wish to hear no more. (SKIF. *crosses away.*) And I had almost
    loved her! Well, it serves me right for being traitor to Rose for a minute. She'll
    be waiting for me. (*Exits.*)

SKIF: All's safe in that quarter. She may go to the devil for all he cares. Bessie goes
    to Benedetto's den. We secure her in a nest of thieves. There's but one escape
    for her, from degradation: and that's to smile on me. I think she'll smile!
    (*Exits.*)
                (*Enter* ROSE *and* FRED.)

ROSE: (*delighted*) I was so afraid you wouldn't get my letter, or that you couldn't
    come; and I should have moped all day. You mustn't mind if I should be wild
    to-day, for this is my birthday-party! Where are we to go? Somewhere that
    I've never been before, mind! It's so delightful to start out for nowhere in
    particular, and bring up anywhere.

FRED: Oh, leave all to me. But you haven't told me what the reason is, you've
    given up your party at home. Has Bessie anything to do with it?

ROSE: Oh, it's Bessie, and pa, and ma, and I don't know who besides.

FRED: Jack Ryver, perhaps.

ROSE: Why, where in the world did you hear of him? Never mind, I'll tell you all

about it as we go. Bless us and save us! don't let's stay here so near the school.
If they should see how happy I look, they'd run out and bring me back.

FRED: Then off we go. Mind, you are not to ask me where we go.

ROSE: No.

FRED: Nor when we shall get there.

ROSE: No, nor when we're to get back. It's so like an elopement, isn't it? If we
read this in a novel, we wouldn't believe it, would we? Let's make a romance
out of it! (*mock heroic*) I am a dismal damsel whom you have rescued from
yonder dungeon! We haste from our pursuers – (*going*) and if they overtake
us – we get into an omnibus.

FRED: (*mock heroic*) And we are saved!

ROSE: (*delighted*) Exactly! (*They run off laughing.*)

Scene 3. *Jacob's Ladder. An all-night's lodging cellar. A resort for sailors, and
immigrants of the poorer class, and thieves. A circular staircase left of center leads
from ground to an aperture in ceiling. At back a row of steps lead to a low door,
set high up in the wall. On right and left are rows of bunks of a squalid character.
Stove on right in a sand-tray, pipe leading off. Kettle on stove. Low stools near it.
The street lamp is supposed to shed a pale light through the aperture in the ceiling.*

*The bunks are all occupied on the left. A sailor is in the upper one, front. The
Dowderry immigrant party are huddled about stove. The boy and girl are in one
bunk on the right.* MRS. DOWDERRY *is preparing the baby for bed, and* TERRY
is standing by. BENEDETTO *is sitting by stove smoking a short pipe.*

MRS. D: Just lift the baby into bed, Terry. (*He takes child.*)

BEN: You pays before you turns in.

MRS. D: Here the money, sir! ten cents aich, and how much for the baby?

BEN: De baby is noting. Dere is four of you, dot is forty cent.

SAILOR: (*gruffly*) Hallo! is there a baby there?

MRS. D: (*bristling*) There is, and what of it?

SAILOR: If I hear a howl from it this night, I'll throw it overboard.

MRS. D: I'd like ye to offer to lay a finger on me child.

SAILOR: (*to others in bunks*) They're going to bunk a baby in here, mates!

ALL: (*in bunks*) Put the baby out – no babies.

MRS. D: Shame on ye, for onmanly devils! Were ye niver babies yourselves? If it
was decent ye were, ye wouldn't be talkin' to a poor widow woman that way.

TERRY: Sure the baby's no harm, and mother'll take care of it herself.

　　　　(*All this is spoken loudly and simultaneously, and is stopped by*
　　　　BENEDETTO.)

BEN: (*Hammers with a club beside him on the floor.*) Will you be quiet? (*Rises and
goes with club to sailor's bunk.*) If you says anoder vord I make babies of
you! Dis is my house (*turning to others*). I lets a hundred babies in, if I likes.
You pays for a bed – by Gar, I no sells de sleep. You get him if you can. (*all
silent*) Dere! now don't let me hear a visper. (*Sits.*)

　　　　(MRS. D. *sits smoking.* TERRY *sits on berth and tries to sleep.*
　　　　JACK *is seen descending the staircase.*)

JACK: (*Looks around.*) Is this old Maggit's place.

BEN: Dis is my place.

JACK: Why, it was old Maggit's, three years ago. He used to tell me, if I were ever hard up, I could spend a night here and welcome. I never thought I'd have to come to it, but here I am.

BEN: I am de successor of old Maggit.

JACK: What! has he gone to another cellar?

BEN: (*Knocks ashes from pipe.*) He has gone furder down den de cellar.

JACK: Dead!

BEN: (*abruptly*) You want a bed, young man?

JACK: (*shuddering*) Thank you, no; I prefer to sit up.

BEN: De charge is de same if you sit up or if you lie down.

JACK: (*Takes seat by stove.*) Who's aboard to-night.

BEN: All honest folks what mind der own business, and don't trouble derselves about oders.

MRS. D: Sure and the good man's right, mavourneen! It's poor we are, but honest. I can't say as much for the spalpeens asleep yonder, for they hate the babies; and thim that hates the only innocent things in human kind, will stand a little watching themselves.

JACK: Why, that's an honest voice (*turning and rising*), and that's an honest face. A party of emigrants, too.

MRS. D: Yes, sir; we're going to Albany to-morrow night.

JACK: Why, so am I.

TERRY: I'd rather go West.

MRS. D: O, if he could only go out on the Pacific railroad, sir! They say there's goold and silver to be picked up there.

JACK: Take my advice and don't.

MRS. D: Why, they told us that the West was the poor man's promised land.

JACK: So it is, but the railroad is not all of it. I've tried it, and I know. If you will go West, seek the spot where you can hew the forest, till the land, and rear your own home in the wilderness. The western farmer lives like a king – the laborer on the railroad like a slave. The one works for himself and rears his children among the laughing meadows, and within the shade of his own plantations. The other toils in the railroad ditch, till the ague seizes on his vitals, and he drops into the grave he has dug. I have seen them! strong, lusty, young and vigorous – fall like logs. They sleep where the rail tracks cover them and the thunder of the engines will never wake them more.

(*Confused babbling outside, and a crowd of little Italian boys clatter down the staircase, with their harps and violins, led by* DAVY.)

BEN: Ah, ha! my little monkeys! You have come, eh? Dat is right. Now, let's see what moneys you have got! (*He goes among them and collects from each.*) Seventeen cents! you is a very dull boy. My heart is broke wiz you. Tree shilling! Dat is a goot leettle boy. You will make your fortune – or mine, vich is all de same ting, so long as you is too leettle to help yourself. Five cents!

---

spalpeen: a low fellow; a scamp or rascal.
monkey: term of affection, applied frequently to small, mischievous boys.

ah, you leettle debbil! (*cuffing him*) You have spent it for candy. You vill go
to de hangman viz dat candy.

SAILOR: (*sitting up*) What's all this rumpus? My eye, if they ain't the Italian
monkey boys!

BEN: Dey is my apprentices.

SAILOR: I say, Frenchy! What'll you take to set 'em going? If I'm to be kept
awake all night, it might as well be with music. Here, old grampus! – here's
a dollar to see 'em caper. (*Throws money.*)

BEN: (*Picks up money.*) Get up you young debbels and amuse his highness.

SAILOR: Start along!

> (*The boys play, sing, and dance. JACK lies on floor. While they are
> dancing, SKIF., disguised in police uniform, heavy beard, and other
> officers in uniform come down staircase.*)

BEN: Sh, boys! de police! (*They stop.*) How do you do, sare!

SKIF: (*gruffly, looking round*) Well, Frenchy, full tonight?

BEN: Yes, sare. Hope dere is no one here you want, sare?

SKIF: O, only a little case of robbery. Keep your pulse down. (*Goes round the
bunks leisurely with lantern.*) Who's here! sailor, eh? (*to another*) Here, turn
round, do you hear? O, is it? (*aside*) She's not come down yet.

BEN: Dere is one more down dere. (*pointing to* JACK)

SKIF: I thought he was one of the emigrants. Well, young fellow, who are you?

JACK: Well, old fellow, what business is that of yours?

SKIF: Where do you come from?

JACK: Everywhere.

SKIF: Look here, my buck, I think you'll bear watching.

JACK: There you're mistaken – I can't bear to be watched.

SKIF: Humph! (*aside, taking* BENEDETTO *away*) Do you know who he is?

BEN: I never see him before.

SKIF: I don't want any strange people here to-night, for I've a little trap to spring
on a young woman. One of your boys will bring her here. When she's safely
in, I'll return and make the arrest.

BEN: O, dat is all right.

SKIF: She expects to find her lover here, that's the bait. Once in, you must keep
her till my men come. Remember! if that fellow interferes, knock him on the
head.

BEN: O, he's a poor debbel, he won't hurt anybody. (SKIF. *goes up staircase at
back, followed by officers. When they are all up.*) Now, boys! get to your
beds, and if you sleeps too much in de mornin', you don't gets your breakfast till supper time. (*Boys go to bunks, scrambling in.* BENEDETTO *sits by
stove.*)

JACK: (*starting up*) What can all this mean? Pshaw! its impossible that it can concern me. And yet that man's words went through me like a knife. (*He goes
up and sits on steps at back.*)

> (BESSIE *enters by staircase, preceded by* PATSY. *She is hesitating
> and pale.*)

BESSIE: O, what a fearful place. Could they have told me the truth? (PATSY *goes
to* BEN.)

JACK: (*coming forward*) Bessie!

BESSIE: (*with a burst of joy*) O, Jack! dear Jack! (*She falls senseless in his arms.*)

JACK: Quick! water there, some of you! (TERRY *runs about in search for some.* BESSIE *recovers and withdraws timidly from* JACK*'s arms.*)

BESSIE: O, Jack, I have walked all day, through miles and miles of streets, to find you.

JACK: To find me! was it really to find me? (*brushing tears from his eyes*) You didn't mean then what you said last night? You *do* care for me! Yes, you must, or you wouldn't come to seek me!

BESSIE: Jack, don't you know why I've come to you? It's to ask you to give me back my peace – my father's love – my honor! (*holding forth both hands to him*)

JACK: Why, Bessie, I'd die a hundred times over for you. What am I to do?

BESSIE: I don't ask you to die for me, Jack. What I ask of you is only to make amends for a fault I know you have repented.

JACK: When? How?

BESSIE: Oh, Jack, don't mock me! Don't make light of that dreadful crime.

JACK: (*taking her hand intently*) Bessie!

BESSIE: You went into my sister's room – and the chain, the gold chain was on the table –

JACK: Chain! I saw no chain.

BESSIE: Father had put it there but a moment before – and no one entered there but you. It was Rosie's birthday-gift.

JACK: (*dropping her hand*) And they accuse me of having taken it!

BESSIE: No – they accuse me.

JACK: You!

BESSIE: I wished to shield you, and I told them no one had entered there but I. Father has called me a thief – has turned me from his door. Oh, Jack, think of my misery! It is my own fault, I know. You were angry, yesterday – but why give up a life of honesty for a moment of revenge. (BENEDETTO *goes silently to back.*)

JACK: And you thought I had stolen it! Oh, Bessie, Bessie! Well, perhaps poverty is next door to crime – but there's a stout wall between them still. May I perish scorned by you, and hopeless for myself, if I have done this deed. To no one else would I volunteer such an oath. (*bitterly*) But it seems that I must justify myself in your eyes.

BESSIE: Oh, Jack, I believe you. (*Gives him her hand.*) Whoever has committed the theft, thank Heaven, it is not one whom I love!

JACK: Whom you love –

MRS. D: (*approaching and whispering*) Sh! Sure, I don't think the old man is up to anny good. (*Points to* BENEDETTO, *who has been fastening the door at back, putting key in pocket, and is watching them.*)

JACK: Ah! the police! I remember!

BESSIE: The police! don't let them – don't let him touch me. That man is bitter and relentless, the more because he once pretended to love me and I rejected him.

JACK: Of whom do you speak?

BESSIE: The detective! I fear him!

JACK: There was a time that you were not afraid when I was by. Let us try to live that happy hour over again. Come! In half an hour you shall be safe. (*He takes her hand; they go towards staircase.* BENEDETTO *has planted himself before it.* MRS. D. *rolls up her sleeves for fight.*) My friend, I wish to pass!

BEN: Not so fast! You must wait for the police!

BESSIE: Oh, Jack, save me!

BEN: (*brandishing club*) Stand back! (JACK *draws dirk.*)

MRS. D: Stand back yerself!

> (MRS. D. *approaches from behind, clutches his arms, throws* BENE-DETTO *off and takes key from his pocket.* BESSIE *runs up the staircase,* JACK *following. A low whistle is heard, and as they begin to ascend, the police, led by* SKIF., *still in disguise, begin to descend. ALL the occupants of the bunks peer out.*)

SKIF: (*midway*) Frenchy, throw down the staircase!

> (BENEDETTO *escapes from* MRS. D., *runs to staircase.* JACK *throws away his knife, clutches* BESSIE, *and as* BENEDETTO *pulls a rope which breaks away the whole lower half of the staircase,* JACK *seizes the centre post and slides down with* BESSIE *in his arms, leaving* SKIF. *and officers above raging and cursing.*)

JACK: Ha! ha! too late, old boy! Terry, take care of that fellow!

> (TERRY *picks up* JACK's *dirk and menaces* BENEDETTO. MRS. D. *has run to steps at back, and opened door with the key she had taken from* BENEDETTO. JACK *and* BESSIE *advance that way as the . . .*)

CURTAIN FALLS

ACT III

Scene 1. *A section of the main deck of Hudson river steamer Daniel Doo. The steamer is seen to be next to the dock. A wide opening right of center shows the dock, which is above the level of the deck, and is reached by a gang-plank. At left of the opening is the entrance to the captain's office; next to it the clerk's window or ticket-office. At right are the doors leading to ladies' saloon. At left the scene represents the midway stairs leading to upper decks. Stored goods of all sorts on the left. The deck is stored with barrels, bales, etc.*

At rise of curtain, porters with trunks, etc., are loading the steamer from the dock, passing in from center and going off left and returning. There is a queue of passengers by the clerk's window, which is lengthened as others arrive and form it. On the dock are orange women, newsboys, etc., offering their wares to those who pass in and out. SKIFFLEY, disguised as a peddler of oranges, is among them. SAM PIDGE, the clerk of the boat, is sitting on a barrel, with freight and receipt book, checking off freight, and signing receipts, as the porters truck it in. Noise and confusion. The last bell of the steamboat, and also another, but distant bell, is heard as the curtain goes up.

SAM: (*checking off*) Smith & Co., 14 bbls. potatoes; for'd. Baxter Bros., butter, 10 firkins – all right! Now then, Pat, easy with them eggs. Hurry up, boys! Ten minutes to six. We must get out before the opposition steams up. Two boxes and a keg for Harris & Sons, Albany; for'd.

          (PASSENGER *knocking at office-window*)

PASS: Hurry up and open this place, will you! Tickets! Tickets!

ALL THE PASSENGERS: Wake up – wake up – tickets!

SAM: (*smoking*) Don't get excited! you'll get your tickets soon enough. One would think you were knocking for supper.

SKIF: Oranges! nice oranges! (*Comes down among passengers.*) Oranges, sir! Shilling a dozen, and six to the dozen. Buy some oranges, sir! (*to* SAM) There ain't a sweet tooth in the whole boat. I wonder if they think I'm selling onions.

          (*A* NERVOUS PASSENGER *comes forward from office-window. He is of a mild and peaceful manner; has a carpetbag and umbrella.*)

NERVOUS: Will you be good enough to tell me (*to* SAM) if your boat goes as soon as the opposition?

SAM: (*not minding* NERVOUS *and speaking to* SKIF.) How much are your oranges?

SKIF: Shillin' a dozen! (SAM *coolly takes one and smells of it.*)

NERVOUS: I beg your pardon, sir, can you tell me –

SAM: (*not noticing him; to* SKIF.) Pretty good! How's trade to-day?

SKIF: Not extra. (SAM *puts orange in his pocket.*)

NERVOUS: Sir! Sir! I asked you –

SAM: (*to* SKIFFLEY) Well, get off the boat – get on the dock.

SKIF: First I'll take three cents for that orange.

NERVOUS: Young man, will you –

SAM: (*Bites orange, then gives it to* SKIF.) Three cents, eh? 'taint worth one. Come, get on the dock. (SKIF. *goes off among* PASSENGERS.)

NERVOUS: (*plucking at* SAM*'s coat*) Sir, I again ask you –

SAM: (*turning sharply around*) I say, what do you mean by dragging onto me that way! Have you got another coat in your trunk to give me, when you've pulled this to rags?

NERVOUS: Confound your impudence, sir!

SAM: No impertinence, sir! You mustn't bully here, we don't allow it.

NERVOUS: I am not bullying, sir.

SAM: You are, sir! You are one of those people who act like tyrants wherever they go, and try to bully the lives out of fellows as is trying to do their duty. But we won't have any swearing around here. What do you want, anyway?

NERVOUS: I want to know –

SAM: Why couldn't you say so right off like a gentleman, instead of walking in here to abuse me! What have I done to you? I never saw you before, sir.

NERVOUS: 'Pon my life, this is cool.

SAM: Now don't try to create any disturbance, for we won't have it. (NERVOUS *retires up, bewildered.*) They think a steamboat clerk has nothing to do but

---

bbls.: abbreviation for barrels.

take their impudence. (*to porters*) Look out there! Mind your eye with those boxes! (*Goes up and off left.*)

> (*The* DOWDERRY *immigrant party enter over gang-plank.* SKIF. *comes forward.*)

SKIF: Not a sign of her yet! Can I have been tricked? No! The old man swore that she hadn't ventured home, and I know from his mad temper that he'd turn her into the streets again, if she had done so. She's not with Jack Ryver, for I've watched him in the stages of a drunken orgie all day. Albany is her only hope of safety. Ha! ha! I don't despair of capturing my pretty thief yet. Oranges! nice, sweet oranges! (*Goes up offering fruit to immigrant party, which comes forward as* SAM *reenters from left.*)

MRS. D: (*to* SAM) Is this the Albany boat, sir?

SAM: Yes, all right – that way. (*pointing left*)

MRS. D: I want to see the captain, sir.

SAM: He's gone up the mainmast with his telescope to look out for Squalls.

MRS. D: And when will he come down, sir, can you tell me?

SAM: He'll come down at eight bells to eat his supper with the midshipmen.

MRS. D: Sure, we've got a letter for him.

SAM: Let's see it.

MRS. D: (*suspiciously*) Are you the captain's son, young man?

SAM: Yes, I'm the youngest but thirteen – all brothers but me.

MRS. D: Sure it's the Irish Emigrant Society has given us a paper to show the cap'n for him to give us a sail to Albany.

SAM: Emigrant Society, eh? Let's see! (*Takes paper.*) Pass Mr. Dowderry and family – (*to* MRS. D.) Are you Mister Dowderry?

TERRY: Sure *I'm* Mister Dowderry.

SAM: Oh, are you? you kept so quiet I didn't see you at first.

MRS. D: You must be a verry young puppy, indade, to be so blind as that. Whin ye're nine days old, ye'll have both eyes open.

SAM: Hem! go for'd!

MRS. D: Go which?

SAM: (*shouting*) Go for'd! There! (*Points left.*) Get out!

MRS. D: Oh, thank you, sir! You're a very polite young man, only no one would find it out by talkin' wid ye.

SAM: Hang your impudence! You've come to America to learn manners, I hope.

MRS. D: Yis, sir! And now we've larnt as much manners as you can tache us, I'll trouble you to send us to a higher class.

> (*All the* PASSENGERS *laugh, and when* SAM *turns angrily on them, they hammer at window and call:* 'Tickets!' 'Here clerk!' 'Open the window!')

SAM: Oh, bother your row! (*Goes up and enters office, throws up window, and commences to sell tickets;* PASSENGERS *pass off left as they get them.*)

MRS. D: Faix, I guess he'll not open his mouth again till he gets his supper.

> (*All go off left with their bundles and boxes, leaving one in center. The steamboat bell, as a warning, rings half a dozen strokes; some ladies enter center and go off right.* BESSIE *appears on dock, and* SKIF. *follows.* BESSIE *comes center, and* SKIF. *steals off left.*)

BESSIE: I wonder if this can be the right boat! They told me on the wharf that
there were two.
(TERRY *re-enters for his box.*)
TERRY: Sure, is that you, Miss?
BESSIE: O, yes, indeed; but what are *you* doing here?
TERRY: I might ax *you* that, Miss, for sure we saw you safe at your father's home,
after we got away from that den, last night.
BESSIE: Ah, my poor friend, you do not know why I have no longer a home with
my father.
TERRY: And didn't he go mad wid joy at seein' ye agin?
BESSIE: He did not see me! I did not dare to show him a face which he despises.
My mother hid me all day until he went out, and I am to go to our friends
who live away in the country where I will never see the dreadful city again.
(SAM *enters from office.*)
SAM: (*aside*) Deuced good looking little piece. (*to* TERRY) I say, Irish, be off with
you! If you dare show yourself out of the steerage, I'll chuck you overboard.
TERRY: Thank ye, sir! Good-bye, Miss (*Exits left with box.*)
BESSIE: Is this the Albany boat, sir?
SAM: Yes, Miss, you are all right!
BESSIE: But are there not two? I should not like to be mistaken.
SAM: There is another boat – a sort of ricketty old concern that bursts her biler
reg'larly once a week. This is the *Daniel Doo*, A 1, leaves before sundown,
and arrives before daylight.
BESSIE: I am all alone, sir. I wish to have a stateroom.
SAM: All right, ma'am – have your key in a moment. (*Goes up as* SKIF. *appears
watching from behind goods on left.*)
BESSIE: How long will it be before the boat leaves?
SAM: Five minutes! Do you expect any one?
BESSIE: (*looking around timidly*) No, no! but I should like to go away from here.
SAM: Certainly, Miss. (*aside*) She's a runaway. I must make her acquaintance
before we get to Albany. (*Exits into office.*)
BESSIE: Every moment I dread to see that hateful face behind me. Skiffley will
never give up pursuit. He will be more persistent because he has been foiled
so often. O, how lonely I am. Every one seems so busy. I see so many young
girls about me who look as though there were no such thing as misery or me.
Even Rose has time to love and be loved. Alas! till this cloud is cleared, there
is no reviving sun of love for my heart.
SAM: (*returning with key*) Here's your key, Miss, stateroom 122. Shall I – hem! –
show you the way?
BESSIE: Thank you, if you please.
SAM: (*Opens door right.*) With pleasure. Just step into the saloon and wait until
the boat starts. I'll be with you in a moment. (BESSIE *exits.*) Deuced good
looking and green – O so jolly green. I must get acquainted. (*Turns and con-
fronts* SKIF. *who has come forward.*)
SKIF: What was the number of the stateroom?
SAM: (*flurried*) Whose?

SKIF: That young girl's?

SAM: What the dickens is that to you? She don't want any oranges, and if she does –

SKIF: You'll take 'em to her yourself. (SAM *cocks his hat and winks;* SKIF. *pokes him in the side.*)

SAM: (*offended*) Get out, or I'll have you chucked overboard. (*Enters office quickly.*)

SKIF: Luck! luck! I've just the pick of every good fortune, and when I'm down flattest, luck lends a hand, and I'm up again. She's here! alone! not a friend – no Chauncey, no Ryver, no interference! I've got the warrant safe in my pocket, and when we're afloat she'll be safe in my power. (*He is going towards center, when* FRED *and* ROSE *appear on the dock.*) The devil! What's this? That fellow and the other sister! They'll spoil all! I must mix in this somehow. (*stands off*)

ROSE: (*coming down,* FRED *following*) Don't say a word, it's too bad! not a trunk – not a box – not a sign of expressman. What can be the matter?

FRED: We'll have to go on and telegraph from Albany. They'll reach us at Saratoga. Don't be out of spirits, my darling. The truant trunks will return in safety, and the lost band-boxes will be restored.

SKIF: Oranges, sir! – nice and sweet!

FRED: (*disgusted*) No, no! (*Looks at* SKIF. *with glass.*)

ROSE: Are you one of the boat hands?

SKIF: Hem! yes'm!

ROSE: Where are our trunks? we sent them by express and we can't find them.

SKIF: (*aside*) Good! I have it! (*aloud*) Can't be possible they're gone to the other boat.

ROSE: (*aghast*) Other boat! You miserable creature, is there another Albany boat?

SKIF: Another! I should think so! a rival – goes out at the same hour – fights with us for the same channel – races with us all the way, and when it can't get our passengers, steals the trunks.

ROSE: O, good gracious, Fred! did you ever!

FRED: The greasy but honest man may be right. How far is the other boat from here?

SKIF: Just one pier down.

ROSE: Fred, I'm going after those trunks! (SKIF. *is delighted.*)

FRED: But, my dear Rose!

ROSE: Now, Fred, don't say any more. I can't run away with only one suit of clothes, and that on. What was the use of making you buy an outfit, if we are to leave it all behind! O, dear, did any one ever hear of such a misfortune! (*Turns to go.* FRED *is about to follow.*) Don't you come, stay and get the tickets. (ROSE *goes up gang-planks.*)

SKIF: Better let the lady have her own way, sir. I'll go and show her the pier. (*Follows* ROSE *up.*)

FRED: Get out, fellow! (*He is about to follow* ROSE, *when* BESSIE *appears at the door of the saloon. They see each other for a moment, and* BESSIE *disappears instantly.*) Bessie here! What can she be doing? Who is with her?

(*Goes up, looking after* ROSE; *then comes down.*) I must see her – see where she goes, and with whom! Rose and she must not meet! not just yet, at least. (*Exits right.*)

        (JACK *appears on the dock, slightly tipsy, and comes over gangplank.*)

SAM: (*entering from office*) There's Jack Ryver, at last! and tight; now that's too bad. Look out there, Jack, or you'll chuck yourself overboard.

JACK: I'm in time! I knew I'd be in time!

SAM: In time! Yes, and in condition, too! Do you expect to be able to tend to the furnaces in that state? You'll blow us up before morning.

JACK: Well, what if I do? What's worth living for, I'd like to know!

SAM: Is that the way you go back on a feller that's got you a place?

JACK: Sam! I'm no more a man than if I walked on four legs, instead of two. I deserve your anger; but you don't know what it is to – (*Stops, looks at him, and turns off laughing wildly.*)

SAM: To what?

JACK: To be in love – madly in love – to think that you are loved again; to wring half a promise from her lips in a moment of danger, when your aid is wanted, and then to have her say, when it's all over – 'Good-bye, Jack, God bless you for what you've done, but try and forget me!'

SAM: (*sympathizing and indignant*) Well, all I've got to say is, that any girl who'd do that –

JACK: (*savagely*) You've got nothing to say about it.

SAM: Oh, deuce take it! If you're as drunk as that, I'll have you chucked overboard to sober you down.

JACK: Where's my station? Where's the engine room? Where's the furnace? It's time to go to work – (*taking off coat, and throwing it down*) and I'm ready for it! Fire up there!

SAM: (*nervous*) He'll scare all the passengers! Now, Jack, come. Lie down for an hour – just to take the fever down. Then you'll be fresh and wide awake.

JACK: I am fresh.

SAM: (*aside*) I should say you were. (*aloud and soothingly*) Oh, yes, I know – all right, old boy! Now come with me. (*Steam whistle is heard.*) There's the starter. (*Leads* JACK *off left and returns.*) Now, then, all aboard! All ashore that's going!

        (*People saunter in at left. Boat-hands come from dock, and prepare to haul in gang-plank.*)

SAM: Now then, boys, lively! Haul her in!

        (*The plank is hauled in and flung upon the stage. The engineer's bell is heard to strike. The rope is hurled in from the dock, and laborers coil it.* FRED *enters from right. The dock commences to pass away.*)

FRED: She's nowhere to be seen! Concealed herself, no doubt. But where is Rose? Hello! Here! I say – there! I must get off!

SAM: Too late, sir!

FRED: Confusion! What will become of Rose!

SKIF: (*outside*) Halo-o-o! Stop her! Stop her!

SAM: (*Returns to gang-plank and looks off right.*) There's that inevitable last man! Never left dock yet that he didn't come along. (*Hands all jeer and laugh at SKIF., who appears at right, running. He is deeply disguised as an old gentleman, with broad hat, umbrella, and carpet-bag.*)

SKIF: (*blowing and puffing*) Hi! hi! Stop for me! (*Flourishes his bag and umbrella.*)

SAM: Go it, old one! Jump for it! Look out, boys!

> (*Hands all laugh. The boat appears to move more quickly, and SKIF. makes a wild jump, his hat flying, his bag and umbrella swing in the air. All shout and laugh.*)

Scene 2. *View of section of Grand Salon of steamboat, showing three state-rooms. They are numbered from right to left: 122, 124, 126. The panels and doors are handsomely gilded.* SAM PIDGE *enters, followed by* BESSIE.

SAM: (*at No. 122*) This is your room, Miss. Just let me have your key, and I'll open it for you. (*She gives him key.*) You see, I've taken good care of you. You're just aft the wheel, and the safest place in the boat. (*Opens door.*)

BESSIE: Thank you, sir. When shall we reach Albany?

SAM: Five o'clock in the morning, Miss. It'll be flood-tide, and we shan't be stuck. Is there anything I can do for you?

BESSIE: (*entering room*) Nothing, thank you.

SAM: (*aside*) She don't seem disposed to give a fellow a bit of encouragement. (*aloud*) Hem! I say, Miss!

BESSIE: (*at door, with bonnet and shawl off*) Well?

SAM: Of course you'll want supper? They'll sound the gong as soon as it's ready, and then –

BESSIE: No, I shall not take any supper. (*Retires.*)

SAM: (*aside*) Brought sandwiches in a bag, I suppose. How confoundedly selfish! If she'd only let me take her to supper now.

BESSIE: (*re-appearing*) You are forgetting to leave me the key.

SAM: I beg pardon! so I did – there. (*Puts key in door outside.*) Now it's all right!

BESSIE: (*Takes key from outside and puts it inside of door.*) Now it's all right. (*Retires.*)

SAM: (*aside*) She's a regular flirt. She wants to draw me on. (*aloud*) Miss, I say Miss!

BESSIE: Oh, are you there yet? Well?

SAM: You'll sit up, of course. No one goes to bed 'till ten o'clock. It's moonlight, too. I can get you a nice arm-chair on the deck.

BESSIE: Thank you, I can enjoy the moonlight from my window, here.

SAM: So you can, and your window looks out on the promenade. In an hour I shall be disengaged, and I can walk around to your window.

BESSIE: Ah, I'm glad you told me, for then I'll know when to shut it.

SAM: (*faintly*) Ha! ha! That's good! I say – (*The door is shut and locked.*) She's rather good looking, but not a bit of style – not a bit. Very stupid, too. Not a bit bright – oh! no! (*Exits left.*)

> (FRED *enters right.*)

FRED: Her room's in this saloon, I know. I saw her led here by the clerk – but that confounded tipsy-looking fellow kept watching me so intently that I was afraid to follow. (*Looks off.*) The deuce! There he is again! Ah! some one has stopped him! I never saw him before – who can he be? Oh, pshaw!

(BESSIE *opens her door cautiously, and looks out, at the instant that* FRED *is turning back to go left. She recognizes him, and closes the door instantly. He appears to recognize her.*)

FRED: That was her dress! (*Runs to the door.*) Bessie! (*Knocks.*) Bessie – it is I!

BESSIE: (*opening the door*) Why do you seek me?

FRED: Because I find you alone and unprotected – and I would befriend you.

BESSIE: I was alone and unprotected yesterday, and you turned from me in contempt.

FRED: But here, evidently courting a concealment which –

BESSIE: (*bitterly*) Which is very natural for a thief!

FRED: No! I find it impossible to believe what I have heard.

BESSIE: I thank you for those words, Mr. Chauncey, although I have not tried to
justify myself to you, nor to anyone. I have been accused – I shall not try to
excuse myself.

FRED: Who accuses you?

BESSIE: I have no wish to say.

FRED: But your father –

BESSIE: It is he that I fear the most.

FRED: Your lover then –

BESSIE: I have no lover. I do not love anyone. Oh, sir, I am not worthy to be the
wife of any man. Two days ago my heart was capable of all tenderness, of all
devotion. I might have given it to Jack then, but there was a moment that I
thought – (*turning away*) I cannot speak it. No – no – no! it is too late. I have
told Jack it is too late, and he hates me.

FRED: (*partly aside*) I have been unwise to trifle with this gentle heart! (*to* BESSIE)
it is I that have been criminal, but I can repair my fault, and I will –

BESSIE: No, you must not feel a single self-reproach. (*resting her hands on his
arm*) It is all my error – and yet we do not lead our hearts – we follow them!

FRED: You shall yet be re-united to that honest heart which beats for you.

(JACK *appears at left and starts back on seeing them.*)

FRED: Dear Bessie! I cannot see a life but just begun, ended in this gloom! All the
joy, all the love for which you are designed, you shall possess.

JACK: (*interposing*) She shall – but not with you!

FRED: (*coolly*) Who is this?

JACK: The man whom you must answer, rich as you are!

FRED: Answer what?

JACK: I loved this girl with all my heart. I left her with her last kiss wet upon my
cheek, to strive for fortune and the right to marry her. I came back – to find
her – how? The eye that was so loving turned away, the clasp that was so
warm grown cold.

FRED: I see. You are Jack Ryver.

JACK: And you – you are the rich Chauncey, who found this humble beauty
please your fancy – and made her false to me.

FRED: Now come, my good fellow, your declamation is entirely thrown away on me, for I decline to become your rival.

JACK: It is a lie!

FRED: (*irritated*) Stop! You are going too far!

JACK: Then why do I find her here, flying from her father's home with you! Her hand upon your arm, your tongue painting the happiness you pretend to give her.

FRED: That may be explained. If in a moment of folly –

JACK: A curse upon that folly of the rich, which works such misery to the poor!

FRED: I can make reparation –

JACK: Give me back the love you have destroyed!

FRED: That must be another's gift.

JACK: But there is a recompense *you* shall yield – your treacherous blood!

BESSIE: (*kneeling*) Jack! For Heaven's sake – I only am guilty!

FRED: (*raising her*) Stop, Bessie! let the consequences and the blame be mine.

JACK: Dispute between you for the honor of having wronged me – but I will right myself! You were bold enough to lay your hands on all that poverty could spare me – an innocent love – are you bold enough to answer for your act?

FRED: What is this? A challenge! Really I didn't know there were such things in these days.

JACK: Call it what you please. I am a desperate man. Life without her love is value-less to me. You have taken the one – I mean to offer you the chance of taking the other.

FRED: Will you listen to me –

BESSIE: (*interceding*) Oh, Jack!

JACK: I will listen to nothing. Only tell me how I can lash you into courage. What insults I can heap on you to stir your coward heart.

FRED: (*rushing at him*) Insolent rascal!

JACK: Aha! (*Meets him and they close.*) I have touched you, then!

BESSIE: (*Shrieks and runs to right.*) Help! Help!

(SAM *enters left.*)

SAM: Hello! Oh, here Jack! What the deuce are you up to now? Oh, confound it, let go of the man, or I'll chuck you overboard. (*He separates them.* JACK *is furious.*)

FRED: I am exceedingly obliged to you. (*arranging his collar and cuffs*)

BESSIE: Mr. Chauncey, please go away.

JACK: You are safe! but don't think you have escaped me!

SAM: Come! you don't know what you are doing.

JACK: We have twelve hours before us, caged together in this boat; if you elude me, *still* there is a lifetime to seek and find you in. Our next meeting shall be the last for one of us on earth, remember! I swear it! (*He is hurried off by* SAM.)

BESSIE: Avoid him! Promise me to have no quarrel with him.

FRED: Sleep in peace, Bessie! Whatever shall result; – it is the curse of Providence on that thoughtlessness which men like me so often suffer to mislead us. (*He kisses her hand tenderly.*) Good night! (*He leads her to the door No. 122.*) Good night!

BESSIE: Good night! (*Exits into room.*)

FRED: Now, if Rose were only here, she'd set this matter right, and persuade that fool of a fellow not to enjoy with such satisfaction the idea of spilling blood. By George! I wonder how Rose likes our separation! Hang this fellow's fighting propensities! it comes of his running about with fire engines, I suppose, and punching people's heads. (*Lights a cigar.*) I suppose I must find him and try to explain this affair – that is, unless he cuts the matter short by 'chucking me overboard', as our friend here says.

(*As* FRED *is passing out left,* SAM *enters with* SKIFFLEY, *disguised as in previous scene.*)

SAM: (*to* FRED) It's all safe, now, sir. I've had our friend taken down stairs, and he'll be perfectly quiet after awhile.

FRED: Ah, very good. (*Exits right.*)

SKIF: (*imitating senile dribble*) He! he! young men fighting, eh!

SAM: Yes, about a young lady in this room. If they commence it through the night again, don't be frightened. Let's see the number of your room. (*Looks at key in* SKIF.'*s hand.*) 126! Here you are. (*Unlocks and opens door.*) Now you're all right.

SKIF: Stop, young man! (*Takes him by coat as he is going away.*)

SAM: Well, what now?

SKIF: Is this room perfectly safe?

SAM: Perfectly! – right over the boiler.

SKIF: Then I want another.

SAM: Can't get it – all taken.

SKIF: But I've never been used to sleeping over the boiler.

SAM: Time you began then – old man like you. It's all right. (*pushing him in*) If you're blown up you can sue us for damages (*Shuts door on him.*) – if you ain't too much damaged to do it. I must look after that girl. I knew she was a case. Wonder who she is? Wouldn't speak to me, and flirting with that swell; tried to pump Jack, but you might as well try to get an explanation from a soda water bottle, he's so full of pop! (*Exits right.*)

(*The instant he goes off,* SKIF. *protrudes his head from door 126, undisguised, as in Act 1.*)

SKIF: He's gone. Tricked 'em all. (*Steps out.*) And now for the last strike! Ha, ha! quarreling among themselves, were they, as to who should protect her! *I* say nothing, but attend to the whole matter myself. Now's the time! (*Takes out handcuffs and handkerchief, and steals to* BESSIE's *door. Listens, and then knocks.* BESSIE *opens it instantly, and is about to step out, when she stands paralyzed at sight of* SKIF., *who grasps her wrists and handcuffs her in a moment.*) Don't cry out, or I'll gag you; besides, raising an alarm won't help you.

BESSIE: What do you intend to do?

SKIF: Only take you next door, to a temporary jail. You're in custody mind, under a warrant. No one can take you from the hands of the law.

BESSIE: Then heaven has deserted me.

SKIF: (*Leads her to 126.*) No, Skiffley's got you, that's all. I'll just bring you in here, and for fear you should hammer at the door and disturb any one, I'll fasten you to the bed. (*Takes her in.*) There! (*Comes out, closes door and locks it.*) Victory! (*Sees* BESSIE's *door open.*) Ah! I mustn't forget to lock that too. (*Fastens door 122.*) Now I can go to supper. It's astonishing how hungry a man becomes when his mind is once easy. (*Exits left.*)

Scene 3. *Section of Steamer Daniel Doo, showing the engine room, the furnace room, and part of the steerage. The furnace room is fully seen in a recess right of center, in which is shown the great furnace, its double doors, with coal bin, shovels, etc. On left is the engineer's room. A part of machinery is seen working. On right are stacks of freight. As the curtain rises, and through the scene, is heard the regular sound of engine and machinery. A couple of firemen are standing smoking short pipes by the furnace. The* ENGINEER *is seated in his room reading.* JACK *is lying in front of the furnace room.*

FIREMAN: Pretty well up to the mark?

ENGINEER: All the way up. She oughtn't to carry more'n twenty, and we've got to that, with only three to spare.

FIRE: The other boat's gaining on us.

ENG: Can't help it, if she was neck and neck with us. This boat is at the top of her speed now. (*resumes paper*)

        (*Enter* MRS. DOWDERRY *and the group of emigrants, from right.*)

MRS. D: Sure there's no harm in our creeping near the fire a bit. It's cowld, this night. (*to* ENGINEER) I'd be axin' ye, sir, if we might sit here a bit, near the fire?

ENG: Why certainly. Is that your family?

MRS. D: Every one of 'em, sir.

ENG: You can fix yourselves comfortably over there. (FIREMAN *rakes fire and it emits flame.*)

MRS. D: Sure that's the fire to cook supper wid, isn't it?

ENG: Ha, Ha! well, yes, to cook supper for the engine here.

MRS. D: Murther, now! and does that thing ate? and sure what does it ate, anyhow, sir?

ENG: Well, hem! I don't know that it devours anything but time and space.

MRS. D: And you're there to see that it don't make a hog of itself and take too much?

ENG: You've hit it. If the boiler were to get the indigestion we'd all feel pretty sick before morning. (*Resumes paper;* TERRY *and children go towards center.*)

MRS. D: Murther, now! and thim young men's watching the kittle. (*Goes to center, sees* JACK *on floor.*) Look at him now, fast asleep by the fire wid the glare upon him. (JACK *starts up to sitting posture.*) Sure it's the lad we saw at that den.

JACK: (*as if waking from a dream*) Bessie! ah, where am I?

MRS. D: Where are ye? why sleeping in the blaze of the fire, for all the world – Lord between us and harm – like a divil in mortial blazes.

JACK: Well, I am a sort of devil, I half believe. I dreamed just now I dragged a man into the seething lake, and though the fiery bubbles shrivelled up my heart strings, I saw him writhe in agony, and was happy.

MRS. D: The Lord be merciful!

JACK: It was but a dream. I woke and recollect that he sleeps safely, with his crime unpunished, my hate unsatisfied and powerless to harm.

MRS. D: (*to* ENGINEER) It's out of his mind, he is. (JACK *throws himself down at center.*)

ENG: Crossed in love, they say. Well, I'm not so old but I remember when for a woman's smile I'd walk through fire, and for her kiss I'd stay in it.

MRS. D: (*to* TERRY, *who comes forward with girl.*) Terry, acushla! give us a bit of a tune, my son. The poor lad's troubled within, but there's nothing evil can come to him when the voice of the heart is heard.

SONG, by TERRY

Young Larry stood upon the deck, his Mary on the strand,
    A long farewell, a parting kiss, a pressure of the hand:
He's gone across the sea to work, she's stayed at home to weep;
    Until the emigrant returns, his plighted word to keep!
America beholds his toil, while Erin sees her tears;
    'Tis hard to fight for fortune, and 'tis hard to wait for years!
But Heaven blesses energy, and watches over love.
    He comes at last to seek his bride, his constancy to prove!

But not alone he sails for home, and anchors in the tide –
    The soldiers of the Union are a' standing by his side;
Bold lads that in America had set the bondmen free,
    Now draw the sword for Ireland, 'gainst British tyranny!
Alas! the tale is known of how they nobly fought and fell,
    And broken-hearted Mary comes to Larry in his cell.
'Twas glory in another's land for liberty to cry;
    But for fighting for Old Ireland the patriot must die.

      (*At end of song, a loud shout of triumph is heard without, and the* ENGINEER'*s bell rings three times.* SAM *enters from right.*)

SAM: I say, Tom, look a here! The Vonderbilt is gaining on us!

ENG: Then the Vonderbilt will burst up, that's all I've got to say.

SAM: (*to emigrants*) Here you! go to the steerage. (*They exit right.*) See here, Tom, (*to* ENGINEER, *confidentially*) there's no shutting it out of sight, this here's *a race*! The passengers are crowding on the decks of both boats, shouting and going on like mad, as either of us seems to shoot ahead or drop down. It's a question now of win or lose – we must win!

ENG: If we can.

SAM: I tell you we *must* win! The opposition are almost making our time, they're getting our passengers – they're getting our freight. They mean to pass us to-night, and if they do –

ENG: What does the captain say?

SAM: He says we must not be left behind.

ENG: But the pilot knows we are at the top of our speed, look at the dial.

SAM: How much margin have we?

ENG: If I was to leave this place, or drop down dead, and you let the index reach 25, why you'd get to kingdom come before you got to Albany!

SAM: Why, it's past 21 now.

ENG: I must let her off.

SAM: (*interposing*) Stop!

ENG: Your're mad! (*bell heard, three times*) What! more speed!

SAM: I tell you what, old buck, you're behind the age. This is the day of fast riding, fast sailing, fast steamboating. (*shout heard outside*) Listen to that! it's the passengers. We've gained on the opposition, and they're delighted. What scares you – what's the danger?

ENG: This is the danger – the boat is old, the engine is old, the furnaces are patched in a dozen places; come here. (*Goes to furnace.*) Do you see that plate up there?

SAM: It looks solid enough.

ENG: If you add twenty degrees to this heat that plate will melt. I know the iron, and I know the parsimony that placed it there, instead of better.

SAM: Well, that's not the boiler.

ENG: No; but the woodwork is not a foot from it.

SAM: We'll have the hose ready. Go to your engine.

ENG: Remember, there are two hundred souls on board this boat!

SAM: I know there are two hundred heads aboard, into which I don't intend to let the idea creep that we are the beaten boat in a race.

ENG: (*looking at dial*) By Jerusalem, 23! she's run up again! (*Pulls out valve – noise of escaping steam heard.*)

SAM: You're letting the steam escape.

ENG: I'm guarding the lives of the people in my care.

SAM: But they will pass us! (*shouts and groans outside*) You hear! our people are furious. (*Bell strikes rapidly, three or four times.*) Shut off the valve!

ENG: Not while I'm engineer here.

SAM: If I had another man to take your place, you shouldn't be engineer ten seconds longer.

ENG: Here, men! put this puppy out!

SAM: (*Turns and sees* JACK.) Let 'em try! Hallo, Jack! you're just the man! You can manage an engine, can't you?

JACK: Well, what of that?

SAM: Come, take this old woman's place!

ENG: If he does I'll brain him.

JACK: (*struggling with* ENGINEER) Don't be foolish. Go and settle this matter with the captain. (JACK *shuts off steam.*)

SAM: (*contemptuously to* ENGINEER) You're too conscientious for a North River steamboat. You ought to be engineer on a canal tub somewhere.

ENG: Young man, will you take a place from which an honest man has been cast out, to let in hazard or death?

JACK: What does it matter to me, I have sported with both. (ENGINEER *goes right, passing his hands across his eyes, with emotion.*)

SAM: (*Looks at him amazed.*) Well, if you ain't soft. (*three bells heard*) Fire up! don't you hear that order?

        (*Firemen open doors and shovel coal into furnaces.*)

SAM: Now, Jack, you keep her to it, and I'll go and chuck this old grampus overboard.

VI *A Flash of Lightning.* Fred and Jack fight in the furnace room (Act III, scene 3)

ENG: (*pleading to* JACK) Mate, we've a hundred lives in our hands. There are men and women about us, lying down to sleep in peace, because they believe they can trust to you and to me. There are little children, whose innocent prayers have gone up *there* to-night, in expectation of a happy morrow – shall we destroy them?

JACK: (*deeply moved*) Not a hair on one babe among them shall be harmed.

SAM: (*uneasy*) I say, Jack, you are not going back on us, are you?

JACK: There's one man aboard this boat with whom I'd jump into that furnace, or sink beneath the sea. Were he and I alone upon this plank, I'd send him to destruction, and fear no man's judgement on my deed. But I will not seek to reach him through so many innocent hearts!

SAM: Why, this is rank mutiny! I'll see about you two fellows. (*Exits right hastily.*)
       (*A murmur is heard above. A slight smoke appears in woodwork right of furnaces.*)

ENG: (*to* JACK) Mate, your hand! while we drive this engine, with power of life and death in the movement of a finger, we can afford to spare a thousand enemies!
       (*The murmurs grow louder. All look off right. The emigrant party runs in.* TERRY, *carrying the baby and leading the girl,* MRS. DOWDERRY *leading the boy.*)

MRS. D: There's something mighty quare going on above. (*The bell is heard to ring once.*)

ENG: There's the order to stop the engines! (*Looks round and sees smoke.*) Great heaven! look at that smoke. Get the hose! come men! the water! (*He and firemen exit left.*)

MRS. D: Murther, sir! what's the matter?

JACK: Matter! don't you see! (*A tongue of flame follows smoke.*) The boat is on fire!

MRS. D: Fire! what will become of us! God be merciful to us all this blessed night! O, murtha! murtha! (*Exits with emigrant party, left.*)
       (SAM *reenters right.*)

SAM: Jack! Jack Ryver! what is wrong? The saloon is filled with smoke!

JACK: (*running and opening the furnace doors*) Save yourselves! We are burning!

SAM: Well, this is a pretty mess! Water there! (*calling off left*) Where's the water? (*Exits left.*)
       (FRED *runs on right.*)

FRED: The boat is on fire! (*Sees* JACK.) Madman! what are you doing?

JACK: Ah, you have come! (*springing towards* FRED) I have waited for you!

FRED: This is no time for such a quarrel. We shall be burnt alive!

JACK: Then we will die together. (FRED *is borne down.*)

FRED: Help! help! (*Firemen and hands enter left.*)

FIREMAN: Hallo! I say, let go of that man! (*They make a movement to pull* JACK *off.*)

JACK: Mates, one word! This man belongs to me! he robbed me of my love, and then deserted her for another. Now I have him under my foot! Will you stand between us? (*Men take off their hands.*)

FRED: Will you desert me?

FIRE: Every one for himself, that's my motto. (*They go off right, sullenly shaking their heads.*)

JACK: Now for your last of earth! (*Drags him up to furnace.*)

FRED: What would you do?

JACK: Give you to a fire as fierce as that which you have kindled in my breast!

FRED: Hold! if not for my sake, then for the girl who is still dear to you?

JACK: Don't name her –

FRED: She is helpless! will you let her perish?

JACK: (*Stops.*) Perish! Bessie helpless! God! I forgot! (*throwing him off*) Take your miserable life! I give it you – for hers! (*Exits right, and FRED rises on one knee, clutching the coal mallet, as scene closes.*)

Scene 4. *Section of saloon, as before. Stage dark; red glare thrown from the right. The murmurs are still kept up. Several boat hands and the two firemen enter right, carrying bundles, coats, etc., in disorder. They are very noisy.*

FIRE: Ha, ha! boys, come along! Here's another door, see what's in there!

NED: (*trying door 122*) It's locked!

FIRE: (*drinking from bottle*) Locked, is it?

NED: Yes, let's burst it open!

FIRE: Burst away! (*They force door and drag out BESSIE's things; her shawl falls in the doorway, one-half out.*) Hurry, there's no time! if we don't make haste we'll be cut off from escape. Woman's fixin's, eh? I don't want 'em.

NED: Nor I. Where's the whiskey?

FIRE: (*giving bottle*) Draw it mild, now. (*It is passed among the others.*)

NED: Let's go!

FIRE: Well, I've got all the pickings I can carry.
　　　　　　(SAM *enters right.*)

SAM: Hurry boys! the fire's catching up to our heels. Have you got everybody out?

FIRE: O, the decks are clear.

SAM: (*pointing to bundles*) What's that you've got there?

FIRE: What's that to you?

SAM: How dare you answer me that way? Obey orders, or I'll have you chucked overboard.

FIRE: How dare we? Don't you know when the ship's sinking or burning, the first thing 'chucked overboard' is order. Come mates! (*All go off left noisily, pushing SAM aside.*)

SAM: Well, this is a first class, A 1, pretty how-de-do, and no mistake. Drunk, every one of 'em. Broke into the bar-room the first thing, and now they're going through the other rooms to pick up what they can. (*calling off left*) Here, you – you there! get out of that! put down those trunks!

NERVOUS PASSENGER: (*inside, right*) Here – I say, I say!

SAM: (*turning*) Eh, what?
　　　　　　(NERVOUS PASSENGER *enters right with a broken life preserver.*)

NERVOUS: My good sir, my dear sir!

SAM: What's the matter? you are all right, you've got a life preserver – tie it round your waist and chuck yourself overboard.

NERVOUS: But I can't tie it, it won't tie, it's broken. O, what shall I do – what shall I do!

SAM: (*Takes it.*) Look here, its not blown up.

NERVOUS: Dear me, no! (*Takes it and blows frantically.*) It won't blow up.

SAM: (*grasping it*) You've got no bellows; let me try it. I can blow. (*Tries to blow it, but it won't expand; they in turn tear it from each other, and try to blow it up, in a state of nervous excitement; at last, when* SAM *is blowing, the* NERVOUS PASSENGER *takes hold of the other end and exclaims.*)

NERVOUS: The wind all comes out of this end – it's broken!

SAM: Eh? so it is! Hang the boat! The engine blows up, and the life preserver won't. Go get another, I can't be bothered, get out! (*About to go left,* NERVOUS PASSENGER *clutches his coat-tail with both hands.*)

NERVOUS: Don't leave me – I can't swim!

SAM: (*calling off*) Here, Jim! (*A big boat hand enters drunk, left.*) Chuck this old rooster overboard! (*Points to* NERVOUS PASSENGER *and exits right. Boat hand throws* NERVOUS PASSENGER *over his shoulder and staggers out left.*)
        (*The murmurs heard.* JACK *enters right, hurriedly.*)

JACK: Not a sign of her! all the passengers have taken to the boats. Bessie must have fled. She could not sleep with all this uproar about her. (*A distant cheer is heard.*) They are going! they are saved! I am left alone! But I must find her; there is but one way to do, door by door, to burst them in till I find her. (*Sees shawl on floor.*) Ah, what's this! luck! it's her shawl! (*pushing open door*) Empty! (*closing it and falling on his knees, kissing the shawl*) She is saved! She has dropped this in her flight. Now life is precious to me, since I can share it with her! (*As he goes off,* BESSIE *is heard to give a piercing scream. The scene closes.*)

Scene 5. *View of the broadside of the burning steamboat; she is lying motionless in the river. The sky and waves lit up with lurid reflections. The entire stern and portion of wheelhouse, smoke chimneys and cabins seen, and the hull of boat continues off at left. A row of closed windows of staterooms seen. The fire is burning from left to right. From windows left, flames issue. The upper deck is burning also.* FRED *is seen in a small boat which floats in front of the burning steamer, towards the right. He is much disordered.*

FRED: Bessie is not aboard. She must have escaped in the other boats. Now I can face Rose with a clear heart.

JACK: (*within*) Help! one moment! help!

FRED: What voice is that?
            (JACK *appears on deck from left with a fire-axe in his grasp, his appearance smeared and burned.*)

JACK: Help! all the boats are gone freighted to the water's edge.

FRED: Jack Ryver, there is no room in this boat for *you*!

JACK: I can perish! Fire has been my toy, I don't fear it – but for her!

FRED: Who?

JACK: Bessie! She is there within a wall of flame.
            (*A scream is heard.* BESSIE *dashes her manacled hands through the*

VII *A Flash of Lightning.* Jack rescues Bessie from the burning steamboat at the end of Act III

window under JACK's *feet, as a tongue of flame bursts from the*
next window.)

FRED: Great Heaven! She is imprisoned in the state-room – she is lost!

JACK: Not while this heart beats!

(JACK *cuts through the deck on which he stands to reach* BESSIE.
FRED *propels his boat to the stateroom window, and dashes it in as*
flames shoot out. JACK *draws* BESSIE *out of the opening he has*
made.)

CURTAIN

ACT IV

Scene. *The chamber of* ROSE *in* FALLON's *house. It is an attic, with deep-set*
roofed window. This is supposed to be the room in which the robbery had taken
place. A window in the center recess, opening on view of housetops. An easy chair
left of window, a small table near it, in front of window, overturned. A flower-pot
on floor near table with a withered branch. Another flower-pot with bright flowers
on the left of window-sill. A neat bed left of window. At right a grate fire-place,
with shovel, tongs, etc., on the upper side. On lower side a matchbox on floor full
of burnt matches. An old-fashioned nursery fender in front of fire-place. A bell
rope hangs by fire-place, at right. Bits of broken bell-wire trail along the wall at the
top into the recess, and then pass down under the window and off left; the main
piece attached to the rope falls to the tongs, etc., to which it is carelessly hitched.
There is a door at right. On wall at right, there is a broken picture-cord, which
dangles loosely. The picture, broken, with a piece of the cord, lies on the floor at
left of door, beside a chair. There are two doors at left and one at left in the rear,
which leads to the passage, and is the only entrance to the apartment; the other
leads to a small closet.

At rise of curtain, music, as of quiet and peace after the storm and passion. MRS.
FALLON *is discovered kneeling by the door at right, as if conversing with* BESSIE,
who is supposed to be inside.

MRS. F: Try to sleep, my darling. It must soon be over. Your father is not as he
used to be. (*rising*) Heaven be praised! she has been spared to me.

(ROSE *enters, dressed in a pretty morning robe.*)

ROSE: Dear mother, how is poor Bessie?

MRS. F: Fretting still, but I don't wonder at it.

ROSE: Won't father see her yet? Have you spoken to him this morning?

MRS. F: I can get nothing from him but the old story: 'If she is innocent it will
come out – if she's guilty, it will be found out.' And he has locked her in
her room 'till one or the other is proved.

ROSE: He acts like a brute. He won't even listen to me now, or I might reason with
him. But, thank goodness, we shall have an end of all this morning. Fred says
he has seen the detectives and they are to make their inspection.

(ANN *enters, carrying a bushel-basket of coal.*)

ANN: (*putting down basket by door and fanning herself*) Phew! Me back's broke
wid it, an' that's the truth.

MRS. F: Carry it to the grate, Ann!

ROSE: Why, what in the world is she doing?

ANN: It's carrying coal I am like a dray-horse. I'll want my wages raised if I'm to carry coal from the corner grocery, down the street, and up all these stairs another day.

ROSE: And why should you do that? Isn't the coal in the cellar.

ANN: An' isn't it the masther has locked it up and kapes it as if it was lumps of gold. (*Lights the fire, then dusts about the hearth.*)

MRS. F: I fear, child, that your father's brain is turned. He has taken a most extra-ordinary fancy about the coal. It only came to him the morning after the robbery. First he locked up the scuttle which was lying there by the fire – then he went down to the cellar, brought up some lumps from the bin, went out in a twitter of excitement, and, when he came back, forbade us to touch any coal we had in the house.

ROSE: Then that accounts for his nonsense last night about the coal stocks, and coal mines, and coal speculations! He's crazy! Pa's certainly crazy, ma! I'll speak to Fred about it.

ANN: Won't I put the room to rights now, Miss Rose – Mrs. Chauncey, I mane?

ROSE: No, no. Nothing must be disturbed. Fred and pa say so. Everything in the room must remain as it was found on the evening of the robbery, so that the detectives may examine and clear up the mystery.

ANN: Well, it's quare anyway. I think the place might be made dacent at least, and strange men coming to look at it. (*Exits with basket.*)

(FRED *passes in.* ROSE *runs to meet him.*)

FRED: Dear Rose! (*kissing her*) You see, I've hurried! Good morning, mother! I've learned to call you that already. I was motherless – and though, in law, nothing that belongs to my wife, belongs to me, I mean to claim her mother for my own.

ROSE: Well, have you found a house?

FRED: Found it and leased it. If you like it, I'll buy it. It's not a stone's throw from the Institute. The school-girls pass it every day.

ROSE: Did you select the location for the sake of the girls going to school?

FRED: Why not? They will always recall our first meeting – our sudden elopement – and the marriage, of which it was the happy cause.

MRS. F: Well, now-a-days girls do everything in their own way; but why you should have run away to do it, when we were all so willing –

ROSE: Oh, ma! (*Crosses to* MRS. FALLON.)

FRED: The detectives are to be here at ten. It's near that now – and who do you suppose has the matter in charge? Guess who! Skiffley! Skiffley, the vaga-bond!

MRS. F: He still!

FRED: So it appears, but it was impossible to prevent him. They say at headquar-ters that no one else can interfere. It's his job – yes – that's what they call it. It's embarrassing, isn't it, to have one's sister-in-law called a job?

ROSE: Bessie will owe her life again to you! Now, ma, isn't he a darling!

FRED: Oh, give the credit where it is due – to Jack! She belongs to him, and I shall be the first to persuade her to think so.

MRS. F. (*Crosses to back.*) Some one's on the stairs. It's your father. Oh dear, he'll be in another tantrum. He forbade any one to come into this room 'till the detectives had finished with it, and here we are.

> (ROSE *and* MRS. FALLON *go up left,* FRED *following.* FALLON *enters, – in a brown study, dress careless, vest unbuttoned, necktie loose, hands in his pockets. He kicks open the door. Eyes on ground. Comes upon* FRED.)

FAL: Mornin' to you, sir. (*Looks around and sees others.*) Mary, what are you doing up here? Go down stairs, both of you.

ROSE: Did you ever see such a bear! Come, Fred.

FAL: I want Fred. Go along with you. (MRS. FALLON *and* ROSE *exit. Then after seeing them out, cautiously to* FRED.) You know all about stocks – now – bonds, stocks and that kind of thing, don't you?

FRED: Well, slightly.

FAL: Do you know anything about coal stocks?

FRED: Coal compa? ⸱⸱ stocks? A little.

FAL: About coal mines! Where they dig coal! (FRED *looks at him surprised.*) Damn it, they *do* dig coal, don't they?

FRED: They do. There's no doubt about it.

FAL: (*mysteriously*) Did you ever hear of a gold-mine being near a coal-mine?

FRED: I don't think I ever did.

FAL: (*impressively*) Did you ever hear of a mine where gold and coal were mixed?

FRED: Never.

FAL: But there might be gold in a coal-mine – or near it – or a gold-mine and a coal-mine might get mixed, eh?

FRED: I hardly know. Gold is the most universal metal, existing almost everywhere, but not always in sufficient quantities to pay for mining.

FAL: (*turning*) Ah! (*reflecting*) Well, that's all. (*Turns away.*)

FRED: And now will you permit me a word, Mr. Fallon, about Bessie.

FAL: (*crossly*) What about Bessie?

FRED: Her extraordinary sufferings and perils must surely have softened your disposition.

FAL: Softened! And haven't I softened? Three days ago I forbid her my house – but didn't I, like an amiable parent, let her be brought here yesterday from the steamboat, and haven't I consented to let her stay 'till this investigation is over? Upon my life, I think I've been softened to no end of a degree.

FRED: Yes, you've behaved like a tender parent, we all know. You have locked her in that room, and threatened her through the keyhole, that she mustn't think you had forgiven her.

FAL: And wasn't that right? There's this one fact yet – a chain that cost me four hundred dollars is gone – that we know! There is another fact – somebody took it – *who*, we *don't* know and that's to be found out.

FRED: And the sooner the better!

FAL: As you say, the sooner the better. Good morning!

FRED: (*sharply*) Good morning! (*Exits.*)

FAL: (*locking door after him*) Good luck to you! You're rich! Your father was rich before you. But I'm richer than you! Rose shall inherit enough to make her your equal. (*Looks around carefully, takes paper from his pocket, unwraps it, and discovers some pieces of partly gilded coal.*) Gold! rich, shining gold! In lumps! What a wonderful thing to dig out of the bowels of the earth! I've found the dealer that sold us the coal. I've bought his whole stock out. I've found out the company that mines the coal. I'm in treaty for their stock. To-day I'll investigate the cellar. If the rest is anything as richly ored as that in the scuttle, I've got a fortune even in the house. (*Goes to closet and unlocks it with key from his pocket. Looks around cautiously, then takes out the coal-scuttle filled with gilded coal. There is a fissure in lower part of scuttle and its side is bulged.*) Not discovered yet! What a mortal blessing that that servant is a raw bumpkin and didn't know the difference between gold and coal. Here it is! (*Turning over two or three pieces of the coal partly gilded.*) I've had it analyzed! Gold, they say! Pure gold! (*Outer bell is heard.*) Who's that? (*Puts away scuttle, turns key in door, but forgets to remove it.*) It's the police. (*Goes to* BESSIE's *door.*) Here are the officers, you degenerate girl! Oh! Cry away! If they prove you guilty, you'll have something more to cry for. (*Unlocks door at left.*)

       (JACK *enters.*)

FAL: Oh! it's you, is it? Come expecting to be thanked for having saved Bessie's life, I suppose?

JACK: No! at least not by you. I did not save her for you.

FAL: And for whom, then?

JACK: Myself.

FAL: The devil you did! And when you used to save women and children from fires, did you always consider they belonged to you?

JACK: Let all that pass! Heaven creates honest love and protects it! For three days it has directed me to the very scene and very spot to save Bessie from death or worse. I loved her long ago, as you know. I love her still, and when I bore her from the burning boat she took my hand and kissed it, though she uttered not a word. I asked her then if she could love me as she used to do, and I swore to her that, good luck or bad luck, riches or poverty, I would love her now and forever – and be a better man! I've come to ask you for her.

FAL: What? while she's suspected –

JACK: A thousand times more on that account.

FAL: And what will you do with her? You can't support her.

JACK: Why, I've a good trade, and since I went away I've studied, and now I've got a profession.

FAL: A profession? Which? Profession of coals and cinders?

JACK: Of civil engineering.

FAL: Very good, then Mr. Civil Engineer, you can't engineer your little plan here! No girl of mine weds a poor man, no matter what he professes, nor how civil he may be!

JACK: Then, I'll do without your consent. (*Door-bell rings.*)

FAL: You will? You dare!

       (MRS. FAL. *enters.*)

MRS. FAL: Garry, here are the officers.

       (SKIFFLEY *and another officer enter.* SKIF. *is dressed with great care, the other very jauntily. Also* ROSE, *who goes behind her mother, and* ANN *enters and stands by the door at left.*)

SKIF: (*Comes down.*) Good morning! good morning, ladies! (*They shrink from him.*) Humph! Ah, Ryver! Not run away yet, eh? Very good, if you stay in the city much longer I'll have to find you a suitable lodging. (*to* FALLON) Your daughter is still in your custody?

FAL: Yes, in that room – her room!

SKIF: And now, if you please, I should like to see the apartment from which the chain was stolen.

MRS. F: This is the room. Just where you stand.

FAL: It has not been disturbed since the robbery.

SKIF: In no particular?

FAL: In no particular.

SKIF: And these things overturned?

FAL: I found them so, as I entered after the robbery.

SKIF: And what time elapsed between your placing the chain here and your discovery of the theft?

FAL: Hardly ten minutes.

SKIF: (*to officer who is writing in note-book*) Got that down? (*Officer nods.*) All right. (*importantly to all*) You see it's plain the thief must be some one who knew that you had the jewel, and the exact spot that you put it. Now show me where you placed the chain.

FAL: (*going up*) This table, which you see overturned, was standing before and close to the window. I laid the chain upon it.

MRS. F: And this flower-pot was on the window-sill.

SKIF: I see! (*going up leisurely*) Now let's look at the window. (*Goes to it, examines it, looks out,* FALLON *following him about.* MRS. FALLON *and* ROSE *come down right to* JACK, *all observing* SKIF.) Thirty feet from the yard. No one could climb that. Alley on each side of the house – no connection with any other building. It's plain the thief doesn't enter there.

ROSE: We all know that. How could he?

SKIF: (*not heeding*) Now for the fire-place. A grate, eh? (*Goes to it.*)

ANN: 'Tis, and dirty as blazes. I'm like to be choked with soot every day.

SKIF: Very good! The thief couldn't have got in there.

ROSE: What are you trying to find out by all this?

SKIF: The thief! Your mother says that it is some robber who obtained access to the apartment unperceived. *I* say it's some one that *lives* in the house. But I'm willing to be convinced. Now let us see. This is your daughter's room. (*rapping on* BESSIE's *door*) Is there any egress or ingress except through here?

ROSE: None. Bessie always passes through my room.

SKIF: (*Crosses, followed by* FALLON.) So much for that. Now what door is over there? (*indicating closet*)

FAL: (*hiding nervousness*) A dark closet, that's all.

SKIF: Then it's plain the thief must have come through the door by which we all entered – the door which leads directly into the room below, and which your daughter Bessie was watching the whole time of the robbery.

FAL: Well.

SKIF: Did any one hear a noise, as of a man running about at the time of the robbery?

ANN: Sure we couldn't hear anything but the thunder and lightning!

FAL: The girl is right. The storm was raging so as to drown every noise, and the Lightning nearly struck me blind!

SKIF: Now, I've had a little experience in these matters, and it guides me to a pretty straight conclusion. This robbery was committed by a woman.

JACK: (*Comes down.*) You have said that from the first. The victim of your persecution is in yonder room. We are waiting to see your proofs.

SKIF: They are all around you. (*to* FALLON) Excuse me – do you understand anything about female nature?

FAL: Well, hem! I've been married.

SKIF: Exactly! Now the first thing about women that leads to their detection when they commit a crime is – they always take too many precautions. They wish to hide their tracks – they hide them too much!

FAL: And you mean to ascribe such artfulness to Bessie! – a young girl scarcely eighteen years old!

SKIF: Bless you, some women are sly from their cradle. You'll pardon me, ladies! I speak of psychological facts.

FAL: Go on and never mind the ology.

SKIF: Now, let us suppose a young girl, dazzled by the beauty of this chain – or, if you please, jealous of her sister possessing it – determines to possess it herself! The first idea in her mind is to deceive everybody as to the real thief.

ROSE: But Bessie attempted to deceive no one. She never uttered a word when she was accused.

SKIF: I don't mean by words, I mean by circumstances. The deception here is very clever. She wishes to give the idea of a man-robber! – a big, burly, boisterous, swash-bucklering robber! for young girls forget that thieves who enter houses to steal, tread like cats, and move noiselessly as the air! Well, what does she say to herself? 'If I make a great disturbance, it will certainly look as if a *man* had been here. I will pretend that he got *in* by the window, and got *out* by the window. If he gets *in* by the window, he will certainly knock over the flower-pots.' So she throws one of them down, as you see! (*Indicates flower-pot on floor.*) Then she says: 'This big, burly robber will, of course, as he *is* a big, burly fellow, overturn the table,' – so, bang, over she turns the table, – and, as robbers always fear interruption, she cuts the bell-wires. (*Showing hanging wire near window, crosses.*)

FAL: I see! I see!

SKIF: Then she looks about and she says to herself – 'This isn't enough damage for a robber to commit,' and she pulls at the picture on the wall, breaks the cord and down it comes. (*Goes up, takes picture to which a piece of the cord hangs, and comes down, all around him.*)

JACK: But this cord is not broken!

ROSE: (*Crosses to* MRS. FALLON.) No, nor cut!

SKIF: Of course it is not cut! Observe, if you please, this cord is *burnt*! There was a very easy way to fix it. She lit a match, got on this chair and burned it through. See if there are any matches there!

ANN: (*Goes up to the mantel and picks match-box from floor beside it.*) Sure' here's the box on the flure, and all the matches in it burned off at the top.

SKIF: Exactly! in her haste to set fire to all of them, she was young, you see, and nervous. All young girls are more or less nervous, particularly about matches.

FAL: It seems clear enough.

SKIF: Now mark the difference. If it had really been a thief from the outside, he could have entered cautiously from the door below; but your daughter would have seen him, and she says she saw no one! He would have taken the chain from the table without disarranging so much as a pincushion near it! Look at this pretended disorder! No, no! it was a woman, artful, intelligent, but inexperienced, and if you ask me to name her, I say it was the young woman who is imprisoned in that room, whom I found in a low den where thieves resort to sell stolen property, the night after the robbery, and who, if justice is to be done, should go to jail.

FAL: It is enough! I knew it would be so! (*Going to* BESSIE*'s room.* MRS. FAL-LON *and* ROSE *kneel before him.*) Stand aside! No thief dwells in my house –

JACK: (*vehemently*) Stop!

FAL: What's the matter with you?

JACK: The matter is, that you are an easily gulled man, deceived by a tissue of non-sense. And a hot-headed man about to do an act of infamy!

               (SKIF. *smiles and looks away.*)

ROSE: I thank you for that.

JACK: The matter is that this fellow (SKIF. *turns savagely.*) with his clever detec-tive art, his suppositions and his tricks, is an ass.

ANN: Begorra, I thank ye for *that*, Misther Jack!

FAL: You insolent pauper!

JACK: (*dignified and calm*) One word, sir, before you do anything wrong. *I* have also inspected this room and I have formed my opinion.

SKIF: And pray, what is your opinion?

JACK: That you don't know what you are talking about. *You* say no man entered this room or leaped from that window! I say that there was such a man.

SKIF: Your proof!

FAL: Yes, the proof!

JACK: *I* am the man. (FALLON *falls back with* SKIF. MRS. FALLON *and* ROSE *delighted.*)

ROSE: (*to* MRS. FALLON) I knew he'd not suffer Bessie to be injured in order to save himself.

JACK: In the middle of the storm I came here (*to* FALLON) to see your daughter. (*to all*) I found her in the room below. I did not wish to be seen. Rose's entrance prevented me from leaving by the front door. I knew the house well, ran up-stairs and sprang through that window. That leap was nothing to a fireman of the old force. In my flight I must have overturned this table.

FAL: Then, you rascal – you stole my chain! (*Makes a rush at him.*)

JACK: Easy, easy! It doesn't follow that because I jumped through the window I carried anything with me.

SKIF: Pooh! It's an evasion. He wishes to save the girl by accusing himself.

JACK: I do wish to save an innocent girl, but I do not accuse myself.

FAL: It won't do! Arrest him! (SKIF. *crosses to* JACK; *the other officer advances also.*)

JACK: Hold off a bit! Suppose, before you arrest anyone, we look for the real thief?

FAL: You mean to say – ?

JACK: I mean to say, that in order to oblige Skiffley and his mate here, I intend to find a thief for them to arrest.

SKIF: (*taking out a pair of handcuffs from his pocket*) Proceed!

JACK: (*up by window*) *I* see certain tracks here, which you, with all your cunning, left unnoticed.

SKIF: I should like to see them.

JACK: First, it did not strike you that there is something remarkable about these flower-pots. (*Picks the one from floor.*) In yonder one (*Points to the one in window.*) the leaves are fresh and green, the flowers are blooming. In this nothing but a withered stump remains.

ROSE: It was my beautiful geranium.

JACK: And when you saw it on the day of the storm?

MRS. F: It was green and flourishing that very morning.

        (FALLON *takes the flower-pot and examines it critically.*)

JACK: Fact number one! Now here is another mystery, which my clever friend did not try to penetrate.

FAL: What is that? (*following him attentively*)

JACK: The bell-wire! You see it is broken here (*pointing*) as well as by the window, and here is a piece carried – why it's carried away over here and twisted over the tongs and shovel. (*Goes quickly to fire-place.*)

MRS. F: We found it so that night.

        (JACK *is tracing some imaginary line, and* FALLON *and the rest are watching.*)

SKIF: (*sneeringly*) Pooh! That's nothing!

FAL: Shut up! Don't interrupt!

SKIF: Oh, very well.

JACK: (*on his knees, examining hearth*) No trace. Yes! here in the soot, and then down through the hearth, and into the flue and so down.

FAL: (*dropping on both knees, almost into grate*) Down – down what?

JACK: (*Rises, yet still pre-occupied.*) But a link is missing – something has been removed. (*to all*) Something must have been standing here (*indicates floor near tongs*) which has been removed. Do any of you know what it was? (FALLON *confused*)

ANN: Sure, there was the coal scuttle!

JACK: The coal – yes! Where is it?

FAL: (*Rises, confused.*) It's gone – taken away.

MRS. F: Why it's in the closet.

        (JACK *runs to closet.* FALLON *tries to interpose.* JACK *unlocks closet and takes out scuttle.*)

FAL: Stop! stop!

JACK: Here! (*Holds scuttle up and looks at bottom.*) I have found it.

ANN: The thief.

JACK: Well, no. But the place where he got out. (*Points to hole.*)

SKIF: Oh, come!

FAL: You are making fools of us! I should like to see the thief that could get out there!

JACK: You shall see him in the moving clouds! His time for work is in the tempest, and his mission is swift, sure and terrible! You wish to know his name – it is Lightning!

ALL: Lightning!

JACK: While you shuddered at the thunder, his aim was accomplished. In the turning of a thought, this robber came and was gone! Mark his footstep! See how it shrivelled up the leaf in one vase, while it spared the other – cut with its sword of fire the cord on the wall and severed the wire of the bell – then, conducted by the path it had made, (*Indicates wire that reaches from the wall to the tongs.*) attracted by the iron and steel, it struck *this* (*Points to scuttle.*) and, passing through the hearth into the flue – was gone.

FAL: (*stupified*) The Lightning! But the chain?

JACK: (*turning up the gilded coal*) Look here! Your chain pleased the lightning, my friend – which took it up, fashioned it to suit it's own fancy – and dropped it here!

FAL: If this be true –

ROSE: (*who has been examining the coal*) Here is a little piece of pearl!

FAL: (*taking it*) There was a pearl clasp to each end of it, and this is one.

JACK: See the proof!

FAL: (*suddenly remembering*) Oh, Lord! Four hundred dollars worth gone! – and I, like an infernal fool, bought up a whole coal yard and dreamed of a goldmine! But I'm glad! Here, Bessie! Bessie, forgive your brute of a father! (*Runs, unlocks* BESSIE's *door and opens it.*) Bessie – empty – gone.

        (ROSE *runs off through door at right.*)

ALL: Gone?

ROSE: (*Re-appears with letter.*) She has lowered herself from the window, and this is all she has left. Oh! (*crying*) Sister Bessie – somebody read this. (*Gives it to* FALLON.)

FAL: (*Reads.*) 'I have no other resource but death! Father, God forgive you! Tell Jack!' (*Drops paper and sinks on chair weeping.*)

MRS. F: (*Crosses to him.*) Oh, Garry, Garry! What has become of her?

JACK: Your cruelty has done its final work. Old man, you have driven her to the grave.

        (*A low murmur outside.*)

FAL: (*starting up*) What sound is that?

SKIF: (*at window*) It is a crowd, bringing a body here.

MRS. F: (*Runs to door.*) My child! My Bessie! where is she?

        (*Two or three men and women appear, then* FRED, *bringing in*
        BESSIE *insensible. She is placed in chair;* JACK *kneels beside her.*
        MRS. FALLON *takes* BESSIE's *head to her breast.* FRED, *with*
        ROSE. FALLON *and* SKIF. *and* ANN *are at back with crowd.*)

FRED: She is only insensible. Thank heaven, it was no worse. I was just in time.

ROSE: Where did you find her?

FRED: I saw her just as she escaped from the house. In another moment it would have been too late.

MRS. F: She wakes softly! Bessie, darling!

FAL: Bessie, can you forgive me? I have been a brute – but I am punished in my own heart.

BESSIE: And Jack?

FAL: Here he is! Jack, damn it, why don't you speak to her?

JACK: Bessie, darling, we shall never be parted again. (*She places her hand feebly on his shoulder. All surround the group.*)

SKIF: Well, my friends, as there is no possibility of doing any good here, I suppose I ought to withdraw. I would have been happy to have captured the thief that took the chain, but although the Metropolitan police stop at nothing, the lightning is one of those vagrants it can't arrest. Good morning! and a happy wedding. (*Exits, followed by officer.*)

JACK: Bessie – once more snatched from death – promise me to live now for me! (*She smiles.*) There – don't speak! That smile tells me I may hope – don't speak!

BESSIE: If you don't let me speak – how can I say 'yes'?

CURTAIN

HORIZON

An original drama of contemporaneous society and of American frontier perils. In five acts and seven tableaux

First produced at the Olympic Theatre, New York, on 21 March 1871, with the following cast:

ALLEYN VAN DORP, just from West Point with his first
    commission. Dispatched to the Far West   Hart Conway
COKE BALLOU, ESQ., A gentleman, who professes what he
    practices; i.e., The law; crusty as coke and dry as a whip   C. Warwick
SUNDOWN ROWSE, ESQ., A distinguished member of the
    Third House at Washington. Owning a slice of every
    Territory, and bound for the Far West to survey his new
    Congressional Land Grant, which lies just this side of
    the Horizon   George L. Fox
THE UNATTACHED MR. SMITH, not a member of the
    Joint High Commission, and unattached to the British
    Legation at Washington   H. R. Teesdale
JOHN LODER, alias Panther Loder, alias White Panther –
    One of the reasons for the establishment of 'Vigilance
    Committees' in the peaceful hamlets of the Plains   J. K. Mortimer
WOLF VAN DORP, one of the sort the West opens its
    arms to receive   J. B. Studley
ROCKS OF TENNESSEE, The Mayor of Rogue's Rest,
    one of the magic cities of the West   O. B. Collins
'UNCLE BILLY' BLAKELY, An enfranchised citizen of
    that enterprising town   G. A. Beane
MR. MACKENZIE, otherwise known as 'Sandy Mac,' –
    another   J. L. Debonay
JUDGE SCOTT, the chairman of that Bulwark of
    Western Liberty: – the Vigilance Committee   E. T. Sinclair
SALERATUS BILL,   F. S. Wilbur
GOPHER JOE,   More of 'em!   Mr. Tyson
CEPHAS, A Fifteenth Amendment   I. Pendy
THE HEATHEN CHINEE, who does not understand   H. H. Pratt
SERGEANT CROCKETT, One of Uncle Sam's Police
    of the Prairies   Frank Chapman
WANNEMUCKA, The civilized Indian and 'Untutored
    Savage' who dwells with the white settlers in their
    villages   Charles Wheatleigh

WAHCOTAH, The friendly Indian who stops among the
  white soldiers at their Fort   W. H. Pope
GUIDE   Mr. Atkins
MED, White Flower of the Plains   Agnes Ethel
MISS COLUMBIA ROWSE, The Belle of *Both Houses*
  and fascinator of the Lawmakers   Ada Harland
MRS. VAN DORP, The Abandoned Wife   Mrs. J. J. Prior
THE WIDOW MULLINS, Emigrant parent, of undoubted
  extraction   Mrs. Yeamans
RHODA, her daughter   Fanny Beane
ONATA, a prairie princess   Lulu Prior
NOTAH, The little papoose, who'd became the spoil of
  the stranger   Jennie Yeamans
ALICE, of the Van Dorp Household   Flora Lee

Citizens of Rogue's Rest, Indians, Indian Maidens, Soldiers.

ACT I

Parlors in the VAN DORP *city house, Waverly Place, New York. Elegant saloon divided by arches, center. Windows at back, looking upon Washington Park. An Apartment seen off right, through another arch. Hallway and main entrance right. Mantel at right with framed picture above it, the face turned to the wall. Table left with lamp, books, etc., inkstand and pens, blotting paper, legal paper. Elegant furniture of various patterns about, in each apartment.* MR. BALLOU *is discovered sitting at table, pen in mouth, pressing blotter on paper. He takes up paper and reads:*

BAL: Hum! I think that's about what she wants. A full and particular exhibit of the property, real, personal and mixed, belonging to Margaret Van Dorp. Now, whosoever gets it at her death, gets a very snug fortune. (*Folds paper up, puts it in his pocket with a number of others, which he takes from table, then looks at his watch. Bell, as if of street door, heard.*) Hallo! Some other visitor! We shan't have an opportunity for a private conference after all. (*Rises and crosses to mantel.*)

>   (ALICE *shows in* CAPT. ALLEYN, *who enters with hat, travelling-bag and light overcoat.*)

AL: Glad to be home again. That I am. All night on train. Just stopped at the hotel to fix up – ran over after breakfast. (*Gives hat and bag to* ALICE.) No one here? (*Sees* BAL.) No! Why, Mr. Ballou! (*They meet and shake hands.*)

BAL: This is an unexpected pleasure.

AL: So it is. I've just come from Washington, by the Owl Train. Where's mother?

BAL: Mrs. Van Dorp – I've not seen her yet.

AL: (*to* ALICE) Will you announce me to mother, and ask if I shall attend her in her own room, or here?

ALICE: Yes, sir! (*to* BAL) I have already told her you were waiting, Mr. Ballou. (*Exit.*)

BAL: Oh, it don't matter about me. Lawyers can wait. We always charge for that, eh?

AL: I hope so.

BAL: Especially when we are sent for on particular business. (*Sits.*)

AL: You lawyers have easy lives. You jog about from house to house, from court to court. Now as to us soldiers –

BAL: (*yawning and laughing*) As to you soldiers!

AL: You may laugh. You think there's no duty for us now.

BAL: No! Thank the Lord!

AL: (*quizzically*) What do you think of the prospect of a war with England?

BAL: Bosh!

AL: Well then, nearer home; how about the Indian troubles?

BAL: They don't hurt us, they're a thousand or two miles off towards sundown.

AL: That's the very spot.

BAL: (*interested*) What spot?

AL: Where I'm going!

BAL: (*jumping up*) You?

AL: (*taking* BAL's *vacated seat*) Ye-e-es! (*yawning*)

BAL: And you are to fight the Indians?

AL: Unless the Indians run away.

BAL: What will your mother, I mean Mrs. Van Dorp – pardon me, she regards you as a son; what will she say to this?

AL: I wrote and told her the whole news. I start tomorrow to join my company.

BAL: (*slapping his forehead*) An idea strikes me! She sent for me because you are going away. I see it all!

AL: Oh, you consider yourself a good substitute for me, eh? (*Sits on ottoman.*)

BAL: Badinage aside. Mrs. Van Dorp, ever since she adopted you as a son –

AL: Twelve years ago –

BAL: And two years after her husband disappeared, so cruelly taking with him their infant daughter, Mrs. Van Dorp, I repeat, has spoken to me about making her will –

AL: Then I don't want to hear anything more about it – (*Crosses to table, sits.*)

BAL: (*Takes* AL's *seat.*) Don't be afraid. I'm not going to reveal her affairs, for she never told me how she meant to leave her property.

AL: All right then. Fire away! (*Sits by table.*)

BAL: She has sent for me a dozen times, and a dozen times has put off the deed. I remonstrated, but her only excuse was: 'we will wait yet a little longer.'

AL: Poor mother! She referred to the expectation she had, that her husband would return and bring back her little girl.

BAL: Her husband took his precautions well. If he meant to leave his wife forever, and to punish her, he succeeded.

AL: To punish her? For what?

BAL: Family history! Family history! He was poor and proud, she was rich and proud. They were both aristocrats, but his family, I think, was a little the older, just a little; that is to say, he could count more Knickerbockers for ancestors than she could.

AL: You are severe!

BAL: As I have had the genealogy searched up, I know. Well, they belonged to the first families, she, the richer. They were married. Marriage, my dear boy, is called a union of souls; when it is, it is doubtless a good thing; but when it is a union of pride, passion and violence, it – well – well! They lived a wretched life for five years. They had one daughter. The husband would not bow down to his wife, so she kept him on short allowance of money; he tried to go into business, failed, got dissipated, reformed, broke down again – and was locked out of his wife's house, (*Rises.*) by the way, this very house.

AL: (*Rises, sadly.*) Yes, I have heard.

BAL: (*Crosses, sits.*) He watched it; tried to get in to see his child, little Margaret. Was prevented. Laid his plans accordingly, and one night gained admittance by force, and seizing the child, carried it off.

AL: Yes, so I've heard. And the next day a letter was delivered which told her –

BAL: Her child was lost to her forever. His vengeance was complete. At one blow

---

Knickerbocker: an original Dutch settler of New York.

he deprived her of her only pleasure, and closed her doors forever to the gaiety and revelry she loved so much.

AL: The spiritless, cowardly villain, who lived on her bounty and abused her goodness! (*Sits.*)

BAL: Oh, of course. But the world says, she was to blame.

AL: She, the kindest, most generous of women?

BAL: Yes, to all but a husband. There are some girls who never ought to marry. She was one, she had no patience to bear the failings of a husband.

          (ALICE *enters.*)

ALICE: My mistress is coming, Mr. Alleyn. (*speaking outside*) Come in, John!

          (SERVANT *enters with a step-ladder, which he places against mantel.*)

ALICE: Now, then, get up right away and turn the picture.

          (SERVANT *mounts the steps, but before he can turn the picture,* MRS. VAN DORP *enters.*)

ALICE: Too late! Stop! (JOHN *descends ladder, as* MRS. V *goes to* AL, *who runs to meet her. She kisses his forehead.*)

MRS. V: My boy! (*to* ALICE) Never mind at present, Alice. Leave the ladder. You can go now.

ALICE: Yes, ma'am! (*Exits, with* JOHN.)

MRS. V: My dearest Alleyn! I have looked for you so anxiously. (*Crosses.*) Mr. Ballou, I beg a thousand pardons for keeping you so long. But you know how whimsical I am.

BAL: Oh yes, I know. You have made me run many a wild goose chase before.

MRS. V: (*to* AL) You see how he scolds me.

BAL: It's my privilege as your legal adviser.

MRS. V: (*Sits in chair, which* AL *places for her.*) And you always advise me well.

BAL: You are at last resolved to make –

MRS. V: (*Stops him by raising her hand.*) No!

BAL: No? Then why am I here?

MRS. V: Perhaps to have one more proof of a woman's inconsistency. I sent for you determined to do – (*Stops, then to* AL.) Alleyn, my dear, will you see if the windows are closed in the reception room yonder?

AL: Certainly, mother! (*Goes up and off.*)

MRS. V: (*quickly to* BAL) Say nothing more about this matter. I have changed my mind.

BAL: Again, and why?

MRS. V: I am ashamed to confess it. You know my old reason.

BAL: You used to say, it was because you cherished a very vain hope –

MRS. V: What if I tell you, that hope revives again?

BAL: It is insanity to encourage such fancies.

MRS. V: Enough then! Being in unsound mind, I cannot make my will.

BAL: But, madam –

MRS. V: Be satisfied with this. By the time Winter comes, I may send for you again. Till then, say nothing.

BAL: But your –

MRS. V: (*rising*) Of that I will never speak to you again.

BAL: (*crossing*) Then for the twentieth time, I put my memoranda in my pocket, and take my leave.

MRS. V: Stay! You will arrange with the bankers to have Alleyn's allowances sent to him in the West, wherever he may be stationed.

(ALLEYN *enters at back.*)

BAL: Oh, that's easily arranged. Nothing more?

MRS. V: Nothing more!

BAL: Good morning, then. (*Bows, goes up and meets* AL.) Well, my dear boy, take care of yourself.

AL: Going? Good-bye! If I'm scalped, I'll beg the ferocious Indians to send you a lock of my hair. (*Both laugh.* BAL *exits.* AL *comes down quickly.*) My dearest mother!

MRS. V: My son! (*She sits, and* AL *brings an ottoman and sits by her side.*) I haved wished so much to see you. Your letter told me all, but not all the little things I wished to know. And so you are a Captain, and you have made influential friends in Washington?

AL: Yes! I wrote you about the best of them, didn't I? The eccentric Mr. Rowse?

MRS. V: Rowse! An odd name, not very distinguished.

AL: Oh, he's better than his name. A bluff, unpolished, generous heart. A shrewd fellow, but an honest politician, I'll be bound.

MRS. V: What is his profession?

AL: Why, a politician!

MRS. V: Is that a profession? What do they do, these politicians?

AL: Why they, let me see – they take care of the public's interests. You know the public interest must be cared for. The old adage is: 'What's everybody's business is nobody's business.' Now the politicians do everybody's business, and account to nobody for the way they do it. That's Rowse's way. He got me my commission.

MRS. V: He must be a very influential man.

AL: Very. He is interested in several railroads – not yet built, and he owns immense tracts of public lands, granted him by Congress to build the railroads on. His daughter, Miss Columbia Rowse, says, he owns a slice of every Territory in the West.

MRS. V: (*coldly*) His daughter?

AL: Why, yes. Didn't I speak of her in my letter? How ungallant of me. She is the belle of the western country; sets the hearts of all the Territory beaux in flames, and is adored by the House of Representatives.

MRS. V: (*stiffly*) A very charming person.

AL: And remember, her father made me a Captain, and – oh! I quite forgot another.

MRS. V: Another daughter?

AL: No. Another friend, whom I have also invited – Mr. Smith.

MRS. V: Mr. Smith! What a name!

AL: The Honorable Arthur Wellesby Vere de Vere Smith.

MRS. V: (*interested*) From England?

AL: An English nobleman, mother. Sixth son of an Earl, poor, but a good fellow, and no snob. He's not attached to the British Legation at Washington, and he goes with us out West to see life.

MRS. V: They must stay with us to dinner.

AL: Thanks, my dear mother, I now –

MRS. V: And now, my dear Alleyn, give me but a moment of your time, while I tell you – you, to whom alone I can confide it, a foolish old woman's troubles. Alas, my boy, I had thought never to see you again.

AL: How? You alarm me!

MRS. V: I have been ill, I thought dying.

AL: And you never wrote, that I might fly to your side.

MRS. V: It was a sudden shock, too sudden, too sudden to call on any human being for aid. Last night –

AL: So lately –

MRS. V: You remember that this is the anniversary of a terrible day to me. I had not the courage to suffer the servants to do, what on this day I have for thirteen years permitted: that picture to be turned from the wall. Go, Alleyn, let me look once more – (AL *ascends ladder, and turns the picture.*) The picture of the man, who was once my husband, and the father of my child.

AL: (*at foot of ladder*) I know it well!

MRS. V: Little Margaret loved him! loved him more than me. God forgive us all.

AL: (*going to her and kneeling*) Poor mother!

MRS. V: Alleyn, I saw his face last night.

AL: Last night? In a dream?

MRS. V: It must have been, but it seemed real. Listen to me. It seemed that you were in some wild Western place – huts scattered here and there – a sparse and ruffianly crew about you. Among them was that man.

AL: Your husband.

MRS. V: He was unchanged – he looked the same. A man of deadly purpose and cruel eyes. I was by your side. He said to me: 'Madam, you have come here to seek me. You have found me. But your child you will never see again.' He turned to disappear into a hut. I could not move. I heard a voice, my little Margaret's voice, crying out: 'Mother, save me!' She was struggling to be free. Her cries grew fainter, then ceased. I fell in a swoon to the earth. When I awoke, I was upon the floor of my own room, alone, and cold as death.

AL: (*Sits.*) It was but a dream.

MRS. V: Was it not rather a divine light cast upon the mystery that fate has wrapped around my child's destiny? I feel it to be so. And I say to you now, that I am certain your mission to the Far West is to be the means of restoring her to me.

AL: I pray it may be so, with all my soul. (*ring at door*)

MRS. V: Your friends! (*crossing to door*)

AL: Will you see them now?

MRS. V: Certainly! one finds good friends so seldom, that yours shall be heartily welcomed at all times.

> (ALICE *enters with two cards on a salver, which she hands to* MRS. V.)

MRS. V: (*reading*) Mr. Smith – Miss Rowse.

AL: I wonder where papa can be? This is the daughter, and accompanied by the unattached scion of nobility.

MRS. V: (*to* ALICE) Ask them in here. (ALICE *exits.*) Is the Honorable Mr. Smith likely to become attached to Miss Columbia?

AL: Stranger things have happened.

(ALICE *ushers in* MR. SMITH *and* MISS COLUMBIA.)

AL: (*advancing*) Very happy indeed to see you.

COL: We came, you see!

MR. S: (*shaking hands with* AL) Thanks – very much.

AL: Allow me to present you. Mrs. Van Dorp, Miss Rowse. Mr. Smith. (*salutations*)

COL: I'm sure, delighted. What an elegant house. Quite an old family mansion. Just like the old Knickerbockers. Delightful people.

MR. S: Charmed to have the opportunity. Yes. Van Dorp has spoken of you so much. Yes.

MRS. V: You have just arrived in the city, I believe.

MR. S: This morning. Yes. We came –

COL: We came by the Owl Train. All of us. Pa, and the Honorable Mr. Smith, and I. We look like owls ourselves, I dare say, – railroad travelling is so scary.

MRS. V: I suppose we shall have the pleasure of seeing your father. Pray be seated. (AL *moves stool.*)

MR. S.: (*All sit.*) Yes. Thank you. Mr. Rowse said he would –

COL: Said he'd come on after us. Pa is always so full of business. He's got to see at least a dozen prominent men here this morning. Most of the prominent men are in New York now.

MRS. V: Indeed.

COL: You know pa never has any business with any but prominent men. Pa knows all the prominent men. All the prominent men know pa. I know as many prominent men as pa does.

MRS. V: It must be very pleasant.

COL: Oh, no! Prominent men are not at all pleasant. You think they are great things till you know them. When you find them out, there's nothing particular about them, except that they are prominent.

MRS. V: Your opportunities of judging are very great, no doubt.

COL: Oh, very! Pa and I have been in Washington every session for five years. All the prominent characters come to Washington. I know them all, from Maine to Texas.

AL: Ha! ha! Have you any preferences as to States, Miss Columbia?

COL: Not as to States. But the Territories are not nice.

MRS. V: (*surprise and inquiry*) The Territories?

COL: The prominent men of the Territories. They come to Washington, but they lack polish, – no refinement. I have no sympathy with them. I know all the prominent characters of the Territories; they don't compare with the States. But what I do admire, is the old families.

MRS. V: Your acquaintance there is also quite large?

COL: Oh, yes! The old families come to Washington too. Many Knickerbockers. As soon as I heard you son's name, I told pa he was a Knickerbocker. You have a real Knickerbocker name. I've read Washington Irving all through, and I know all the names.

Washington Irving: (1783–1859). Daly refers to *A History of New York From the Beginning of the World to the End of the Dutch Dynasty* (1809), presented as the work of a fictional character called Diedrich Knickerbocker.

MR. S: It must be awfully fatiguing to remember them all.

COL: Oh dear no! I've practiced on names. Pa and I never forget a name. We have to remember them. A prominent man never forgives you if you forget his name. I tell the Honorable Mr. Smith he will never rise in America, because he forgets names. Don't I, Honorable?

MR. S: Eh? Yes! Oh, yes! Miss Rowse very often says so. I can't always recollect. I get them mixed, particularly the colonels, and the generals, and the judges.

COL: Yes, it was so funny. One day he called the Governor of Montana Colonel, and the Governor's Secretary he called Judge, and Judge Jones he called Governor, and he nearly defeated one of pa's bills. Didn't he? (*to* AL)

AL: I believe something happened.

MR. S: It was distressing. I was very sorry. Yes. But I apologized to the Judge, and the Secretary, and the Governor, and it came out all right.

MRS. V: That was fortunate.

AL: I believe Miss Rowse's powers of fascination had to be exercised.

COL: Oh, you bad fellow! (*to* MRS. V) But it's a fact. Pa had to give a dinner, and I had to do the agreeable, and play euchre with the Governor. It's a dreadful thing to be the daughter of a public man, Mrs. Van Dorp. (AL *moves stool.*)

MRS. V: It must be indeed. (*door bell*)

COL: Oh, that must be pa now. Pa can't be very punctual, but he never breaks his word. In Washington the members say: 'Sundown Rowse has given his word he'll square things; we'll go for this bill.' If pa broke his word once, he'd never get another bill through.

        (ALICE *enters.*)

ALICE: Mr. Rowse.

MRS. V: Show Mr. Rowse in, Alice. (ALICE *exits.*)

COL: It's a real holiday for pa to get away from Washington, he enjoys it so much.

ROWSE: (*outside*) All right, never mind me, I'll find the way.

        (ROWSE *enters.*)

ROW: Ah, here I am, you see. I knew Columby'd be here before me! Ah, Captain! (*to* MR. S) How de do again, Honorable.

AL: Allow me. (*Presents* ROW *to* MRS. V.) My mother, Mr. Rowse.

ROW: Glad to see you, ma'am. Warmish day for the season. Run almost to death. Came straight here from the Fifth Avenue Hotel. (AL, COL, *and* MR. S *withdraw, looking over portfolio of pictures.*)

MRS. V: Allow me to thank you, Mr. Rowse, most warmly for the kind interest you have taken in my son, and the great service you have done him.

ROW: Don't mention it, ma'am. It wasn't much. I had a cousin wanted the commission, but he didn't like to go and fight the Indians. Your son jumped at the offer. My cousin backed down, asked me if I thought he was a chicken to go for the Chickasaws, and told me, I might go myself and keno the Kiutes.

Chickasaw: tribe of the southeastern United States.   *keno*: gamble on.
Kiutes: this tribe (and its variant, Caiute, on p. 145) is an invention by Daly. Perhaps it was created from Kai and Ute, two real North American Indian tribes, though neither appropriate in locale. Other possibilities are Kaiyau (a California tribe), Cayuse (a plateau tribe of the Northwest), Paiute (a tribe of the West and Northwest), or Kiowa (a Plains Indian tribe of the Southwest).

MRS. V: Alleyn is very courageous, and believes a soldier ought to fight.

ROW: He's a trump. I appreciate pluck. I come of a fighting family. They were the first settlers of Kansas. Perhaps you have heard of Hefty Bill Rowse of the Prairies?

MRS. V: I never had the pleasure.

ROW: He was my father; one of the original border ruffians; as honest a man as ever lived. He cleared the settlements, and was elected Mayor twice by thirteen majority. Your son will get some notion of Western life, when he goes out.

MRS. V: (*going to* AL *and putting her arm about his neck*) My hope and belief are, that Alleyn will never forget he is a Christian, even among the lawless settlers of the West.

ROW: Oh, I know him. He's a little soft here, perhaps, but he'll get hardened. Men must be hard out West, ma'am. I was too mild myself for it, and father sent me to Washington to dicker. I had a brother, who loved glory and stayed home. He was killed in a fight the very day I got my first bill through Congress. We buried him on my first land grant: two thousand acres near Silver Creek.

MRS. V: (*returning*) There are many persons from the Eastern States, who settle in the West, are there not?

ROW: Thousands! Whole families! Single men – single women – double men – and double women, husbands and wives, you know, – everybody.

MRS. V: Do they ever change their names, when they settle there?

ROW: If they are absconders, they mostly do. If there ain't no debts, nor no trouble about the law, they don't. I know one town where every inhabitant's got another name. They take ranks there according to the amount of debts they ran away from. The worst insolvent is elected Sheriff.

MRS. V: There are many too, no doubt, who go West to escape domestic troubles.

ROW: Oh, yes. The most part of the single people out there are divorced. It's a healthy country for domestic troubles.

MRS. V: And the place Alleyn is detailed for, what is it called? Is it much settled?

ROW: Fort Jackson! Well, it's pretty well out towards the Horizon.

MRS. V: You are familiar with the locality?

ROW: (MRS. V *and* ROW *sit, pulling out a map.*) Here's the map. I know it, because my grant takes it in. I run from here on the west bank of the Big Run River down to Dogs' Ears, that's the name of another settlement, then out to All Gone, that's an Indian camp, and then to Hollo Bill, that's a traders' settlement. Queer names, ain't they?

MRS. V: (*sitting*) And the inhabitants of these places?

ROW: (*folding map*) Queer lot! Native Americans with a sprinkling of the Injun and the least speck of the Chinee. I expect to locate several more towns, when I get out there.

MRS. V: You are going too?

---

dicker: negotiate, barter, haggle.

Fort Jackson: apparently fictitious. There was a Fort Jackson in Alabama, famous for the Treaty signed there, ending the Creek Indian War (1813–14).

ROW: Oh, yes! I'm off with the Captain. C'lumby's going too, and the Honorable
    Smith. I'm going to prospect for the first hundred miles of the Fort Jackson
    and the Big Run branch of the Union Pacific Railroad, chartered by Act of
    Congress and subsidized with twenty thousand acres, well adapted for farms
    and settlements.

COL: (*coming down*) What on earth are you doing, pa? Boring Mrs. Van Dorp with
    your everlasting railroads and maps. Put 'em up.

ROW: Well, C'lumby, I –

COL: Put 'em up, I say. This ain't a committee room.

MRS. V: Your father has been giving me most valuable information.

COL: All about his land grants, I suppose?

MRS. V: (*significantly to* AL, *who comes down with* MR. S) About the people of
    the West.

MR. S: I'm really anxious to see the great West. Yes. The aboriginal red men and
    the real original white settlers.

AL: And I to see that noble territory, destined to be the cradle of a greater republic.

COL: And I'm dying to see whether the place has grown any since I was a girl. The
    Honorable Smith is going to hunt buffaloes and bison, and I'm going with
    him. Ain't I?

ROW: Well, after I've located my railroad –

COL: Bother your railroad. It's like a grand picnic. We'll go over the prairies on
    wild horses and camp out in the woods.

MR. S: And eat buffalo steak cooked by the camp fire. Just as they do in the
    romances.

MRS. V: And the danger –

AL: Danger, mother! What danger?

MR. S: Danger! Is there danger, truly?

MRS. V: The lawless inhabitants of the settlements. I have heard such stories of
    violence.

MR. S: We'll call in the police. Besides, I'm protected by the British flag.

AL: They can offer no insult to a soldier of their own land.

COL: At least they will respect the softer sex, won't they, Honorable?

ROW: Well, if the worst comes to the worst, I'll stand by my Act of Congress and
    retire behind my land grant.

MRS. V: But the Indians –

MR. S: Aw – yes – the noble savage. I'll speak to him as his paleface brother. I've
    read the Leatherstocking stories, and I think I can manage 'em.

AL: No quarter to the savages, who murder women and children. But to the weak
    and oppressed, I may be a friend. Duty commands no more.

ROW: Well, I'm going to take a case of dollar store jewelry out with me, and trade
    it for furs with the simple-minded red man. There's nothing like carrying
    civilization into the Far West.
    (ALICE *enters.*)

ALICE: Dinner is served, ma'am.

Leatherstocking stories: series of five novels (1823–41) by James Fenimore Cooper that follow
the career of Natty Bumppo from his youth to his death.

MRS. V: Come, gentlemen. Come, Miss Rowse.

ROW: Dinner – really – bless me – I've half a dozen appointments.

AL: Oh, you must!

ROW: But I've so many engagements.

COL: Let them wait for once.

ROW: But we start at eight.

MRS. V: And so, at least, we can spare one hour in saying farewell to friends we may never see again. (*All surround* ROW, *and preceded by* MRS. V, *they go up.*)

CURTAIN

ACT II

The town of Rogue's Rest – sixty miles from Fort Jackson – one of the wooden cities of the West. Hotel of primitive order at left, with portico, etc. Sign: 'Occidental Hotel, on the European plan.' Opposite, a building of two stories, upper windows practicable, and reached by door and steps facing audience, over which hangs a lamp and painted thereon 'The Clarion of the West.' Lower floor with signs, etc., denoting Pacific Express office. At back is a low fence, partly concealing a house and low shed. Gate in fence near left. At the rise of the curtain ROCKS OF TENNESSEE, *the landlord of the hotel, and late Mayor of the town, is seated on piazza in a wooden arm-chair, smoking, in a loose lined duster.* WANNEMUCKA, *the Indian, is lying, in front of hotel, pretending sleep. In center is a group of rough settlers, some sitting, others standing, engaged in loud discussion. Among them is* BLAKELY, GOPHER JOE, *and* MACKENZIE.

BLAK: Why won't they hang 'em?

GOPHER: Quick work, I say!

MAC: No gal's work for us.

CROWD: No nonsense! Clear the settlement! Give us a chaw of terbacker!

ROCKS: Give us a rest, boys, do! What's the use of a row! If the job's to be done, it will be, and there's an end.

BLAK: It oughter been did afore.

MAC: Two months ago.

ROCKS: Well, ain't you satisfied now? You've tilted me out of my lawful authority as Mayor of this settlement, and you've taken the law into your own hands.

BLAK: No disrespect to you, boss, you know.

ALL: Oh, no!

ROCKS: I know it, boys, and I'm much obliged. The civil power wasn't able to control. The settlement got overrun with blacklegs, horse-thieves, and other alibis and aliases, as we say in the law books, and so the citizens unite to clean the town themselves.

BLAK: (*to others*) That's it, like a book.

ROCKS: You've formed a Vigilance Committee, and the Vigilance Committee cleared the streets effectually.

---

blackleg: swindler, especially in gambling or racing.

BLAK: Not quite, governor. After the clearing two weeks ago, a few specks of dirt still stuck to us.

ROCKS: You mean Loder, the gambler?

BLAK: Yes, and Wolf!

ROCKS: Old Wolf? Why, he's only a nameless old sot. He sleeps his day in that shanty yonder, more like a pigsty than a house. (*All look back at house.*) I'm agin turnin' him off, for the sake of his gal.

BLAK: Let 'em go somewhere else. We're hard-fisted, hard-working men. Mac, pint yer pistol. (*Takes dram from bottle produced by* MAC.) Empty again. That's the fourth time today. Reform is powerful dry work. I say, Mr. Mayor, have her filled up. (ROCKS *catches bottle and throws it inside.*) Clear 'em all out, I say, and begin with the Injun.

MAC: Oh, the Injun will go, if we kick him out.

ROCKS: Boys, it seems to me there's an almighty powerful talk here by the jury, right afore one of the condemned. (*Points to Indian.*)

BLAK: Oh, he's drunk, as usual.

MAC: Not so early.

ROCKS: Listening, I'll swear! (*Significant nod to boys, as he rises and draws pistol.*) Boys, the Injun might as well go at once. I've got my blotter handy, and we might as well wipe him off the records now. I'll just pint his ear and blaze. (*Goes to* WAN, *cocks his pistol audibly, then points the muzzle first at his head, then over it, and fires. The Indian doesn't stir.*) Dead drunk!

ALL: Oh, he's all right!

　　　　　(ROWSE *appears at window of hotel and looks out.*)

ROW: Hallo! you there! (*Crowd look up.*)

BLAK: Hallo yourself! Who are you, stranger?

ROCKS: It's all right, gentlemen. There's a party come in last night on their way to Fort Jackson. This is one of them. Mr. Rowse is all right. Let me introduce you to some of our citizens, leading citizens. Leading citizens, Mr. Rowse! Mr. Rowse, leading citizens!

ROW: How are you, leading citizens! What are you holding a town meeting for?

BLAK: Stranger! The free and independent residents of this place don't usually explain their business to folks from other settlements; but if you want particularly to know, why, we've formed a Vigilance Committee, to reform the character of our population.

ROW: A what? A Vigilance Committee? (*calling inside*) I say – Smith – here!
　　　　　(MR. SMITH *appears at window.*)

MR. S: Good gracious! What is it?

ROW: Did you ever hear of that peculiar institution of the Far West, called a Vigilance Committee? Here's one, you ignorant Britisher; take a look.

MR. S: Vigilance Committee! Good gracious, yes! Some kind of animal. Where is it?

ROCKS: The Committee is meeting in the newspaper office. (*Points.*)

ROW: Ah! The head of the animal is across the street. This is only the tail.

MR. S: Yes! Good gracious!

BLAK: Strangers! The Committee is a scary animile, and mustn't be riled. If you ain't got proper respect for it –

ROW: (*loudly*) Respect for it! (*blandly*) Will you kindly excuse me for a brace of shakes, until I can come down stairs.

ALL: Oh, come down out of that!

ROW: Thanks! Honorable, let's descend. (*They disappear.*)

BLAK: (*to* ROCKS) Who are these suckers?

ROCKS: Very influential man, Mr. Rowse, from – Washington. Eh, here he is!
　　　　(ROW *and* MR. S *enter from hotel. Crowd observes them sulkily.*)

ROW: Happy to make your acquaintance. May I ask what this Committee is met for?

BLAK: To sit on the live bodies of our parties that must get out or be put out.

ROW: You propose to expel four of your fellow-citizens?

MAC: (*savagely*) Yes, we do!

ROW: I beg your pardon! How are you? (*Shakes hands with him.*) And may I ask whom you propose to put out?

BLAK: First – an old drunken sot, Whiskey Wolf they call him, he hangs out over there.

ROW: And what's he done?

MAC: He's drunk and disorderly. (*Passes bottle around 'mongst crowd.*)

BLAK: Secondarily – A scoundrel that calls himself Loder – a gambler and worse, if there can be! (*Takes off hat to wipe face, pack of cards fall out.*)

ROW: He's very offensive to the community, I suppose? More so than Whiskey Wolf, eh?

MAC: Oh, Wolf's only a boozer.

MR. S: A what?

ROW: A boozer! From the verb to booze, one who boozes. (*to* MAC) When does he booze particularly?

MAC: All day. Loafs all the time. Never does a day's work. Then there's the Chinee.

ROW: You haven't got a Chinee here? Not a regular Heathen Chinee?

BLAK: Yes, we have. The varmin!

ROW: And what does he do?

BLAK: Why, he works for half-pay. Steals the bread out of honest men's mouths.

MR. S: You condemn one fellow because he don't work, and another because he does.

BLAK: Stranger! We clear out every feller as don't do as we want him to.

MR. S: Yes, I see!

BLAK: Lastly – That Indian yonder – lying over there drunk.

ROW: Oh, that's one of the criminals! Where are the others?

BLAK: I reckon you'll find Whiskey Wolf in thar. (*Points to fence.*) The Chinee is sent for. He's down in the hollow, making chairs out of swamp rushes, and the boys are laying for Loder down by the Tree Tavern.

ROW: Very good! Now, my fellow-citizens, you can leave this job as fast as you please.

ALL: (*starting*) What!

ROW: I say you can get an extension of time to perform this contract, and go home with your minds easy.

---

brace of shakes: a few moments.

BLAK: What do you mean?

ROW: I mean this. From what I see, the people you mean to turn adrift on the plains are no worse than the average crowd that's necessary in pretty nearly every well regulated city. And they may as well stay here, as go to other settlements to steal. (*murmurs by the crowd*)

BLAK: Stranger, was your parents particularly long lived?

ROW: They stood the chills pretty well for their time of life.

BLAK: Well, they never had sich powerful shakes as you'll have, if you don't get into your shafts and travel pretty quickly.

MR. S: Good gracious! What does he mean? Get into your shafts! He takes you for a horse!

ROW: All right, gentlemen! I see you want things done regularly, and the papers produced. (*Takes out map.*) Do you see this map? Here's Fort Jackson, there's All Gone, and there's Rogue's Rest – the flourishing city, where we now stand to inhale the breath of freedom.

ALL: (*looking over his shoulder*) Correct!

ROW: You observe a red line, which takes in the various localities aforesaid and stretches out to the top of Coyote Hill.

ALL: (*as before*) Correct!

ROW: Then, here's a copy of the grant by which the Government of the United States has conveyed to me the whole of this purchase, including your populous city. In other words, I'm the owner of this here settlement, the landlord of the premises, and proprietor generally. In a few words more, I won't have any mob law, and no Vigilance Committee, and no riots, and no games of that sort on my land. How's that for turning up a bower? Do you pass?

BLAK: (*drawing pistol*) No, stranger, I order it up.

MR. S: Good gracious! Where are the police?

BLAK: Boys, shall we give them a taste of our productions?

ALL: Clear 'em out. (*They draw knives, pistols.*)

BLAK: Take up them papers! Put them up, I say! (ROW *gathers map nervously.*) Now git!

ROW: But I say –

MR. S: Don't touch me – I'm a British subject. I'm under the protection of the British flag.

MAC: (*Knocks* MR. S*'s hat off.*) Oh, scissors! (*Hat kicked about.*)

ROW: You'll hear from me. I'll – (*The two are hustled toward the hotel.*)

ROCKS: Now, gentlemen, – (*interposing*)

                (SALERATUS BILL *enters, running.*)

BILL: I say, boys, Loder and the Chinee have gone down by the Gulch. Slater thinks they are skedaddling.

BLAK: The devil they are. After 'em, lads. Don't let 'em slope till we get through with 'em!

---

shakes: chills and fever accompanied by trembling.
shafts: parallel bars of wood between which an animal drawing a vehicle is hitched.
bower: the right bower is the highest trump card in the game of euchre.
oh, scissors!: indicative of disgust or impatience.
slope: escape or run away.

(*The mob run off, headed by* BLAK *and* BILL, *crying: 'This way',
'All right', 'Go it', etc.*)

MR. S: (*picking up hat, which the mob have given a final kick*) It's an outrage. It's
a blarsted country, altogether.

ROW: I'd like to know the good of an Act of Congress, if it ain't respected out
here.

(ALLEYN *enters, gaily.*)

AL: Hallo! What's up? You look flushed.

MR. S: Flushed? Yes! By Jove! Just look at my hat, that's flushed.

ROW: Cap, you're just the man I want. How long will it take you to bring a company of soldiers from Fort Jackson and put out my tenants?

AL: Why, I haven't got as far as Fort Jackson yet. We were not to start until this
evening.

ROW: Well, just start at once, and bring your troops over, won't you? I want this
town blown to the devil.

AL: Why, I thought this place was your property.

ROW: And can't I do what I like with my property? Blow it to the devil. I'll stand
the loss.

AL: What's the trouble? I like the place. I've just seen the prettiest girl you can
imagine. A backwoods Venus, lovely, young, delicate. Miss Columbia and I
met her down by the post office. A perfect Venus.

ROW: Don't talk to me of Venuses. I want Marseses, the gods of war. Alleyn,
there's a Vigilance Committee here and they're going to –

AL: Not harm you or Smith?

ROW: No. To turn some poor devils out.

AL: Oh, that's nothing; they're always doing that.

ROW: But I won't have it on my property. Won't you stand up with me and stop
it?

AL: We two against a hundred – nonsense.

ROW: Then you won't –

AL: (*looking off*) Sh! Yonder comes the girl I spoke of.

ROW: (*angry*) Hang the girls. A man is no use to the community till he's married.

AL: There she goes with Miss Columbia. What a charming step! Smith, just look.

MR. S: Ah, yes! Miss Rowse, monstrous fine girl.

AL: No, the other!

MR. S: Ah yes, so she is! Introduce me!

AL: (*taking his arm, impetuously*) Come along, we'll meet them; hurry up; she may
turn off into some of the houses. (*Exit, dragging* MR. S.)

ROW: Here. Don't go off! What the deuce were girls ever made for? Who'd have
thought there'd be a girl out here to turn a chap's head. (*Sees Indian asleep.*)
There's one of the poor devils the committee's after. He'll be shot while he's
drunk and never know it. (*Touches Indian with his foot.*) Hi! you! Indian!
Wake up and let me scare you to death! (WAN *jumps up and confonts* ROW,
who jumps back.) Hello! that's early rising. What kind of whiskey do you
drink to freshen up so quick after it?

WAN: Injun no drink whiskey. Stranger think Wannemucka drunk?

ROW: It looked like it. What did you say your name was?

WAN: Wannemucka! Wannemucka chief! Big chief! Tribe far away! Down there – sunset!

ROW: If your tribe's down by the sunset, they're luckier than you are.

WAN: Wannemucka safe. Ugh! White man think injun sleep. White man talk – injun's nose (*Imitates snore.*) asleep, injun's eyes (*closing them*) asleep, but injun's ears awake.

ROW: Oh, you've been playing possum and listening. Then you've overheard them. Why don't you run for your life?

WAN: Wannemucka, no fear. (*Shows dirk.*) Wannemucka got this.

ROW: Oh, you mean to fight for it, eh? But they'll kill you if you resist.

WAN: (*Goes to bush behind express office, shows rifle, which he replaces.*) Wannemucka not go alone.

ROW: You want to go with the sots and blacklegs, eh? Don't, injun; go back to your tribe in decent company.

WAN: (*stealthily approaching*) White stranger ever love?

ROW: Did I ever love? Not much, or if I ever did, it's gone clear out of my head. What of it?

WAN: Wannemucka love! She here! Wannemucka take her, or never go back to his tribe again.

ROW: The deuce. Some squaw of yours here, eh? More girls! Even the injun won't save his own bacon, but risks it for a girl. Well, you're a plucky bird anyway. I wish you joy and well out. There's my hand. (WAN *takes it reluctantly, and then, drawing near, fingers* ROW's *chain.*)

WAN: Ugh! nice!

ROW: You like it, eh?

WAN: Heap o' skins to buy that?

ROW: Yes, injun, it would take considerable coon skins to reach.

WAN: Injun like it! Injun want it!

ROW: (*Draws back, takes revolver from pocket.*) Stand back! Do you want to rob me, you unsophisticated redman?

WAN: No. Injun play for it.

ROW: Play for it?

WAN: Poker! (*Takes greasy pack of cards from his pocket and shuffles them.*)

ROW: Moses in the bulrushes! Who'd have thought of this romantic injun sporting a deck and offering to play poker. My feelings are hurt. If you had offered to scalp me, you red rascal, I might have forgiven you. But poker! That knocks the romance, and I despise you!

> (LODER, *who has entered at 'My feelings are hurt', and carelessly looked on, now comes down.*)

LOD: (*to* ROW) You won't take a hand then, stranger? (*Laughs and sits on back of chair, pulls out a pencil, commences to whittle it.*)

WAN: Ugh! White panther here! (*Puts up cards.*)

ROW: Take a hand? I'm sorry I shook hands with him. I'd rather have seen him carry a tomahawk than a pack of cards.

LOD: That's civilization, my friend! When the noble savage was in his native state, he went for the hair of your head. Now he's in the midst of civilization, he carries the weapons of enlightenment, and goes for the money in your pocket.

ROW: I'm sorry for it. I don't want things so progressive on my lands.

LOD: P'raps not. But it's just as well you didn't play with him. Injun is a prime hand at poker. You can't beat him. Why he almost comes up to me. (*Rises, crosses to* WAN.) Don't you, injun? (WAN *grunts.*)

ROW: And who may you be?

LOD: Me? Oh, I'm no account. I travel.

ROW: Oh, a traveller!

LOD: You've put it right. My business is to leave. I'm an outpost of progress! I open up the great West to the march of mind. When things get settled about me, I go on! (WAN *plucks his sleeve.*) Eh? What's up?

WAN: Something to tell.

ROW: (*curious*) Eh?

LOD: (*to* ROW) I reckon your friends are looking for you.

ROW: Eh?

LOD: (*to* ROW) I reckon your friends are looking for you.

ROW Eh?

LOD: (*coolly*) I reckon your train's about to start.

ROW: My train?

LOD: (*sternly*) I reckon you are staying here to mix up in domestic secrets, and worry my mind. Your train's waiting. Get aboard!

ROW: Oh, you want me to go! Why didn't you say so? Well, for a new country which belongs to me, and inhabited by people who don't pay me any rent, this is the most impudent – (LOD *points for him to go.*) Oh! This town will certainly have to be blown to the devil. (*off into hotel*)

LOD: (*whittling*) Now, Injun, what is it?

WAN: Sh! (*Points to Vigilance Committee room.*)

LOD: Well!

WAN: Committee!

LOD: Vigilance? (WAN *nods.*) How do you know?

WAN: Injun sleep there! Crowd! Talk much! Must go, or – (*Imitates hanging.*)

LOD: So soon, and only here four months. (*Puts up knife, puts pencil away calmly.*) And no money to speak of. Just getting into luck too. Well, if I must, I must. So I'm the marked man?

WAN: Injun, too!

LOD: You? You poor, pitiful sneak! To turn you out! It's a damned disgrace to John Loder to be walked out of a town with a greasy injun!

WAN: More! Old man! (*Points to wall at back.*)

LOD: (*excited*) What! Wolf and his daughter?

WAN: All go!

LOD: (*deeply moved*) She! By the – it will kill her! What has she done? But what the devil am I standing here for? Come! (*excitedly*) In with me. We must wake him. We must agree upon some plan. Come! (*Rushes to the door in wall.*) Oh, the cursed wretches! (*looking back at Vigilance Committee's house*)

If I! – Oh, get in, and don't waste time. (*Pushes* WAN *and exits after him.*)
   (ALLEYN *and* MED *enter; he carries her little basket.*)

MED: This is as far as I go.

AL: I wish – I wish it were a mile further.

MED: A mile further, and I so tired!

AL: Pardon me, I didn't think of that. I was only thinking of the pleasure to myself.

MED: And why would you be so pleased? Though I used to love to walk, to run, to
  play all day in the woods.

AL: Won't you sit down? Just for a moment! Right here. I love to hear you talk.
  (*He gently presses her to sit on seat.*) You are a real backwoods girl, ain't
  you?

MED: And you are from the city?

AL: Yes! Ever so far away.

MED: It is beautiful in the cities where you come from – is it not?

AL: Very. Wouldn't you like to leave such life as this, and go to the splendid city?

MED: Yes, and I will too, if I live.

AL: If you live?

MED: Yes! Didn't I tell you? No, I told her. They say I'm very sick.

AL: You look delicate and pale – but a little rest, a little care – why don't you see
  the doctor?

MED: We never have doctors come out here. But there are agents always travelling
  about with patent medicines. (*Laughs.*) Oh, it was so funny to see the settlers,
  big fellows, six feet high, who never knew what it was to be sick, coming into
  father's cabin with big bottles and little bottles, that cured everything – so the
  agent said – and making me try them all. I think they made me worse, don't
  you?

AL: (*Sits beside* MED.) But, now – surely you are not ill now?

MED: No, I do not suffer now; but the feeling is like – as if the struggle were over.

AL: Oh, if I could only do something for you!

MED: Yes, that's what they all say.

AL: Who are all?

MED: Oh, everybody! That is, some particular ones.

AL: Who are they? Not lovers! (MED *nods and plays with his buttonhole.*) Lovers!
  You! Why you are only a little girl!

MED: Ain't I big enough to love?

AL: Yes, now.

MED: And I suppose yesterday I wasn't? Oh, that's not true. I've had so many.
  Everywhere we went, father and I, somebody was sure to say: 'I love you.'

AL: And you – what did you say?

MED: Oh, your necktie is all loose.

AL: No, no! Tell me what you said?

MED: Let me fix the necktie first.

AL: Yes, on condition that you tell me. (MED *ties it while he speaks.*) What did
  you say when they told you they loved you?

MED: I said – I said: 'I love you, too.'

AL: (*vexed*) You did? (*about to rise*) Well, you shan't fix my necktie any more.

MED: (*pulling him down again*) Nonsense! Let me fix the necktie.

AL: (*pause, then looking up into her eyes*) Do you know, you're a little witch?

MED: (*Rises, and goes down stage.*) No! Witches never get sick.

AL: When I get to Fort Jackson, I'll send the surgeon over to see you.

MED: (*archly*) I don't want to see the surgeon.

AL: (*quickly*) I'll come with him.

MED: No, indeed, Mr. Assurance, I didn't mean that. But will you come to see Meddie, truly?

AL: Meddie? What an odd name! What does it mean?

MED: Why it means me.

AL: Then it's just the name you ought to have.

MED: But will you come – truly – ever so truly?

AL: Yes, indeed, I will.

MED: And when are you going away?

AL: This very day. (*looking at watch*) By George, within half an hour! (*Starts up.*) The guides and horses are waiting for me.

MED: (*Rises.*) And the pretty lady who is coming yonder – is she going with you?

AL: Oh, no! She and her father, and the tall gentleman are going to take the boat down the Big Run River, to explore his grant.

MED: I know the river. Wannemucka's tribe belongs there. Only think, an Indian loved me, wanted me to be a princess. (*Laughs.*) I didn't tell *him* I loved him. I told Loder, and Loder knocked him down.

AL: What perils surround you, poor little thing!

MED: I'm so glad the pretty lady is not going with you.

AL: Why?

MED: Because!

AL: Nothing could make me ever forget Meddie.

MED: You are sure.

AL: I know it as I know –

> (*Puts his arm about her waist, when* COLUMBIA *and* MR. SMITH *enter.*)

MED: Oh! (*Runs up and disappears through gate in wall.* AL *does not see where she goes to in his confusion.*)

COLUMBIA: Oh, Captain! Caught you in the very act.

MR. SMITH: Yes! Very act of besieging the fortress of Beauty.

COL: Yes! The very act of throwing the lines of circumvallation around her waist.

MR. S: Where did she go?

COL: Must have run down the street.

AL: (*aside*) Gone! But I can run over from the Fort and see her, and I will, if I have to –

COL: Oh, Captain, don't be so silent. I knew you were struck by her, as soon as we met her. And that was the reason I took the Honorable Mr. Smith around the settlement, while you had a chance to chat with her.

AL: You were really so good and amiable to –

COL: To get out of the way and leave you two alone?

AL: Oh, I don't mean that! But she really is a charming, original little thing, just the little angel to –

COL: To chat with once, and then forget. Nonsense! A puny, sickly little back-woods girl! I'm astonished at you! Come! To Fort Jackson! There's your guide, now.

(*Enter* GUIDE.)

GUIDE: The horses are saddled, Captain. We only wait for you.

AL: Baggage all right?

GUIDE: Yes, sir! Mr. Rowse is down by the Tree Tavern, waiting for you. We'll have to start soon, to get over the ford before dark.

AL: (*Crosses.*) Then I'm off.

MR. S: (*to* COL) We'll see him off, eh?

COL: Certainly. We'll see you safe out of here, for fear any other original and charming little girls should detain you.

AL: Ah! Spare me this time. It's my first and only flirtation. Perhaps I shall never see her again.

COL: Oh, how solemn!

MR. S: By Jove, it's heartrending! (*Laugh, and take him off between them.*)

(LODER *enters from the gate, pulling* WOLF. *His daughter,* MEDDIE, *follows, clinging to him in fear. After a while,* WAN-NEMUCKA *follows them out moodily.*)

LODER: (*as he enters*) I tell you, governor, it's neck or nothing. The town's up, and we've got to go!

WOLF: (*staring about him*) Go! (*vacantly*) Where?

MED: Oh, anywhere from this dreadful danger. Father, father, do try and think. Rouse yourself! Do try and understand our peril.

WOLF: Ps'h! My throat's as hot! – Have you a drop in your flask, Loder?

LOD: Don't think of liquor now, governor. Brace up! Be a man!

WOLF: I'm past it. I'm a gone body, Loder. I feel it here (*head*) and here (*heart*). Nothing in me. Let 'em kill, curse 'em. I've travelled thousands of miles, like a madman, for years. Perhaps I'll get a madman's rest now. (*Points to ground.*) The grave!

LOD: If you can't take care of yourself, think of your daughter! If you stop here, they'll shoot you, maybe. I've tried the obstinate dodge, and nearly squalled for it. If you're dead, what becomes of her?

WOLF: Margaret! Meddie! Dear little Med! You won't leave me?

MED: Never, father, while I live. You will go with us. It may not be far. We may find another and kinder settlement; if not, we can go to the Fort.

WOLF: I'll not budge a foot. I'm a desperate man, and I'll dare 'em to do their worst.

LOD: And your daughter? You told me often that you loved her. You won't trust her to strangers?

WOLF: You coward! You'll desert us, will you?

LOD: Look here, governor, I'm not a coward when I have a show. But I don't fight mobs. Besides, I'm tired of this place. It's getting too civilized for me. When civilization steps in, it's time for John Loder to make a move higher up. I mean to put for some infant settlement a little nearer the Horizon, and give it a lift. (*Goes up.*)

WOLF: Go then! Back out! Leave us!

WANNEMUCKA: (*coming forward*) Wannemucka friend! No leave old Wolf to die by the dogs. Injun honest! Take care of young white girl. (LOD *starts, looks around.*)

WOLF: You! Trust my child to you!

WAN: Indian honest! (LOD *regards him coolly.*) Wannemucka chief of tribes. Take white maiden there. Be a princess.

WOLF: You copper-colored scoundrel! You dare to think of my daughter – a lady – (*Strikes him.*)

MED: Oh, father, don't! Let us fly together! Oh, Heaven, what will become of me?

LOD: (*approaching*) Whatever happens, little girl, no harm shall come to you, while I have breath and blood to spend. (*Noise of voices and mob heard.*) Come, old man, will you start?

WOLF: No!

LOD: Then put your girl in the house before the pack is on us.

WOLF: Take her!

MED: Oh, bring him with us! (*to* LOD) Do not leave him!

LOD: Don't fear, I'll do what I can.

> (*Stage growing darker. Voices heard nearer.* LOD *leads* MED *to gate, she exits, he closes it. Voices louder. Windows of the newspaper office open and the heads of* SCOTT *and others of the Committee, appear. Mob enters, headed by* BLAKELY, MACKENZIE, *etc.*)

BLAK: (*as he enters*) Here they are, all together! Bring along the other scamp! (*The other,* CHINEE, *is thrust forward among exiles.*)

SCOTT: (*as crowd yell*) Gentlemen, order! Order!

BLAK: Silence, boys – for the Committee.

SCOTT: Gentlemen, the Committee has decided.

MACKENZIE: Three cheers for the Committee!

SCOTT: (*Puts on glasses, reads from paper.*) The Committee having proceeded according to law and the traditions of the Border, have found the following persons guilty of the following crimes: (*turning to another leaning over him*) Colonel, will you jest oblige me by moving your everlasting elbow out of my back! (*Resumes reading.*) John Loder, gambler and fighter!

BLAK: Stand out, Loder!

LOD: Anything to oblige, Judge! I say, Scotty!

SCOTT: Well! (*Looks down.*)

LOD: You couldn't give me a reference to the next place, could you? (*Mob laugh and shout: 'Good boy!' 'Game!'*)

BLAK: Order! Order!

SCOTT: Wolf Van Dorp, drunkard, gambler, and nuisance generally!

WOLF: (*rousing up*) Stop! What name was that?

SCOTT: Your own name, I reckon.

WOLF: It's a lie! Strike it out!

SCOTT: Not while the evidence is before the Court. (*Packet is handed him from inside.*) A bundle of old letters, newspapers cuttings, etc. found in your house.

WOLF: You robbed my house, you thieves!

SCOTT: I reckon we took an everlasting squint about your premises, while you were drunk last night, and found it. But the Court's done with it. You may take it. (*Flings it out.* WOLF *grasps it eagerly, looks over it, then puts it in* LOD*'s hand, and whispers to him.*)

SCOTT: Wannemucka, Indian, gambler and horse-thief, as the Committee suspects! (WAN *folds his blanket and grunts.*) Chinee, heathen and mean-spirited furriner!

CHINEE: Me? No, Melican, me no bad! Love Melican! Work – no play – no gamble – no drunk – poor Chinee man!

SCOTT: Judge, will you give that critter an all-fired squelcher! (BLAK *attends to Chinee.*) The sentence of the Committee is that the aforesaid persons, all and singular, git up and git out of this settlement within thirty calendar minutes from the reading of this verdict. (*The mob cry out and menace the group.* SCOTT *folds up paper.*) What do the prisoners at the bar say?

LOD: Gentlemen, for my part, I always bow to the will of the people. The population having unanimously elected me to represent them in some other settlement, I beg leave to thank them, and gracefully retire.

WOLF: (*Whispers to him.*) Don't fail me, lad! That packet to Med. In your charge I leave her, remember!

LOD: Trust me! (*Bows to mob.*) Gentlemen, good evening! (*Exit.*)

WAN: (*who had listened*) Injun remember too. (*aloud*) Palefaces! Wannemucka glad to go to his tribe! (*Stalks off, and during the ensuing scene creeps back stealthily and takes his rifle, then goes off behind houses.*)

SCOTT: Clean out the rest. (*The* CHINEE *is hustled out and the crowd return to seize* WOLF.)

WOLF: One moment! (*All stop.*) You may kill me, but I don't go!

CROWD: Hang him! Hang him!

WOLF: Well, you can't hang me but once!

>   (*The mob rushes at him with a yell. One of them,* MAC, *makes a noose, when* ROWSE *enters, and interferes.*)

ROWSE: Stop, you fellows! Am I in time? No one hung up yet, I hope?

SCOTT: Who's this?

ROW: I'm the landlord here, and I want to know, who gives notice to quit, while I'm about?

BLAK: (*to* SCOTT) He's crazy!

SCOTT: Then clean him out! (*Mob advances.*)

ROW: (*Draws a pair of revolvers, crowd halts.*) I thought not. Now fellow-citizens, listen to me. What are you going to do with this old man?

SCOTT: He's been ordered to leave and he won't.

ROW: Well, what then?

MAC: Then he must be strung up.

---

squelcher: a heavy blow.

ROW: (*shaking hands*) Oh, how are you again, neighbor. (*Crowd murmur.*) You won't hang him till he's tried, will you? The committee, as far as I can get at it, only agreed to turn him out. He must be tried before he's sentenced to be hung, mustn't he? (*Mob murmur.*)

SCOTT: That's so, gentlemen. The stranger's correct; we must try him for refusing to go.

ROW: (*Takes off his hat, puts it on ground, and mounts chair on stand.*) Fellow-citizens: Let us not be irregular, let us not proceed to mob law, let us give the prisoner at the bar a fair shake before he steps out on the rope-walk and misses his footing in the circumnambient air; is that law? (*Mob assent among themselves.*)

SCOTT: (*blandly*) I beg pardon. What is the gentleman's name?

ROW: (*blandly*) Rowse! Sundown Rowse, of Washington, District of Columbia!

SCOTT: (*to mob*) Gentlemen, allow me to introduce Mr. Rowse, of Washington. Mr. Mayor, a glass of water for the speaker. (*Canteens, bottles and flasks are passed to* ROW.)

ROW: Thanks! Gentlemen, we are here proceeding according to law. Not the musty statutes of effete systems and oligarchies of the Old World, but the natural law implanted in the bosoms of man since our common ancestors were washed, wrung out and hung up to dry by the universal flood.

MOB: Hear! hear! Go in! (SCOTT *and committee clap their hands.*)

ROW: What do I find? I find the public characters of the town are called upon to do justice to their fellow-man. In such cases, in my experience, it is not un-common to ask any prominent citizen from another, and friendly settlement, Washington or New York, for instance, to meet with the committee and form a general High Commission to settle all disputed points. Am I right, or am I not?

SCOTT: (*who during the proceeding has consulted with the committee*) Mr. Rowse is correct. Such has been generally the practice. The committee respectfully invite Mr. Rowse to step up and jine the deliberations. (*All applaud,* ROW *is handed down, his hat is given him and is escorted to door.*)

ROW: Thanks! fellow-citizens! Thanks!

SCOTT: The committee also invite all citizens to keep their feelins suppressed for ten calendar minutes longer, while the deliberations is going on. (*Disappears.*)

BLAK: All right, governor! Boys come in and see what old Tennessee Rocks has got. (*shout from crowd, who press forward and exit into hotel*)

WOLF: (*alone and eagerly*) They mean to do their worst. Life is precious after all. (*Picks up a flask which one of the crowd has dropped and drinks.*) It gives me new courage. I am not too late. I can yet fly with my child. (*Runs eagerly up to gate. Shot heard from behind.* WOLF *falls.* WANNEMUCKA *appears, throws gun down near body, jumps up on shed.*)

WAN: Now injun have white princess!

(LODER *and* MED *appear at gateway.*)

LODER: You red devil! Come and take her!

(*The mob rush from hotel. The committee and* ROWSE *appear at windows.*)

CURTAIN

ACT III

SCENE 1 – *The stage represents the head of flatboat navigation on Big Run. Fort Jackson is supposed to be situated here, and on the right, up stage, a low, one story store shed projects, surmounted by a flagstaff and colors flying. The bank of the river extends from right to left. At back is a view of wild country, through which the Big Run winds its course. A flatboat is moored in the stream, a little to the right, and is approached by a sort of gang-plank from the bank. The time is afternoon. The curtain rises upon a scene of bustle.*

    SERGEANT CROCKETT *is directing soldiers, who are loading the boat with bags, barrels and bundles from shed, right, and* CEPHAS *and other darkies are loading it with wood from left.* CEPH *carries a single, very small log for each load, singing or whistling with each trip. The* HEATHEN CHINEE, BLAKELY *and* WAHCOTAH *are playing cards on the ground by left lower entrance. A sentry is on duty at back on bank. The curtain rises to a chorus of the darkies loading up.*

CEPHAS AND DARKIES: –
> 'I'm proud to be in the service of the Lord,
> And I'm bound to die in his army.'
>> (*As darkies go off for another load,* CEPH *comes down and leans on his stick of wood, looking over the group of card players.*)

CEPH: Hi! dars de way dem trash has of musin' derselves. (*to* CHINEE) Hi! you, play de ace, you cussed fool.

BLAK: Play the ace? Why, not him! He's tried five aces on us already.

CHINEE: Me no understand!

BLAK: Don't understand, eh? Well, what you *don't* understand would furnish brains for a mosquito.

CEPH: Hi! golly! Chinee wipe nigger out, eh?

BLAK: Well, for 'Ways that are dark and for tricks that are vain.' Why he's won all my terbacker already! Ain't you, Chinee?

CHINEE: Me poor chap! No understand Melican. (*sudden grab at trick* BLAK *is about to take*) Mine, Melican!

WAHCOTAH: (*throwing down his cards*) Ugh! Cheatee!

BLAK: (*drawing a dirk*) That's the sixth ace in this hand; let me go for that heathen. (CHINEE *starts up, runs towards shed.* BLAK *after him, stopped by* SERGEANT.)

SER: Come! none of that! Let this poor devil alone. Get aboard with you! (BLAK *goes off muttering into boat.*) Come, African, lively with that wood there.

CEPH: All right, massa sejiant. (*Sings as he goes off into boat:*)
> 'I'm proud to live in the service of the Lord,
> And I'm bound to die in his army.'
>> (MR. SMITH *enters from left, looking back. He is dressed in Western prairie fashion, but with silk hat, gun and bag.*)

MR. SMITH: Yes! This way! come along.

WIDOW MULLINS: (*outside*) Heaven bless your honor, that's what I say. (WIDOW MULLINS *enters, followed by a young girl, her daughter, and a little girl.*)

SER: Well, Honorable, what sort of game is that you've got?
> (COLUMBIA *appears on boat.*)

MR. S: Game! Yes! you know – oh! there Miss Columbia! By Jove – good morning!

COL: Good morning! Here, you boys, give me a hand.

SOLDIERS: That we will, Miss! (CEPH *again comes. Two men run forward and help her across gang-plank.*)

COL: Thanks! (*Comes down and confronts* WIDOW *and others all laden with packs on their backs.*) Mercy, who are these?

SER: You must ask the Honorable, miss, he brought 'em in.

WIDOW: Faith, an' he did – long life to him and more whiskers if he wants 'em.

COL: Irish! Irish out here?

WID: Irish! out here; faix ma'am, an' did iver ye go anywhere ye didn't see the Irish?

MR. S: Yas! I was surprised myself. You see I was out trying to start some game, and all in a minute I came out on the place, about three miles yonder, where these poor people live.

SER: Oh, you are the Mullinses?

WID: Yis! We are the Mullinses! This is my daughter Rhody, ma'am, an' this is Molly, sir! and we were sitting by our house – more by token, it was no house at all, seein' it had been knocked over by the Indians – crying our eyes out, whin this gentleman come up –

RHOD: Thrue for ye, mother.

COL: Your house knocked over?

SER: By the Indians? When?

MR. S: Last night, they told me.

RHOD: Thrue for ye, sir!

COL: Must be the same party Capt. Alleyn has gone after with pa! I hope they'll catch 'em, the red ugly things.

MR. S: When did they go?

COL: Just after you left this morning. A scout ran in and told the captain about a party of Indians who had been seen in force along the river.

MR. S: Then, by Jove, I've had a narrow escape. It's well I came back so early with these poor people.

WID: It's well ye did, sir, for if the Indians got ye, they'd make elegant work of that fine head of hair of yours.

MR. S: By Jove, they might have scalped my whiskers.

RHOD: Thrue for ye, sir!

COL: But why did the Indians attack you?

WID: (WAH *listens quietly.*) Faith, they were looking for firearms and 'munition, they said. An' whin I tould 'em I was only a poor widdy and my husband was dead wid the chills and fever, and divil a gun we had, dey just knocked over the shanty and left us cryin'.

SER: How many were there?

WID: Faith, I was so worried I couldn't see; a thousand I'm thinking.

RHOD: Sure, mother, there was only three.

WID: Now, Rhody, how can ye say dat?

RHOD: I obsarved 'em and heard them speak of a larger party they were going to join.

SER: Ah! They were scouts then. We'll soon find out when the captain comes back.

RHOD: (*to* COL) Please, ma'am can you tell us what we're to do? We've got no home now, 'an sure we're afraid to go back.

COL: What do you want to do?

WID: Sure, ma'am, we want to get near some settlement where we'll be snug and safe.

COL: We're all going down the river this evening, about thirty miles to a settlement. We go in the boat there; would you like to come?

WID: Sure and that we would, ma'am. (*Distant gun heard.*)

SER: (*going up to boat*) That must be the captain now.

COL: Oh, there comes my pa, then; I'll get him to find room for you, and you shall go with us.

WID: Heaven bless ye, ma'am!

RHOD: Bless ye, ma'am! Thank the lady, Molly.   (*Together*)

SER: (*on boat, looking off*) Yes, there's the party.

MR. S: Any captive Indians?

SER: No! eh? (*looking off*) Something very odd. Mr. Rowse has got something. (WAH *interested*) A dog, I think, is following at his heels.

MR. S: (*to* COL) By Jove, how odd! I go to hunt buffaloes and bag an Irish family. And your father goes to capture Indians and brings back a bow-wow!

COL: Oh, you amusing creature. But don't you like this exciting life? Isn't it romantic? Nothing but alarums, Indians, scouting and scalping – charming!

MR. S: Very!

COL: So delicious. You go to bed at night and never know if you'll ever get up to breakfast again.

MR. S: Yes.

COL: To go and take a romantic walk by the side of a placid stream, expecting every moment to have your bonnet strings cut by a bullet –

MR. S: Delightful!

COL: Let's go and take a walk. We have still time enough, before the boat will be ready to start.

MR. S: (*nervously*) Certainly! with pleasure! and if the Indians surprise us –

COL: You will divert their attention – while I run back for help.

MR. S: Oh, ye-es! (*Both exit.*)

               (ALLEYN *and soldiers and darkey enter. Soldiers enter shed.*)

SER: (*Salutes.*) Captain!

AL: No luck so far, sergeant. We must have a party to scour the river bank to-night. It's not safe to send the boat down unprotected.

SER: Indians really about, sir; this poor family were surprised last night by three scouts, and they spoke of a larger party.

AL: We came on the trail of an Indian family, and found an old squaw with her child. The woman fled, leaving her infant.

SER: That's what we saw with Mr. Rowse then, sir!

AL: (*laughing*) Yes, he seized the infant, not knowing what he was doing. She has clung to him ever since, and he's rather annoyed at it. Where is the friendly Indian you spoke of this morning who hangs about the fort?

SER: (*Calls.*) Wahcotah!

WAH: (*advancing*) Injun here!

AL: What tribe is it that surprised this poor family?

WAH: No tribe. No warriors, only boys. Indian boys love fun.

AL: Are you sure? But the squaw and child were found today –

WAH: Wahcotah not know. Many squaws. Many papoose. (*Waves his hand to take in the whole country.*)

AL: You are friendly to us, I understand?

WAH: Yes! Injun friendly!

AL: Are there any warriors in this neighborhood?

WAH: No!

AL: It is safe for the boat to go down the stream to-night?

WAH: Safe!

AL: All right, then. (*to* SER) We'll send a double force out since this friendly Indian is sure there is no danger. Is every one in? (WAH *retires.*)

SER: All in but two, Captain. The young girl and that gambler chap from Rogue's Rest.

AL: The young girl. Where is she?

SER: Miss Rowse said they'd be back before night.

AL: If they don't, the boat must wait for them.

SER: Wait for them? They can easily overtake the boat.

AL: A weak, delicate little thing like that?

SER: No better than the rest of the lot I'm afraid, sir!

AL: What do you mean?

SER: Why, she belongs to the worst crowd in the place. I've seen her often at Rogue's Rest. You don't know Western people, sir, like us old hands.

AL: Perhaps not. But as for her I'd stake my life – ! Hem! no matter. Look after the boat. (SER *goes up.*) These fellows will laugh at me. (*Exits into shed.*)

SER: The captain's struck with her, sure. Well, he ain't the first. I was that way myself when I saw her last, but hallo! (*looking off left*) Here's Rowse and his little injun sure enough.

> (ROWSE *enters in great confusion, followed by* NOTAH *clinging to his coat.* WAH *watches.*)

ROW: Oh, bother, you young sarpint! get out.

NOT: No – no – no – no!

ROW: You confounded little imp! What do you mean by hanging to me for? I don't want you.

NOT: Oona gow ga tcheka!

ROW: What?

NOT: Oona gow ga tcheka – poo!

ROW: Stop swearing! I wonder what she means by that? If she could only speak English, I might reason with her. I don't know any Indian. What's your name?

NOT: Oona gow ga tcheka! Chun ge gah! Bees mah!

ROW: Bismarck! It can't be possible! I say, why don't you go home?

NOT: (*impatiently*) Ugh!

ROW: Won't you please go home to your family. I never was a mother, and I don't know what to do for you.

NOT: (*same*) Ugh!

SER: You've got a nice captive there, sir!

ROW: I wish I hadn't. I took hold of the little devil when her mother ran away, just to look at her, when she caught hold of my coat-tail, and hasn't let me go since.

SER: (*to* NOT) Wont-ee come-ee to me-ee?

NOT: No – no – no – no!

ROW: Oh no! All of 'em have tried that.

SER: Here's an Indian, sir, maybe he can tell you what she wants.

ROW: Eh? Where is he? Here you!

WAH: Injun here.

ROW: What's this little red imp mean by hanging on to me in this way?

WAH: Little papoose belong to Wannemucka's tribe.

ROW: I don't know Wannemucka's tribe, and I'm not an orphan asylum. Speak to her. (WAH *touches* NOT *on shoulder. She starts back and clings to* ROW.)

NOT: Oona gow ga tcheka! Chun ge gah!

WAH: She say – white father got her – white father keep her always.

ROW: The deuce she does!

NOT: Looka nah ta poocha. No!

WAH: She say her father is big chief!

ROW: Then why don't she go back to him?

WAH: Injun papoose cunning. You capture papoose. Big chief father come after you.

ROW: Eh!

WAH: She keep close to you – big chief know you took papoose.

ROW: And what then?

WAH: Big chief kill man steal his papoose.

ROW: Then she's hanging on to my coat-tail so as to identify me as the right man for big chief to kill. (*Shakes* NOT *off.*) Here you, get off! Thunder and lightning, what a prospect! (*Walks about followed by* NOT.) I might as well have a death-warrant pinned to my back at once. I shall have to dye my hair and black my eyes – I mean my face – to avoid recognition. Let go, you little imp. (*Throws her to* SER, *who holds her laughing.*)

NOT: Ah chee mah poo da! Ah chee! Poo da!

ROW: Just hear her swear! I haven't the slightest doubt that's very profane in the Cherokee language.

WAH: Me take all trouble. Me take papoose, carry her back to tribe. White man safe den!

ROW: Will you? That's a good fellow!

WAH: Come! (*about to take* NOT)

SER: Not so fast. We can't let her go!

WAH: No!

Cherokee: Indian tribe that formerly lived around the Great Lakes but then migrated to the Southeastern states. By the date of this play, they had been removed to what is now northeastern Oklahoma during what is known as the Trail of Tears (1838–39). Since Daly is unclear as to the location of *Horizon*, this reference might either locate the play in the Oklahoma territory or suggest Rowse's ignorance of Indian tribes and their behavior. The Cherokees were very civilized and peaceful.

ROW: Why not?

SER: Not while the Indians are up and likely to give us trouble. You've made a lucky capture, Mr. Rowse. I think this is the child of some important chief. If so, we can hold her as a hostage, and it may save somebody's life in the event of trouble.

ROW: So she may. I recollect that rascally Wannemucka tried to steal old Wolf's daughter, and when Loder was too sharp for him, he slunk off, swearing he'd have her yet. We'll block his domino with this little hostage.

WAH: Me no have papoose?

ROW: (*crosses to* NOT) Not till I get safe to Big Run settlement, and leave old Wolf's daughter in safety. Then you can tell Big Chief to send me a receipt in full, and I'll give him the chick.

WAH: But papoose want to go home.

ROW: Does she? We'll see. (*to* NOT) Hanky – panky – hickory – dickory?

NOT: Me – ho – na – watee!

ROW: She says she won't go home till morning, and don't want to be put in her little bed. Come along. (ROW *exits into boat and down hatches.* SER *laughs and goes up right.* WAH *slinks off, and presently reappears in the water, climbs into boat and goes below by opening.*)

　　　　(MED *enters with little bundle, her hand on* LODER's *shoulder.*)

MED: See, we are here at last!

LOD: After a very hard day's tramp for you, little girl.

MED: For me? Why you carried me across all the fords and almost over all the hills. I'm not tired. To-night we will be floating down the river with our friends, and by to-morrow we will be safe in another settlement.

LOD: But your father's last wishes –

MED: (*sinking on mound*) Poor father! Not even a last word for me.

LOD: You weep for him. Well, well, perhaps it was only because he *was* your father.

MED: Why, what do you mean?

LOD: I mean he didn't do a father's part to drag you – you, a lady – through the world like the child of a thief.

MED: But he loved me, and so I cry for him.

LOD: I won't say another word agin him, princess! I don't know what fine feelings are, and so I'll keep quiet.

MED: Yes, you do! You're kinder to me than anybody – ain't you?

LOD: That's why I want to take you home.

MED: Home? Where?

LOD: To New York.

MED: Oh, yes, so you told me. All about that rich lady who is my mother, and who turned my poor dead father out of her house.

LOD: (*taking packet of letters from his pocket*) So these letters say. And a strange story it is.

MED: Do you think my father's daughter would ever enter that lady's house, sit by her side, live in luxury and comfort, and yet dream every night of the far-

---

domino: a knock-out blow.

off town where *he* was treated like a wild animal, shot down like a dog –
and all her fault?

LOD: But you're her daughter!

MED: And he was her husband. If I were married, and the man I promised to love
were the greatest villain –

LOD: (*eagerly*) You could love him?

MED: Pshaw! I don't know what I'm saying. (*turning to him*) Promise me, you
won't speak of my mother again nor of taking me back to New York.

LOD: Where will you go then?

MED: With you. Where you go.

LOD: (*recoiling*) With me?

MED: Can't I go with you?

LOD: (*Laughs.*) Why I'm Panther. That's what I'm called out here in this red wilderness. I can't read nor write. I'm always up at knives' point with some one
or other! I've been shot at fifty times and turned out of three Territories by
Vigilance Committees.

MED: I don't mind that. You are the only friend I have in all the world.

LOD: I tell you, girl, it can't be done!

MED: Why not?

LOD: Your father left you to my care.

MED: Then you must take care of me.

LOD: Yes. I can watch over you day and night. If anything happened to you, I
should see ghosts.

MED: And so, if you take care of me, you can't fight, nor drink, nor go off with
horrible men to gamble. Do you love these things better than me?

LOD: Well no! But I know something of the world. People would say I persuaded
you to stay with me. I tell you, it's no use talking. I'm a scoundrel, and I
must take you to your mother.

MED: If you were as bad as you say, you would not. I don't believe you. You were
always good to me. I know you used often to give father money, just when
you saw my dress was ragged and my feet were almost on the ground, so that
he could buy things for me. Oh, I'm wiser than you think, and I loved you
for it.

LOD: You loved! (*aside*) Oh, if I were only an honest man. But it's getting too hot
for you, Loder. You must think of some damned rascally trick to stop this.
If she would only fall in love with somebody who would marry her and take
her home!

MED: What are you thinking of? Me?

LOD: (*She leans against his shoulder, clasps his arm.*) Oh, ah, yes! (*aside*) I'll pick
out some decent chap. Some young fellow who don't play cards. I'll put her
in his way; he's sure to love her; who could help it?

MED: I never saw such a stupid, dull fellow as you are.

LOD: Me? Yes! (*aside*) I'll keep out of her sight.

MED: I do believe you hate me!

LOD: Hate you?

MED: Then why don't you love me? I want somebody to love me – now – poor
papa is gone. (*Sinks on mound.*)

LOD: (*aside*) Yes, that's how I'll fix it, and if all turns out well! if she falls in love with him (*moved*) and marries him! and goes back to New York with him! I'll see them safe off and blow my own worthless brains out comfortably.
(ALLEYN *enters.*)

AL: Almost time to start. (*Sees* MED.) Why, my little prairie flower!

MED: (*coquettishly nestling up to* LOD) Is that you?

AL: I have been so anxious about you.

LOD: Who is this?

MED: The young captain from New York.

LOD: From New York? (*Goes up.*)

AL: Who is your suspicious looking friend?

MED: He is my *best* – my only friend.

AL: Oh! (*to* LOD) I say, are you going down in the boat?

LOD: Well, if she goes down, I reckon I'll go down with her.

AL: Then you'd better jump aboard and be lively. (CEPH *and* BLAKELY *appear on boat, getting out poles.* LOD *near* MED *about to go.*) Med! (*She draws back and looks towards* LOD, *he insists on her remaining.*) Just one word, Med. I'm so happy to see you again. I've never stopped thinking of you since that day. (*Takes her upstage.*)

LOD: Curse his soft tongue! He'll capture her heart! Hallo! But that's what I've been wanting! After all it's a hard thing to stand. She said she loved me – and – ! Damn it, I'll take my medicine like a man anyway. (*Goes up and on board and assists the boatmen.*)

AL: (*coming down with* MED) I'm not going on the boat with you, but I take a party of soldiers with me to guard its course for a few miles down the stream.

MED: Oh! I'm safe now. Panther will take care of me.

AL: Panther?

MED: Yes! You saw him just now. You don't like him, but I do, and so good-bye!

AL: But Med –

MED (*running to boat*) Good-bye! Good-bye! (*Runs to* LOD.)
(COLUMBIA *and* MR. SMITH *enter.*)

COL: Now, Honorable! (*to* AL) Is papa on board?

AL: Yes! and everybody else except you and Smith.

COL: Come, Honorable! Take care of yourself, Captain.

AL: I'll try to! (*As she is going up gang-plank, noise heard of* ROWSE's *voice.*)

COL: What's that?
(WAHCOTAH *appears with* NOTAH *at bow of boat, followed by* ROWSE, *who snatches at* NOT.)

ROW: No, you don't you red devil! (*Seizes* NOT *and kicks the Indian over upon bank.*)

WAH: Big chief on the trail! Wahcotah warn him! (*Exit with a run.*)

COL: Why, pa! What have you got there?

AL: What's all this?

ROW: No interference, Cap. I've got this young papoose in safe-keeping. She's a policy of insurance on all our lives. All aboard! (COL *is handed up by* MR. S.) Cast off! (SER *and soldiers draw in gang-plank and draw it off.*) Good-bye,

Cap. (BLAK *and* CHINEE *and* CEPH *commence to pole the boat off and the scene begins to change. Panorama of a river. Scene begins to grow darker.*)

ROW: Be hearty now, boys. I guess I'll go below and secure my captive. A piece of bread and butter will do the business. (*Exits below.*)

AL: Sergeant, get the men in line. Good night! (*Goes off.*)

> (*Group on boat:* MED, *who had taken* COL's *hand, sits in prow with* MR. S. *The top deck is occupied by boatmen.* LOD *sits in stern. The group of Irish are central figures.*)

MR. S: It's very romantic, 'pon honor!

COL: (*to* MED) Are you comfortable, dear?

WIDOW: Faix, can any of ye's give me a light?

CEPHAS: Here you is, old lady.

> (ROWSE *re-appears.*)

ROWSE: Come, boys, push her lively.

BLAK: All right, Cap.

SONG BY BOATMEN

> The boatmen dance, the boatmen sing,
>> The boatmen are up to everything.
> When the boatmen goes ashore,
>> He spends his money and works for more.
>> DANCE – The boatmen, etc.

> I never saw a pretty girl in all my life,
>> But she was a boatmen's wife, etc.
>> DANCE – The boatmen, etc.

> (*The* WIDOW *dances to this music and the song grows fainter as the panorama closes the scene and forms*)

SCENE 2 – *A dense wood and dark night.* WAHCOTAH *moves in noiselessly as if through shrubbery, and looks about him. Two other Indians emerge from scene. The other song merges into music of a march, at first very faint.*

WAH: Where is Wannemucka?

INDIAN: Coming, river side! (*music of march more forte*)

WAH: Sh, soldiers!

> (*The Indians glide back towards right as the music grows louder and* ALLEYN, SERGEANT, *and file of soldiers with rifles enter.*)

AL: How far can we keep the boat in sight from this path?

SER: We can keep within three hundred feet of the river bank for at least twelve miles.

AL: Can we keep up with the boat on foot? At what rate do they pole her down?

SER: They don't pole the boat after they get into the open stream. The current takes them down about a mile, or a mile and a half an hour.

AL: Oh, then it will be easy to keep up with it.

SER: We're half a mile ahead of it now, besides there'll be no fear of any attack to-night, Captain.

AL: I'm not an old Western campaigner, Sergeant, but it seems to me that your confidence upon that point doesn't justify our neglecting any precautions.

SER: Of course not, Captain; but it does argufy that we needn't creep through the woods all night at a snail's pace when we might push on, and keep the road clear by driving the Indians before us.

AL: That's sense. I suppose there's no danger of their closing in our rear and attacking the boat.

SER: All the Injuns in the wackcinity are ahead of us, I'll swear.

AL: Well, we can push them on then. (*The chorus again heard faintly.*) Where did you sight the boat last?

SER: Drifting down behind us safe enough. There! don't you hear 'em?

AL: Sure enough! Well, come, my boys! On! March!

> (MUSIC, *march. All off. Music fainter.* WANNEMUCKA *enters after them. A pause. He throws himself on the ground.* WAHCOTAH's *head appears through bushes; they meet.*)

WAN: Little snake heard the white braves?

WAH: Much talk! White braves talk like Indian squaws!

WAN: Ugh! Boat?

WAH: Boat full. Come slow!

WAN: Who?

WAH: Papoose! Notah!

WAN: Ugh! Prairie Dog's papoose! (*Other Indians creep through branches.*) What white squaws on boat?

WAH: Ugh! Wannemucka's squaw!

WAN: Mine! All mine!

WAH: Panther with her!

WAN: (*Shows knife.*) Wannemucka knows where to strike White Panther! (*Distant and faint sound of song heard, as if from boat.*)

WAH: Boat come. Big chief strike now?

WAH: Bow! Hist! Braves follow Wannemucka! Close! hist! close! (*Exeunt.*)

> (*Singing still faint, but nearer. All the Indians off. The scene gradually begins to open and the dense forest to clear, disclosing the moon, and then a large clearing through which is shown – :*)

SCENE 3 – *A narrow bend in the Big Run River. From the bank on extreme left, a blasted and fallen tree trunk stretches over to right, dipping the water.* WANNE-MUCKA *and three Indians are concealed on this tree.* WAHCOTAH *and another are in the water. Other Indians concealed behind logs and trees.*

The song is heard more plainly. It is MED *and* COLUMBIA *singing, seated in the extreme bow of boat, a low and plaintive ballad. The boat gradually moves on from right to left, passing beneath the fallen tree. Groups on boat same as before. All asleep.* ROWSE *not in sight.* MR. SMITH *not in sight. As it approaches where* WAHCOTAH *lies concealed, he rises from the water and stops it, raising his body out of the water and grinning at the two girls.*

MED: Why, the boat has stopped. Wake, Loder! (*Turns and sees the Indian.*) Ah! (*Piercing scream and starts back.*)

> (WANNEMUCKA *drops from branch of tree on deck and seizes*

MED *and half raises her.* COLUMBIA *rises in alarm on deck.*
WAHCOTAH *threatens her with hatchet.* ROWSE *runs out of cabin
to her aid.* LODER *springs up in alarm, as two more Indians drop
down upon deck. They fall upon* CEPHAS *and* BLAKELY, *who roll
over with them at back.*

MED: Help! help!
WANNEMUCKA: Come!
LODER: Indian, drop that girl!

> (*Indian yell from all sides.* WAN *draws dirk and runs at* LOD.
> WIDOW *seizes* MED *and holds her.* LOD *seizes* WAN *who bends him
> over the boat with the dirk at his throat.* ROWSE *engages the
> Indians, who clamber up sides of the boat, and fights them with a
> bag of meal.* LOD *finally releases one hand, draws a Derringer and
> fires at* WAN, *who leaps up, staggers front and falls. The drum and
> sound of approaching soldiers heard as the -*)

CURTAIN FALLS

ACT IV

SCENE 1 – *A stockade or primitive fort in the prairie. Time – second day from the
incidents of last act. The stage represents the interior of the stockade, or two sides
of it, with the angle in center. All round is the horizon. A closed shed on the left,
within the stockade, beside the walls. Stakes of stockade about ten feet high. Gate,
left. A clump of trees upstage right outside. Rocks and bush growths, left of stage
outside.*

As curtain rises, several groups are formed inside stockade. WIDOW *is cooking
with pot swung on sticks over faggot fire and ladle in hand.* CEPHAS *watching and
blowing the fire.* RHODA *and* MOLLY *looking on. Soldiers here and there in
groups, outside stockade and inside, cleaning rifles.* COLUMBIA *is walking up and
down with* ALLEYN, *his hat on her head coquettishly and carrying his sword.*
BLAKELY *and* CHINEE *looking over stockade at back. They come down presently
and join* CEPHAS.

COL: Oh, you should have seen us!
AL: Terrific, no doubt!
COL: I don't know how many Indians we killed.
AL: Yes, the enemy was so ashamed of the defeat that even the dead men disap-
     peared.
COL: But it's no laughing matter. Indians right up to you in the dead of night!
WIDOW: Faix, you may say that. 'An the diviltry of 'em wantin' to run off wid de
     young creature. (BLAK, CEPH *and* CHINEE *make a dive at soup and are
     caught.*)
AL: If I once lay my sword on Wannemucka I'll make an example of him to every
     amalgamationist in the territory.
COL: So singular that he should be in love with Med.
AL: Hem, very!
COL: You'd suppose now that he'd like a bold, brave woman, something like a

princess. Med is so timid. I used to think I'd like to have an Indian brave fall in love with me – so romantic.

AL: Set your cap for Wannemucka.

COL: I mean a real noble savage, not a dirty, common Indian.

AL: They're all the same.

COL: Somebody like Fenimore Cooper's braves.

WID: Coopers, is it? Faix, all trades is alike, they're all a dirty pack, and coopers is not better nor any of 'em.

>(ROWSE *enters, followed by* NOTAH *from gate.* NOT *has a newspaper cocked hat and rides a stick, but still holds on to* ROW's *coat, as usual.*)

ROWSE: Time to be stirring! All's safe! I've prospected for a quarter of a mile in every direction, and I've come to the conclusion that this is the most desirable spot in the whole country for me to get up and clear from, as fast as possible. I shan't lay the foundation of Rowseville, the future metropolis of the West, in this spot, I can tell you.

AL: Then what direction shall we take?

ROW: Further in towards that little cluster of woods yonder, just on the stream. That's the spot for Rowseville.

AL: Then we must be getting ready. Sergeant! (SER *advances.*) Have the men ready. We must push back to the bend and bring the reams up to carry the ladies and stores. (SER *retires up to soldiers, who rise and file out of gate.*) Mr. Rowse, will you stay here with the ladies, and act as guard till we return?

ROW: Certainly! So will Loder.

AL: No! Loder, or whatever his name is, must go with us.

ROW: Why? Confound you, you young mosquito, do you want to strip me? (*to* NOT)

AL: I have my suspicions about that Loder. Here he is.

>(LODER *enters at gate and looks around, then goes to shed, and sits. He carries a rifle, and is followed by* MR. SMITH *with another.*)

AL: Watch his eye.

>(COL *goes to meet* MR. S.)

ROW: Looks shot. Guess he's been up all night playing poker with your men.

AL: I tell you he's a rascal. I've watched him when he's been talking to –

ROW: To whom?

AL: Well, never mind. But he's not to be trusted. (*Goes up and off among his men, looking suspiciously towards* LOD.)

ROW: (*to* COL) And how's our little patient?

COL: She's been sleeping in the hut there, all the morning. We made her as comfortable as we could with some of the Captain's army blankets. (*Goes into shed.*)

ROW: Ah, that's how Uncle Sam's property is diverted from its proper use, is it?

MR. SMITH: (*to* LOD) I say, old fellow, you've been as dull as the deuce all day.

LODER: Well, stranger, I'm sorry for that, it's not my way always.

>(COLUMBIA *re-appears, leading* MED, *very pale and languid.* LOD *draws back.*)

COL: Try a little walk. There's no danger now.

MED: I'm not afraid of the danger.

ROW: You'd face a dozen Injuns, if they dropped in now, wouldn't you?

COL: Here, some of you men. Give her your arm, and let her take a little walk.

> (LOD *and* AL *both start forward.* LOD *catches* AL's *eye, and draws back.*)

AL: Come with me.

MED: It's so good of you to mind me. But I don't care to walk.

ROW: (*to* COL) C'lumby, I'm afraid those horrid red wretches have scared what little life there was in her out of her.

MED: (*walking to bench by shed*) You are going to leave us?

AL: Only to send teams up to bring you down to the bend. (*They sit.*)

ROW: (*to* COL) Smitten, hey?

COL: Yes, and it's so romantic.

ROW: Well, just you fight as shy of that sort of nonsense as long as you can and not inconvenience yourself, and I'll be just as glad as you can reckon.

> (*Off, followed by* COL *and* MR. S. ROW *looks back just in time to catch them flirting; they all go off with a laugh.*)

AL: You don't think I'd leave you in any danger.

MED: I thought I should never see you again, when the Indians attacked our boat.

> (LOD *crosses quietly at back and leans against upper end of shed, listening to conversation.*)

AL: The danger is all over now. Try and brighten a little.

MED: For what?

AL: Don't say for what? Say for whom?

MED: For whom, then?

AL: For – (*She looks at him.*) For those who love you.

MED: Everyone who loves me, leaves me. All, except one –

AL: And he?

MED: Poor Loder! See, how faithful he is.

AL: You love him, then! (*He rises. She rises, as if to re-assure him.* LOD *makes a step forward.* AL *turns suddenly on* MED *and steals a kiss, she leans on his shoulder, and they turn to go up, when they confront* LOD.) Well, sir! (*sternly*) Are you preparing for the march? (MED *reproves him with a glance, and holds out her hand to* LOD, *who kisses it.*)

> (ROWSE *re-enters, followed by* NOTAH. *As he comes on,* ROW *turns around savagely to* NOT.)

ROWSE: See here, I've had almost enough of this!

> (MR. SMITH *and* COLUMBIA *in doorway*)

MED: Oh, the little Indian. I'm afraid you've captured her heart, Mr. Rowse, and she'll cling to you, for better or for worse.

ROW: Cling to me! I should think so! I'm afraid I'll have to adopt her, unless some of you take her off my hands. Don't you want her, Alleyn?

AL: I – for what? (MED *disengages herself, and goes quietly to* LOD, *whose down-cast look she has been watching. He leans against his gun.*)

ROW: To bring her up as an Indian interpreter.

AL: No, thank you. I'm afraid of the Big Chief.

ROW: Here, Smith, suppose you take her.

MR. SMITH: Aw! Where to?

ROW: Back to England. She'll be Pocahontas, and you'll be Smith, just the very thing.

MR. S: I'd like to oblige, but I'm afraid she don't deserve it. Pocahontas saved Smith's life, but this little creature is likely to get us all killed.

WIDOW: (*coming over*) Sure, the dinner's ready.

ROW: Dinner! That's handy! Come, lads! (CEPH *and* CHINEE *take pot from fire, as directed by* ROW, *and all exit into hut.*)

MED: You look so cross.

LOD: I'm not cross, girl. I'm sorry.

MED: Sorry for what?

LOD: It's a mean thing to confess, but I overheard you talking with the young Captain.

MED: You heard us? Where were you?

LOD: It was wrong, wasn't it?

MED: Yes! It was not like you.

LOD: Yet I wouldn't give away the memory of what I heard for my life itself. Only tell me, is it so?

MED: Is what so?

LOD: Don't trifle, Med! For God's sake, don't. I heard you speaking.

MED: (*bashfully*) Well!

LOD: You spoke of those who loved you – and of one –

MED: That was you.

LOD: Oh, if it should be so. I would die for you any day – or better than that, I would fight for you and work for you. You could make me an honest man.

MED: I want to do that. You know I do.

LOD: And he asked you if you loved me?

MED: (*gladly looking at him and putting her hand on his shoulder*) And you heard –

LOD: No, I heard no more.

MED: I told him 'yes!' I loved you as if you were a dear brother! (LOD *looks at her stolidly.*) And he seemed so pleased. And you are my brother, ain't you? And you shall always be. And that made him so happy, and then he told me that he loved me, not like a brother, you know – oh, far from that –

AL: (*coming over*) Well, Mr. Loder, time's about up. We must leave the ladies here until we return.

MED: Oh, will that be soon?

AL: This evening, perhaps.

COL: (*in door*) Come, Med, have something to eat.

MED: I'm coming. (*to* AL) And you will be ever so careful of yourself, and not fight with the Indians, if you meet them?

AL: No, I'll stand up and be shot. (MED *laughs and runs off, with* COL. AL *is about to go.*)

LOD: Captain!

AL: Well, sir!

LOD: May I have a word with you?

AL: Many as you please, if you're quick about it.

LOD: I'm not one of the drawling sort, stranger, and I say my mind in a few words. You love that girl!

AL: (*angrily*) What is that to you?

LOD: (*smothering his anger*) I beg pardon. Perhaps I was too plain – she tells me –

AL: Then keep what you're told to yourself. (*about to go*)

LOD: Captain!

AL: Hark ye, my friend, if you address me on that or any other subject again, I'll have you left out on the prairie to look after the redskins alone, without any soldiers to protect you.

LOD: Well, Captain, I've fought the redskins – and alone against odds – before now. I'm not a coward, if I am a – pshaw! I only want to say that the young girl yonder was left by her father to me –

AL: Just what a drunken brute might do! And I suppose you consider you've a claim on her?

LOD: Yes! (AL *laughs*) But not what you supposed. I love her!

AL: Oh, I've no objection. I shan't interfere!

LOD: You mean to tell me you don't love her yourself, then! Why you've just confessed it to her.

AL: (*annoyed*) She told you –

LOD: Yes, and you're ashamed of it. You think it good sport to fool a friendless creature like her. You're deceiving her, and you know it!

AL: Whatever you please.

LOD: Captain! I beg pardon again if I'm insulting. But if you only knew all. If I thought you really loved her, I'd be content.

AL: I'm much obliged, I'm sure.

LOD: Another man who spoke to me as you speak, should fight me until one of us was stretched dead at the other's feet. But she loves you, and I dare not harm you. If you will only say to me that you love her! I have one duty to perform, and then you will see me no more. A secret –

AL: A secret! About Med?

LOD: To the man who really loves her, a secret worth the world full of gold. For it tells him she is worthy to be his wife. (AL *approaches* LOD.) Remember, it is to be told to one only – the man who is to be her husband.

AL: Whatever your secret is, it is safe with me.

LOD: But you will not answer me!

AL: Answer what?

LOD: That you love Med!

AL: Well, then be answered, I do!

LOD: Come, then; on the road ask me what you will, and every information which this packet does not contain you shall have. (*Shows* WOLF's *packet.*)

AL: (*kindly*) My good fellow, I was hasty just now. I do love her; there's my hand upon it.

LOD: No, stranger, I can't take your hand. If she had been poor like me, I'd have taken her far away to the wild West, to be mine, and mine only. I give her up now, as the fretful child must give up the star he sees so far above him.

AL: I was going to take you with me, but now, that I can trust you, you shall stay here and watch over her till we return.

LOD: No. I won't be tempted. From this time I speak to her no more. She is to be the wife of an honest man and is to become a lady. I know what I am, and that she is too good for me. I'll go with *you*. They are safe here.

AL: As you will. On the road I will speak with you.

LOD: (*going*) On the road.

> (MED *re-appears.*)

MED: Are you going?

> (ROWSE, COLUMBIA *and* MR. SMITH *enter.*)

LOD: Only a little way.

MED: (*gaily*) Good-bye then.

LOD: (*struggling with emotion*) Good-bye! Good-bye! (*Off.*)

ROW: That fellow's got the worst face I ever saw.

MED: And the best heart that ever beat. (*Goes to* AL.)

MR. SMITH: I understand he's quite a scoundrel.

COLUMBIA: He looks like some member of Congress, whose name I forget. You know, pa!

ROW: Yes! That chap from Maine, that voted against my railroad bill.

AL: Now we must be off.

ROW: So I'm to stay and protect the ladies?

MR. S: Yes! take my gun, it's double barrelled, both barrels loaded. (*Gives it.*)

ROW: I never fired one of these things in all my life.

> (CEPHAS *and* CHINEE *come out from hut.*)

AL: Now, then, Sergeant –

SER: (*outside*) Aye, aye, sir!

AL: (*to* COL) Good-bye! (*to* MED) Until to-morrow, darling! Now for the road.

> (*All off to music.* COL *climbs the stockade, waves her handkerchief.*
> ROW *in gateway.* MED *near* COL. *The soldiers and all men except*
> ROW *file off.* WIDOW *and others waving them 'Good-bye.'*)

ROW: (*coming down*) Hello! Where's that little Indian of mine? (WID *goes up to gate.*)

COL: I don't know, perhaps she's got into your pocket, pa! She's been near it so long.

ROW: That's funny. I've taken such a fancy to her that –

WIDOW: Shure, I saw the little crethur yonder running off towards the woods chasing the butterflies.

ROW: (*laying down gun*) Chasing fiddlesticks. We mustn't let her get away or she'll be bringing some stray Indians here on us. Which way did you see her go?

WID: Straight down to the gully forninst the wood.

ROW: I'll fetch her! (*Goes off running.*)

MED: It's not safe for him to go!

COL: Oh, he's got his gun.

WID: Faix, that he hasn't. Shure, here it is. Rhody, dear, run –

MED: Oh, yes, run – call him – take it to him. (RHOD *takes the gun and afterwards when the door is barred, she rests it against the barred door.*)

COL: (*up to gate*) Pa! pa! Oh, pshaw! he's running so fast and he don't hear. (RHOD *stops.*)

MED: (*looking over the stockade*) He's running down to the ravine. He should keep in the open.

COL: Oh, Pa's wise. He knows what he's about.

WID: Shure, his wisdom wouldn't amount to much if the red divils was about.

COL: Pa's a great boxer! Let him alone! (*coming in*) Come down, you little canary. (*to* MED)

MED: (*looking off still*) Yes, in a moment! (*Sunset begins.*)

COL: You don't expect to see pa *there* do you?

MED: No, I was only –

COL: You were only looking after somebody else. (*Below, looks up at her.*)

MED: (*Above, looks down at her.*) No, indeed, I –

COL: No fibs! Come down, I want to talk to you.

MED: What about?

COL: About yourself and the other one!

MED: Which other one?

COL: Oh, you needn't pretend. I saw you flirting.

MED: (*coming down*) Flirting! what's that? (WID *and others sitting back*)

COL: I know your secret. You love him! Isn't it so?

MED: Yes!

COL: Then why didn't you tell me so that night on the boat.

MED: Because I did not think then he would look at poor little me in such a way as that.

COL: Why, you ain't serious, are you? You don't think of marrying him?

MED: I haven't thought of anything but his love.

COL: Why, he's ever so rich. He's got an aristocratic mother in New York who wouldn't listen to it. Besides he's an awful flirt. He'll forget you for the next pretty face he sees. Oh, I know 'em.

MED: Oh, you don't think him like that.

COL: They're all alike, my dear. But don't cry over it. There, there. I've been in love myself, often; been deceived too, my dear, and all that; oh, it's terrible. There was a member of Congress from Indiana, then there was the assistant clerk of the Under Secretary of the German Minister, he made love to me. He was a Baron. I gave him my young heart's affections, and his wife and seven children, all barons, came out in one of the Bremen steamers, and took him home.

MED: I don't know what will come of it, but I love him too much to doubt. Let us talk of something else. Are you not in love now?

COL: My affections are hardened.

MED: Even to the tall gentleman?

COL: Sh! Have you observed him? He's a nobleman.

MED: He's very tall!

COL: All English noblemen are!

MED: And does he love you?

COL: If any one could restore peace to my solitary heart – (*Darkness deepens.*)

MED: He could –

COL: He could – if he would. But I'm afraid it don't enter his mind. His head is a little thick. He doesn't seem to know what's good for him.

(*Distant cry like an owl's heard, as if a signal. All listen, cry repeated.*)

MED: Did you hear that?

COL: It must be pa! (*Cry repeated.*)

MED: No! (*breathlessly putting her ear towards the ground, as though to listen*)

WID: (*looking over wall*) I don't see anybody at all – at all!

MED: Quick! Close the gate! (*All run to it.*) Bar it!

COL: But if pa comes?

MED: We can let him in.

COL: Why, what are you afraid of?

MED: We are alone and near the woods. If the Indians should have been concealed there!

COL: (*Laughs.*) Ha! ha! ha! You little scared thing. Why, the soldiers were out all the morning. Come! You must be braver!

MED: I was so once. But when I was a little girl father took me far up the Colorado; we were surprised there by the Indians in our hut.

WID: (*Others gather.*) Howly Saints!

COL: Oh, a story! How delightful! Do tell it!

MED: Alone at night. The darkness gathering, just like now. We had barred the door – there were no windows. I was roused from my sleep by a noise, like the stealthy tread of some animal on the roof.

COL: But we have no roof here, and we would see them if they came, and shoot them.

MED: I looked towards the door, the bar seemed to move as if someone pressed against it. (*The gun which* RHOD *has placed against the door falls.*)

COL: (*frightened*) What's that?

WID: Only the gun! (*Runs and places it upright against the hut and runs back.*)

MED: My father started up, but too late. With a wild shout the door was broken down, and the savages were upon us.

> (WAHCOTAH's *head appears above the stockade.* COL *sees him and screams, and points breathlessly while sinking to the ground.* WAH *disappears.*)

MED: What was it? Speak!

COL: Indians! (*Knock heard at gate.*)

WID: We are all murdered!

MED: We can fight for our lives! (*Runs and grasps gun.*)

COL: Oh, don't! don't! You'll make them so angry. (*Knock repeated.*) It is the Indians! Heaven preserve us!

WANNEMUCKA: (*outside*) Open the gate!

MED: 'Sh!

> (*Several blows are heard, as though stones were hurled against the door. Some of the stakes of the upper part are broken. An Indian puts in his head.* MED *fires; he falls. The gate gives way, and the other savages pour in,* WANNEMUCKA *coming last and passing to the front of them. They start back before the gun, which* MED *presents with the crowd of women clustering around her, all kneeling but* MED.)

WANNEMUCKA: White maiden, put up your gun. Indian too many!

MED: Wannemucka! Coward! to attack women!

WAN: Let the white maiden come with Wannemucka, and her sisters shall be free to go.

COL: Never!

WAN: Indian too many. White maiden's gun can kill but one.

MED: Let the *one* who wishes to be killed come forward, then!

WAN: (*after a pause*) Braves no wish to hurt white maiden.

MED: Then go!

WAN: (*turns to speak to Indians.*) Yes! Indians go! Indians not fight women. They seek warriors. (*Parleys with tribe.*)

COL: Oh, if they will go!

RHOD: See, they seem to be quarrelling.

MED: Oh, if they should! There might be a hope!

　　　　　　　(WAN *and tribe seem to disagree. He turns to* MED *softly.*)

WAN: White maiden, Wannemucka is no enemy. His wigwam was cold and his fires unlighted. The eyes of white maiden have warmed his heart, and he would take her to his tribe, their princess! (*Indians murmur.*) Wannemucka would save the white maiden that he loves, and his tribe are angry with him.

MED: I cannot trust you.

WAN: White maiden shall see. (*To Indians, takes a step in advance.*) Warriors! Indian braves fight white braves, not women. Let the warriors of the Caiute follow their chief, and leave the white women in peace.

WAHCOTAH: Ugh! The Caiute knows no difference. Their lodges are hung with the scalps of women. Wannemucka, coward! traitor!

WAN: Wahcotah drunk! Go! Caiute braves know Wannemucka! Go! No harm shall come to white women.

WAH: Wannemucka traitor! Stand by –

　　　　　　　(*Draws knife and attempts to pass by* WAN. *He is stopped. Short struggle, and all the other Indians press forward and strike* WAN; *he falls.* WAH *kneels over him, as if to strike again. Women scream.*)

MED: Stop! Another blow, and this bullet strikes you dead! (WAH *jumps back.*)

WAN: (*faintly*) White maiden, Indian loved you to his death. (*He stretches out his arms.*)

MED: Chief, I forgive you. Creep to me – they shall not kill you! (*He crawls to her. Indians try to press forward, as he falls. She keeps them at bay with the gun.*) Nearer – nearer! This bullet is for him that touches you. Now – now – you are safe!

WAN: Yes, safe!

　　　　　　　(*He crawls to her feet, then suddenly springs up, wrenches the gun from her, throws it to his men, who receive it with a yell, and he grasps her. Indians overpower the rest.*)

WAN: Mine! All mine!

CURTAIN

　　ACT V

SCENE – *A ravine, in which the Indians have camped for the night. High ground at sides and at back, surmounted by bushes and thick shrubbery. A path, quite high*

Caiute: see note on p. 111.

at the back, across from right to left. Paths down from right and left to center at back. Mountainous perspective. Time – the dark hour before daylight. A tent of skins in center, midway up stage. Smouldering embers of a campfire. A clump of bushes at a half eminence behind the tent.

ONATA *and five Indian girls are grouped around the tent, which is closed.* WANNEMUCKA *stands, leaning on his rifle, watching his tent. Irish family,* WIDOW, RHODA *and* COLUMBIA, *guarded by a group of Indians. They are seated on the ground, their heads covered with shawls, handkerchiefs, etc. At the eminence on the right is seated an Indian on guard.* WAHCOTAH *seated in buffalo dress.*

WAN: The day is almost here, but the Caiute warriors may rest until it comes. The flight was long, and the way hard. What says Onata?

ONA: The maidens rejoice that their warriors have returned, but not that they bring white women to the tribe.

WAN: The beloved of Wannemucka need not fear. The white maiden shall be the slave of Onata.

ONA: Onata needs no slave whose face is like the white moon, and shines through all the lodge.

WAN: She is the prize of Wannemucka, and marks his triumph. Go, look upon her. She is weak and frightened. She is ill.

ONA: If she die, the Indian women will be glad. (*Exits into tent.*)

WAN: Let the will of the Great Spirit be done.

WAH: (*Rises and goes to* WAN.) The Great Spirit marks out the time of all things. He scatters the flowers and the buds together. (*aside to* WAN) The herbs have done their work.

WAN: When will she sink to sleep?

WAH: Her eyes close even now.

WAN: Go then! Tell Onata that the white maiden will not see the sun rise.

(WAH *nods, goes to tent, looks in, then goes off.* ONATA *comes out cautiously, looks at* WAN, *who stands stolidly, and glides out after* WAH.)

WAN: Ugh! (*When she is off.*) The white woman makes her dark sister angry. (*Calls to Indian scout on eminence.*) Go!

INDIAN: (*coming down*) All is silent!

WAN: The white men will not find us. They have sought us in our ancient hunting grounds. (*The other Indians rise up and come, surrounding* WAN. ONA *steals in behind them and enters tent.*) My brothers ask for council, the braves shall have their wish. Bring in the paleface. (*The Indian scout goes out.*) The warriors have taken no scalps, and their hatchets are unstained.

(ROWSE *enters, guarded by the Indian.*)

WAN: Loosen the gag. Let the white warrior speak.

ROWSE: I'm much obliged. I haven't had so much in mouth for several years.

COLUMBIA: (*Springs up.*) Oh, pa! is it you? (*Runs toward him, Indians stop her.*) Oh, let me go!

WAN: Let the white maiden go to him. She loves him.

COL: Oh, pa, dear! I was afraid I'd never see you again. Oh, can't we get away? What will they do to us?

ROW: I don't know, my child! But if ever I get back to Washington alive, I mean to turn my attention to Indian affairs. I'll bring in a bill to settle this.

WAN: The white maiden loves you!

ROW: I guess she does. She's my daughter.

WAN: She is fair, she will make a bride for one of our braves.

COL: (*Screams.*) Oh! the wretches! I won't have any braves! I don't want to be a bride.

WAN: The white woman will learn to love the young warriors. She will bake their bread and dig their corn.

COL: Will I? I'll break their heads and scratch their faces.

WAN: Take her away! (*She and* ROW *are separated.*) Now paleface!

ROW: Don't call me paleface! My name is Rowse! Sundown Rowse, Washington, D.C.

WAN: The paleface has a double name! What does his name signify? What rank is Rowse? Is he a chief, is he a warrior among the palefaces?

ROW: (*aside*) I suppose the greater I am, the more consideration they'll show me. (*aloud*) Yes. Rowse big chief! Big warrior!

WAN: Where are the big warrior's hunting grounds? Where does he battle?

ROW: Where do I fight? My principal battle ground is the lobby.

INDIANS: (*to each other*) Lobby! (*Seem puzzled.*)

WAN: Rowse take many scalps?

ROW: Oh, we don't take scalps any more. We don't want any hair – we sleep on *spring* mattresses now.

WAN: Big chief must have killed many.

ROW: Oh, yes. I've killed a great many – bills.

WAN: How he kill them?

ROW: Squelched 'em in the Committee of the Whole, or beat 'em on the Third Reading.

WAN: Rowse great warrior then?

ROW: Oh, I believe you!

WAN: Rowse lie!

ROW: Eh? What's that you say?

WAN: White man lie! Rowse no warrior! Wear no war paint! (*Points to clothes.*) No blue! no gold buttons, no belt for long knife!

ROW: The rascals know a soldier when they see one!

COL: You horrid savages. My father *is* a great chief. He's one of the prominent men of Washington!

WAN: Prominent man! Ugh! Medicine man!

ROW: They're laughing at us, C'lumby. We can't stuff 'em. We'll have to beg off.

COL: It's shameful! and to think you own the whole country too!

ROW: Yes. I'm in the hands of some more of my tenants. They couldn't treat me worse if I'd come to collect the rent.

WAN: (*Consults with Indians, then:*) What says the daughter of the paleface? Does the white man claim the whole country?

COL: Yes, he does! All this land belongs to him!

ROW: Yes, and I've got the grant in my pocket, much good it's done me.

WAN: Who gave our white brother this land?

ROW: Congress, you red rascal!

WAN: Congress give you land and water and trees and all?

ROW: Here, C'lumby, take out the grant and show 'em?

COL: (*Takes paper out of his pocket.*) Here it is! (*Opens it.*) And here's the map! (*Spreads out the map.*)

ROW: Look at that! Every acre of it mine!

WAN: Congress gives it to you. Congress bad spirit! Bad spirit made the lying paper that takes the land and the water from the red man and gives it to the pale-face. (*Snatches papers from* COL.) Burn the bad spirit. (*Gives them to the Indians who carry them to fire.*)

ROW: Here, I say! What are you about?

WAN: Ugh! White man prays for bad spirit. (*The paper is in flames and the Indians shout around it.*)

ROW: Well, curse my luck. My grant gone! my map gone! my hands tied, and three thousand miles from Congress! Oh, you infernal rascals.

WAN: Seize the paleface and prepare the stake.

ROW: What!

COL: Oh, my poor papa! Oh, pa, what do they mean?

ROW: I don't know! I'm very sick. (*At a sign from* WAN, *Indians seize* ROW.)

WAN: Let the paleface pray. When the dawn breaks, he dies!

> (ROW *is carried off struggling.* COL *is kept from him at a sign from* WAN, *who also darts an angry glance at him and silences him until he is quite off.* WAN *advances toward the tent, which suddenly opens and* MED *appears, followed by* ONATA. *The Indians draw back in a cluster about* WAH, *and all look on curiously.*)

MED: Let us go on! See, the sun is up! the daylight has come! the birds are singing.

WAN: Beautiful maiden! all is dark about you. The night is cold. The earth is wet with dew. Go back to the couch of skins, which your dark sisters have made for you.

MED: No! no! see how bright everything is!

WAN: (*aside to* WAH) The herb is making her mad. The Indian women will not hate her now!

COL: (*running to her*) Oh, Med! Med!

MED: Who is this? – Alleyn?

COL: Don't you know me, Med?

MED: You said you loved me! Come, let us go! (*Sinks on ground.* COL *bends over her.*)

COL: She is dying!

ONATA: She is favored by the great Manitou! He has taken away her mind.

WAH: (*Approaches, throwing back his buffalo head.*) Fear not! I will speak to the pale sister! (*He kneels and takes her hand.*)

WAN: Will the maiden grow better?

WAH: She is near the spirit land! Already she beholds it! (*Rises.*)

MED: Alleyn! Dear Alleyn! (*Takes* COL's *hand.*) I told you, you remember, that I

Great Manitou: supernatural force, or spirit, present in all things animate and inanimate, that controlled the destinies of men.

was doomed to die. I did not think so soon! Look! my father! (WAN *turns aside.*) No, father, I will come to *you*. She is not *my* mother and I will not go to her. Dear father, don't turn from me. I am with you! (*Her eyes grow fixed. She is gently laid back by* COL, *who sobs and the Indian maiden takes her.*)

WAH: The white maiden is as the leaf upon the ground – as the fallen rosebud.

COL: Oh, my poor darling!

        (*The women tenderly raise her, and take her into the tent, followed by* ONA *and* COL. *The tent is closed.* WIDOW, RHODA *and* MOLLY *enter.*)

WAN: When will she wake?

WAH: If she sleeps till the dawn, it will be sunset before she opens her eyes to the light. But a little now might rouse her again.

WAN: And Onata?

WAH: I gave Onata the drink. She thinks it poison.

WAN: When the sun rises, our march will be resumed, and Onata will seek the land beyond the hills of the south with the tribe. Wannemucka will then return and enjoy the prize which many moons have still found him pursuing, still hopeless, but undespairing.

WAH: See, the women begin their lamentations.

        (WAH *re-covers his head. The tent is opened.* ONATA *and the women crouch on the ground near a couch, on which* MED *lies,* COL *kneeling near the head.*)

WAN: (*Goes to foot of couch, bends over it.*) As the roses on the stalk droop, when one of their number is plucked away, let the fair sisters of our tribe bewail her. She shall be laid under the prairie grass, where the wolf shall not find her, for her grave shall be as deep as the red man's love!

        (ONATA *and the Indian girls break into the following low chant:*)

  Let us speak of her:

    She was white as the white snow,

  And her spirit went away

    Under the breath of Manitou,

  As snow flees before the sun.

        (*As the chant is dying away, the distant sound of a drum mingles with it, at first unperceived by the Indians. The music dies away, and the drum continues. The Indians listen.*)

WAN: The white warriors! (*All start up.*) Quick, cover the fires!

        (*The tent is covered again, concealing all the women. Indians enter, bringing* ROWSE. *The fire is scattered. All bend low to the earth.*)

ROWSE: Oh, you murdering rascals, you are caught at last!

COL: (*bursting from tent, with* WIDOW, *etc.*) It is Alleyn!

WIDOW: Woroo! We are saved!

WAN: Seize them! (*All are seized and held by the Indians with drawn knives.*) If you breathe a cry, you die!

        (*A party of soldiers are seen crossing the high path at back. Drum outside still.*)

ALLEYN: (*outside*) Halt!

SERGEANT: (*same*) Halt! (*The soldiers pause.*)

       (ALLEYN, SERGEANT *and* MR. SMITH *appear on bridge and look down.*)

ALLEYN: Is there a path down this ravine?

ROW: Oh, if this infernal knife wasn't at my throat!

MR. S: (*looking down*) By Jove, I don't see anything here!

ROW: Oh, *you* never could see anything anywhere!

SER: Black as pitch.

AL: Listen! don't you hear the branches crack?

ROW: I wish someone would sneeze!

MR. S: I can't hear anything!

ROW: Of course you can't, you fool!

AL: Where is Loder?

SER: He took another cut through the woods, more to the south. He thought he found traces of those scoundrels.

AL: Then we had better follow his lead. Come, let us hasten.

MR. S: Ya'as that's what I say. I'll go on through the gully in this direction.

AL: We'll keep on through the wood. Keep the drum beating, Sergeant, so that if our poor friends hear it, they may know we are near.

       (*Drum again, soldiers and all off.* MR. S *on left.*)

ROW: Well, 'pon my soul! They're precious asses to be sent out here to hunt Indians! (*He kicks over the Indian near him.*)

WAN: (*As the drum dies away in the distance.*) The captives may be freed, but let no one speak.

ROW: Now, will anybody tell me the use of having friends, when they walk right over you like –

       (LODER *appears on eminence, pushes aside the branches cautiously and says 'Ah!'* WAN, ROW *and* WAH *repeat the exclamation and turn and see him. A pause. He dashes away,* ROW *following him with his eye, but not moving.* WAN *directs* WAH *to follow* LOD, WAH *draws his knife and glides out. All breathless attention.*)

WAN: (*to Indian*) Quick! Glide by the water course, and stop the flight of White Panther on the north.

ROW: Two to one! Loder can't stand that!

WAN: Silence!

       (*All quiet. A pause.* LODER *enters, dressed in the disguise of* WAH, *and impersonating him. As he enters, looks backward off, wiping his knife, as if of blood.*)

WAN: Ha! You have slain White Panther. (LOD *shakes head.*) No! Then Cayote will find him there upon the ravine path. Hist! (*The Indian enters with* MR. SMITH, *who is impelled forward at point of knife.*)

MR. SMITH: Aw, by Jove, this is what I get for going off on my own account.

ROW: The Honorable, by all that's unlucky! Then it wasn't Loder I saw!

MR. S: Here, I say! Use me gently! I'm a British subject, and the British flag – (*He is bound and cast beside* ROW.)

WAN: (*to Indian*) White Panther fled?

INDIAN: Yes! Fled!

WAN: Then we must break camp! He will bring all upon us. (*to* LOD) Quick, rouse the white lily! She must be carried with us. (LOD *nods and takes rifle.*) No fire! Alarm warriors!

LOD: (*Shakes his head.*) No! Gone! (*He approaches* MED *and bends gently over her. Daylight begins to break.*)

ROW: Smith, we're lost! We'll be taken to the other end of creation!

MR. S: Oh, Lord!

WAN: No! Indians fly! White women fly! White men remain! (*to Indians*) Bind the white captives to yonder trees and pin them with your knives. (*bugle*)

MR. S and ROW: Oh, Lord! (*Indians seize them and yell.*)

> (*The drum is heard faintly again. All silent in a moment.* MED *starts up at the sound.*)

MR. S: They've missed me and are returning.

WAN: (*to* LOD *and approaching* MED) Quick! To the woods! (*drum nearer*)

LOD: (*casting off his disguise*) Indian! Stand back!

WAN: White Panther!

LOD: Aye, Loder, White Panther!

WAN: Spy! (*Springs towards him with uplifted knife. All the savages with a yell spring upon their captives.* LOD *seizes* MED *and fires his rifle at* WAN, *who falls.*)

> (*In an instant the ravine is filled with soldiers.* ALLEYN *darts forward and passes* MED *to him just in time to ward her from a blow aimed by* ONATA *who darts out of the tent.* ROWSE *and* MR. SMITH *floor their guards.* COLUMBIA *runs to* MR. S, *and, on this picture of triumph, the –*)

CURTAIN.

LOVE ON CRUTCHES

A comedy in three acts (from the German of Stobitzer)

First produced in New York at Daly's Theatre on 25 November 1884 with the following cast:

SYDNEY AUSTIN, a gentleman of Leisure, who has Written Something	Mr. John Drew
GUY ROVERLY, a gentleman of Leisure, who has seen Something	Mr. Otis Skinner
DR. EPENETUS QUATTLES, Love's Postman	Mr. James Lewis
MR. BITTEREDGE, 'Interviewer'	Mr. Wm. Gilbert
PODD, a Valet in place	Mr. F. Bond
BELLS	Mr. W. H. Beekman
ANNIS AUSTIN, an Ideal of the Misunderstood	Miss Ada Rehan
EUDOXIA QUATTLES, posing for Martyrdom	Mrs. G. H. Gilbert
MRS. MARGERY GWYNN, inclined to tempt Fate a second time	Miss Edith Kingdon
BERTA, Mrs. Gwynn's Maid	Miss Jean Gordon
NETTY, Maid to Mrs. Austin	Miss Jennie Trevor
Guests, etc.	

TIME. – The Present.
Place. – New York.

ACT I

The scene represents a veranda, fitted up as a conservatory and breakfast-room combined. The house is at the right, and is reached by two doors – an upper and lower entrance. The garden is reached by a stairway at center. The center of the scene represents glass-work and open trellis work. Door left. A table is at the left, covered by a large Japanese shade. A lounge with small writing-table is at the right. Easy chairs are scattered about. A folding screen with a mirror on one of the folds stands above table. The table under the screen is laid for a breakfast for two. The service is quite rich. Everything about the place denotes elegance and taste. The curtain rises to a cheery melody. After a moment, PODD enters, pauses; looks off the balcony at back, – comes down to the table, – peers into the cups, – holds up the toast-rack, – feels the coffee urn and set.

PODD: As usual, not a mouthful eaten. Breakfast untasted! Coffee untouched! Ditto toast! Ditto eggs! (*Goes to door downstage left and listens.*) Mrs. Austin gone to her room. (*same action at door upstage right*) Mr. Austin gone to his. So much the better for us. (*Goes to balcony and calls off quietly.*) Netty! Netty! Hist! (*Beckons some one, and comes down to table.*)

        (NETTY, *a very pert and trim looking Maid, enters.*)

NETTY: What is it, Mr. Podd?

PODD: Will you do me the honor of assisting at breakfast? (*Places a chair, quite after a manner.*)

NETTY: (*affecting elegant manner*) Oh, with pleasure, my dear Mr. Podd. (*Sits.*) Everything untouched, as usual. (PODD *fills her plate, while she serves coffee.*)

PODD: Our young couple feast on love!

NETTY: Or the sight of each other spoils their appetites.

PODD: (*Eats.*) That's good – that's very good.

NETTY: (*tapping his hand playfully with spoon*) I never saw such a couple. Do you know I've never yet surprised them at even one kiss.

PODD: I should sooner expect to surprise them scratching one another's eyes out.

NETTY: No fear! They'd have to get too close for that.

PODD: While they never overstep a certain limit, do they?

NETTY: They never meet but at table.

PODD: And then they always send us out of the room. I wonder why? All the world might hear what they have to say to each other. They don't seem to have a single confidence between them. It beats me. She so fresh and pretty – like a rosy apple, and he shuns her as if she was wormeaten.

NETTY: There's no telling *what* worms feed on the fruit in these aristocratic marriages.

PODD: (*eagerly*) So you suspect? –

NETTY: (*Looks around.*) That Mr. Austin has found traces of the insect.

PODD: Already! and the honeymoon only just over!

NETTY: (*half whisper*) You know her friend, Mrs. Gwynn?

PODD: The young widow –

NETTY: (*Nods her head.*) Whenever *she* calls, I'm sent away, and then commences *such* a whispering and reading of letters, with closed doors!

PODD: (*keenly*) How do you know, if you are sent out?

NETTY: Stupid! are there no keyholes where you come from?

PODD: To be sure! (*as if struck by an idea*) And there's just the same kind of mystery between master and that old doctor, – doctor, what's-his-name, I never can remember it! (*Ring heard.*) Dr. – Dr. –

NETTY: You mean Dr. Quattles.

PODD: Yes, Quattles, a regular old mouser that. Do you know –
(*They lean over the table and whisper, as* QUATTLES *enters.*)

QUAT: Everybody out of the way! Nobody to tell me whether anybody's at home. Ah, I see! The servants' hall discussing the family affairs and the family break-fast together. (*aloud*) Don't move, I beg! (PODD *and* NETTY *bound up.*)

PODD: (*Crosses, wiping his mouth.*) I beg your pardon, doctor. I'll announce you at once. (*Exits.*)

QUAT: The rascal! Lets visitors wander through the house, while he enjoys his master's toast and eggs.

NETTY: (*taking up tray*) Please, doctor – please don't tell on us.

QUAT: (*melting, as he looks at her*) Well, you shall both be forgiven, for the sake of your pretty eyes.

NETTY: The pretty eyes are ever so much obliged to you, doctor. (*Curtseys and darts out.*)

(SYDNEY *enters.*)

SYD: (*smiling*) Do I intrude?

QUAT: No, I was merely doing homage to your taste in the selection of domestics.

SYD: Too much honor. The selection is my wife's.

QUAT: She evidently has no twinges of jealousy.

SYD: Evidently, so far as I'm concerned.

QUAT: Happy man. I wish my wife had as much taste and as little suspicion.

SYD: Sit down. (*Draws chair from table as* QUAT *sits.*) To what do I owe the pleasure of this visit? Business – or – do you come as Love's postman?

QUAT: Both.

SYD: (*rising eagerly*) Give Love the preference. Where's the letter.

QUAT: Business first, pleasure afterwards.

SYD: (*throwing himself back, vexed*) Hang the business.

QUAT: I saw the publishers today. Your novel has reached its tenth edition.

SYD: (*alarmed and drawing nearer*) 'Sh! The walls have ears! So the last edition is sold out?

QUAT: Perfectly staggering. It beats 'Uncle Tom's Cabin'.

SYD: Speak lower. Do you want the whole town to know I'm the author of 'Tinsel'?

QUAT: Not for the world. The success of the novel is due to the mystery.

SYD: (*nettled*) Indeed!

QUAT: People wouldn't take half the interest if its title-page bore the conceited announcement, 'Tinsel: a Novel of Society, by Sydney Austin'. They'd read

---

'Uncle Tom's Cabin': Harriet Beecher Stowe's novel, of course, was immensely successful. 300,000 copies were sold during the first year of the American edition (1852); over one million copies were sold in England the same year. By 1878 it had been translated into at least twenty languages.

it, and toss it aside and forget. But now you hear on every side, who *can* the author be? Who is 'Marius'? The knowing ones say: 'Oh, some hack, trying to make capital out of a new *nom de plume*.' 'Nonsense,' says an enthusiastic admirer, 'Look at the style! Look at his acquaintance with social life! It must be a real swell, – see how he lashes society.' Then the whole chorus joins in: 'Who can it be?' 'Have you read the book?' 'No?' 'You *must* get it!' and so they wonder, – they buy, – they read, and you make the money.

SYD: So my book does not owe its success to its merit. (*Rises and puts away his chair testily.*)

QUAT: Not a bit of it.

SYD: Extremely flattering.

QUAT: No false notions! Success is one thing, merit is quite another.

SYD: I feel inclined to unmask at once.

QUAT: (*Rises.*) And dispel a mystery worth ten thousand dollars to you?

SYD: Yes. I wish to prove that I have other ideals than mercenary ones.

QUAT: No proof is required. I know you have other ideals! 'Diana!' for instance! (*Produces a letter from his pocket.*)

SYD: (*eagerly*) From 'Diana'!

QUAT: To 'Pascal'!

SYD: Give it to me! (*Takes letter.*)

QUAT: Have you considered that this particular ideal will vanish when you reveal your secret?

SYD: (*has paused*) You are right. (*Opens letter and sits to read it.*)

QUAT: There you are, like a moon-struck youth over his first love letter.

SYD: (*Turns.*) And I tell you I am in love for the first time. Everything until now has been a passing fancy, *here* my whole being is possessed.

QUAT: That's a pretty speech for a young husband just out of the honeymoon, with the loveliest wife man was ever blessed with.

SYD: My wife! (*bitterly*)

QUAT: It's the old story. What we haven't got, we want – and what we have got we don't care for! Now, what you have got is the most delicious, the most captivating, the –

SYD: I know, you always rave about her. (*Resumes reading.*)

QUAT: As far as loyalty to my own Eudoxia permits, I do!

SYD: I don't.

QUAT: No you rave over an unknown – a bluestocking in spectacles and false bands, who writes trash by the page.

SYD: (*hotly, rising*) My Diana! (*Shrugs shoulders and crosses to him.*) You're insane!

QUAT: No, *I'm* not.

SYD: Diana a bluestocking in spectacles!

QUAT: I'll wager your unknown correspondent hasn't a tithe of your wife's beauty and spirit.

---

bluestocking: woman with considerable scholarly, literary, or intellectual ability, so called from the informal dress, especially the blue wool stockings, worn by some members of 18th-century literary clubs in England.

SYD: Not her spirit, thank Heaven! – the spirit of contradiction!

QUAT: Well, her beauty.

SYD: The beauty of a statue! It chills me to look at her. (*Sits on lounge.*)

QUAT: Why don't you waken the soul in the statue then, you obstinate pig! Don't be a pig, – be a Pygmalion! (*Sits beside him.*)

SYD: Soul – in her!

QUAT: You'll allow she has some soul?

SYD: (*yawning*) I really can't say.

QUAT: Have you never looked into her eyes and seen the melting tenderness there?

SYD: I've seen the inclination for a precious row there, – that 's all.

QUAT: Possibly. Eyes are mirrors. They reflect what's before them.

SYD: I suppose, now that my wife is *your* ideal!

QUAT: She's the ideal of what a wife should be. But what induced you to marry such a soulless creature?

SYD: I inherited her. She came from my uncle with his money. We were to marry each other, or be cut off. I knew nothing about her, hadn't seen her since she was sent abroad to school. When the will was read, I looked her up, found her pretty, but cool as an iceberg! Thought of the money, looked at her again. Thought we might possibly live on a friendly sort of footing! Asked, was accepted in the same spirit, and we were married. (*Rises and crosses toward center.*)

QUAT: But you tried a little love making afterwards!

SYD: Love! We've got beyond that.

QUAT: What? Distanced Cupid?

SYD: Easily. My dear fellow, Cupid, for us, is not only blind, but lame.

QUAT: I see – on crutches! Eh?

SYD: Exactly.

QUAT: Rather chilly wedded life for a poet.

SYD: Poets never expect to find their ideals! We cry for the moon – but we are content with green cheese.

QUAT: (*Mutters to himself vexedly.*) Green cheese! (*Throws himself on lounge.*)

SYD: I am wrong, of course.

QUAT: Of course you are.

SYD: And yet my ideal lives and breathes. (*Sits beside* QUAT.) One day, after my book began to be talked about, you brought me a letter, which had been sent to the publisher for the unknown author. It was signed 'Diana', the name of my heroine – written in a female hand, apparently disguised – and contained such proofs of admiration – so fresh and yet so well expressed, that my vanity was flattered. The writer wished to correspond with the unknown author: to impart the sentiments his work had kindled, but stipulated that I should never attempt to discover her name, or reveal my own, that she might remain as ignorant of my identity, as I was of hers. There was something so original and mysterious in the proposition that I agreed. With your consent, I suggested that we should forward our letters through you. I wrote. Her answers enchanted me more and more. She discarded her shyness, and gave me such glimpses of a woman's true soul, that –

QUAT: That you quite forgot you had a wife.

SYD: (*Rises, crosses, sits left of table.*) They are not to be mentioned together. The cold and lifeless moon, compared to the life-infusing sun!

QUAT: Oh, now your wife is the moon! A little while ago she was only green cheese. That's the way. You get the moon you cried for, and now you want the whole solar system.

SYD: You think I exaggerate? Look at this letter. In it Diana confesses that she too is suffering under the yoke of an ill-assorted marriage.

QUAT: Oho!

SYD: Stop! Instead of laying the blame on her husband, as thousands of her sex would, she accuses herself; – confesses it is her own pride and self-will, her own coldness and obstinacy that have wrecked her happiness. Can anything be nobler?

QUAT: Well, if Diana says that, (*Sits beside* SYD.) she isn't quite a hopeless case yet. It's the first step to reform.

SYD: (*angrily*) What? You believe *she* is to blame? No. Her humility proves her to be faultless. A man who couldn't live happily with such a woman, is an ass. (*Rises.*)

QUAT: My opinion exactly. There are men who own nightingales and go to parrots for music. (SYD *moves away.*) I know a specimen – a fellow who thinks himself unappreciated by a most excellent wife, and yet won't take the trouble to win her regard.

SYD: (*eagerly*) Exactly the case with Diana's husband. (*Crosses.*) Her brute is evidently unconscious that he is mated to the loveliest and noblest of created beings.

(ANNIS *appears.*)

QUAT: (*Rises.*) And there she is!

SYD: Diana?

QUAT: No, your wife.

SYD: (*sarcastically*) We were speaking of the loveliest and noblest of created beings. (*crossing*)

AN: The loveliest and noblest of created beings? Good morning, Doctor. Who is the happy woman that inspires my lord and master with such enthusiasm? (SYD *pockets the letter, and turns aside.* ANNIS *gives her hand to* QUAT.)

QUAT: Can you doubt who the happy woman is?

AN: You mean me? Ah, what an awkward hand you are at a fib. We have been married five months; after five months an angel would cease to be the loveliest and noblest of created beings in my husband's eyes; and alas – I am not an angel. (QUAT *goes up stage.*)

SYD: (*He and* AN *bow.*) We were merely speaking of –

AN: No matter. It does not interest me in the least to know with whom you were enraptured. (*Moves away.*)

SYD: (*Yawns affectedly.*) Ah!

AN: Did you speak?

SYD: No.

AN: I thought you yawned.

SYD: I beg pardon – it was quite unintentional.

AN: Pray, don't mention it. (*Sits on lounge with a shrug of the shoulders, and sighs.*) Ah!

SYD: What did you observe?

AN: Nothing.

SYD: I thought you sighed.

AN: Really! Forgive me, it was quite accidental.

SYD: Don't restrain yourself on my account.

AN: Thank you.

SYD: (*Bites his lip, and then to* QUAT.) Will you excuse me? I have a letter to write. (*aside*) My answer to hers. (*Makes a sign of caution and exits.*)

AN: (*turning on seat, and affably to* QUAT) I heard your voice, and came in to ask if I should have the pleasure of seeing you at Margery's this evening?

QUAT: Of course. The simmering of a pretty woman's tea-kettle is a siren's song that I never could resist.

AN: And you'll bring your wife?

QUAT: (*leaning over arm of sofa*) Catch her exposing me alone and unprotected to the siren.

AN: (*Rises.*) She is wrong. A woman can do nothing so unwise as to show her affection!

QUAT: Ah! You think so!

AN: Marriage should be considered an armed neutrality: both parties ready for attack and defense.

QUAT: Marriage is generally compared to a haven of rest.

AN: That is where one runs into port voluntarily. Where one is towed in by main force – it is a prison.

QUAT: And the husband is the jailer? Sydney would be delighted to hear that description of his occupation. Do you know, you are –

AN: I am what? (*Sits at table.*)

QUAT: An enigma! A prize puzzle! My first is good, kind and amiable! My second is – quite the contrary! My whole – Forgive an old friend his plain speaking, but I can't bear to see two beings created for each other, embittering their whole existence.

AN: Created for each other! You mean, married to each other?

QUAT: It's the same thing.

AN: My husband is of a different opinion.

QUAT: You are so sensible, so good, so generous –

AN: My husband is of a different opinion.

QUAT: You deserve to be loved –

AN: My husband –

QUAT: You can make him the happiest of men – and he is –

AN: Of a different opinion.

QUAT: (*Sits.*) That's because you pretend to be the reverse of all that you really are – kind and lovable.

AN: I shall not force my attentions upon one who ignores them.

QUAT: He does not ignore them. You won't let him see them.

AN: He could see them, if he were not devoured with his own self-sufficiency.

QUAT: It is not self-sufficiency! It's the self-reliance of a really remarkable man.

AN: Remarkable? For what? I've never perceived it. Or perhaps he conceals his greatness, for fear that such a goose as I wouldn't appreciate him. (*growing agitated*) Does a man's greatness consist in belittling his wife? (*Rises.*)

QUAT: (*shrewdly*) Why not show him that you are his equal. I wouldn't stop 'till I found means to conquer his indifference.

AN: (*vigorously*) Show me the way! Oh, what wouldn't I give to do it!
              (PODD *enters.*)

PODD: Mrs. Quattles, ma'am! (QUAT *throws up his arms, as much as to say: 'I knew it.'*)
              (MRS. QUATTLES *enters.*)

MRS. Q: I knew it. (*Looks at both.*)

QUAT: And I knew it! (PODD *exits.*)

MRS. Q: I never miss my husband but I'm sure to find him tête-à-tête with some pretty woman.

AN: (*giving her hand to* MRS. Q) You are just in time to prevent a declaration of love.

MRS. Q: Declaration of love! Oh, he'll be at it yet. He raves about you. My dear, he's a butterfly.

QUAT: With his wings clipped.

MRS. Q: I had to clip 'em, or you'd have singed them off long ago. (*The skirmishes between Mr. and Mrs. Q are always in good temper.*)

AN: Why, my dear, you are a female Othello.

MRS. Q: No, I'm not, because I don't need an Iago to open my eyes. (*to* QUAT) Ugh! (*He goes up chuckling, the two ladies sit. She continues, aside, to* AN.) It flatters Quattles to think I consider him a dangerous creature – and I make the most of his gratitude afterwards. (*aloud*) Oh, I'm an unhappy woman. (QUAT *comes to her.*) Don't come near me, sir. (*He retreats.*) Yes, you may. I want ten dollars. (*He goes up, taking out his pocket-book. She continues, aside, to* AN.) Remember this little incident, my dear – when your honeymoon is over, and your husband goes the way of all flesh –
              (SYDNEY *re-enters.*)

SYD: (*to* MRS. Q) It is needless to ask after your health, my dear madam – you look blooming.

MRS. Q: Blooming! How deceptive appearances are! I'm wretched.

QUAT: (*Crosses to her, giving her some bank-notes.*) Take one of these every hour till you feel better.

MRS. Q: (*putting notes in her reticule*) He makes fun of me – the monster! (*Rises.*) He doesn't feel the least pang at being a nail in my coffin.

QUAT: How can a nail feel a pang!

MRS. Q: Go on! He don't understand me! (*Throws herself back.*) He never does. I'm a poor misunderstood woman. (*Sits, and sobs.*)

QUAT: Of course! That's the cry! (*Looks from one to the other in rotation.*) The world is full of misunderstood people. All hunting after ideals – chasing illusions – posing for sympathy – and, when plain common sense people give their nonsense its right name, they throw themselves back, and groan at being misunderstood! All humbug – all acting! But if these heroes and heroines knew what ridiculous figures they cut on the scene – they'd gather up their skirts and rush off the stage.

MRS. Q: I'm a ridiculous figure! (*Crosses to* SYD.) See how the monster delights to torment me! (*Goes up with* AN, *and aside to her, vivaciously.*) Not a bit of it, you know. But it's so interesting to be a suffering wife.

SYD: (*aside to* QUAT, *handing him a letter*) Take this, it's Diana's answer.

QUAT: In the disguised handwriting, as usual.

SYD: Of course. (*They go aside.*)

MRS. Q: (*to* AN) You are still in the honeymoon. You have no need to act the distressed wife.

AN: To act it! No, I've no need to act it!
(PODD, *at entrance, announcing*)

PODD: Mrs. Gwynn – Mr. Roverly.

ALL: (*turning towards center*) Ah! Ah!
(MARGERY *and* ROVERLY *enter.*)

MAR: (*laughing*) A general ah! What an encouraging reception! (*Kisses* AN.) See what an honor. Escorted by the famous African traveller – who has not even had time to shake the dust of the desert from his feet. (*Looks at* ROV*'s boots.*) No! It has already disappeared beneath the polish of civilization. What a pity! It would have made you so interesting, Mr. Roverly!
(*During the above, in dumb show* – QUAT *is introduced to* ROV.)

ROV: (*who has bowed to the ladies, and shaken hands with* QUAT *and* SYD) After all, there's not so much difference between the wilderness and society.
(*Crosses to* AN.)

AN: (*Meets him.*) You compare the two?

ROV: Because there are oases in both.

AN: Did you learn flattery from the savages of the Congo?

ROV: I might have done so. They have all the vices of fashionable life.

MRS. Q: Thank goodness, you escaped from them.

ROV: Escaped! I'd give worlds for a chase in which I might be the game instead of the hunter – merely for a change. (*Sighs.*) Life is as much a bore there as –

MAR: Everywhere else. Poor fellow, he went to Africa to escape ennui –
(PODD *at entrance, announcing*)

PODD: Mr. Bitteredge.

SYD: Not at home.

QUAT: (*to* SYD) Oh, you must see him. (SYD *nods to* PODD, *who exits.*) The most successful interviewer of two continents. Inventor of the most astounding conversations ever held. Discoverer of all the sea serpents of twenty years. In one word, special correspondent of the 'Morning Electrifier'.
(BITTEREDGE *enters, shown in by* PODD, *who exits immediately.*)

BIT: Ladies and gentlemen – (*Bows.*)

SYD: (*shaking hands*) You are quite a stranger.

BIT: No time. We poor journalists toil night and day, to feed that voracious monster – the news-devouring public.

AN: (*Crosses to him.*) How I wish we had an item for you. But there's not the least bit of scandal stirring. Stop. You know Mr. Roverly, the tourist and explorer?

BIT: It would be a scandal not to know him. (*to* ROV) I've just come from your quarters. Been on your trail since daylight.

ROV: To what am I indebted for the honor?

BIT: You're just from Africa, the lion of the day: the African lion! The wildest and most unapproachable species – just the game for us.

MAR: There, you have your wish.

ROV: And why do you hunt me down?

BIT: To tan your skin for the readers of the 'Electrifier'. In short, to extract your adventures.

ROV: What! You want me to bore myself twice – first by travelling and next by talking about it? No, my worthy Nimrod, no.

BIT: Bore! You were really bored by your hair-breadth escapes? (*Puts on glasses, and takes out note-book and pencil.*) Allow me to make a note of that. It's fresh and original. 'Bored by his adventures.' Capital head-line!

AN: (*Crosses to* ROV.) What spot on earth did you find most amusing, Mr. Roverly? (BIT *prepares to write.*)

ROV: None.

BIT: (*At first cast down, is suddenly struck, and writes.*) Capital! 'Found no spot on earth so interesting as home.' Another good line. That'll set you right with our readers at the start.

SYD: He didn't say that.

BIT: (*to* SYD) I must enlarge a little. Privilege of the Press!

AN: I mean, where did you find the most occupation?

ROV: Where the mosquitoes were thickest.

BIT: (*Sits, writes on table.*) Immense! 'Sanguinary conflicts with the natives.'

SYD: Another expansion.

BIT: (*to* ROV) They were savage mosquitoes, of course? – gave no quarter!

ROV: No, nor took none. They wanted the whole. (*All laugh.*)

AN: How intellectual!

ROV: (*Crosses to* QUAT.) In these climates there is nothing intellectual. You go to sleep.

MRS. Q: Well, we'll wake you up here.

AN: (*dropping down behind* MAR) We have a few pretty women to plague you.

ROV: A very good substitute for mosquitoes.

QUAT: These have claws. Beware of them!

MRS. Q: Claws! I wish we had, wouldn't I scratch you.

QUAT: My dear, no one comes up to scratch quicker than you do.

AN: Don't mind him. A while ago he extolled marriage to the skies.

MRS. Q: He told me this morning, that marriage was the grave of love, and woman the stone that marks it. He forgot to observe, that husbands were the grave-diggers.

QUAT: (*injured*) You wrong me, Eudoxia! I compared marriage to a garden of roses.

AN: Really!

QUAT: Yes. We pluck the buds in the morning, and get stuck by the thorns ever after. (*Retreats up the stage, pursued by* MRS. Q *round table.*)

BIT: (*Comes forward with* ROV.) If I don't throw a fat morsel to the public every morning, they'll eat *me*, and I don't want to give them the dyspepsia. At this very moment I'm hunting a bit of news that our readers are starving for – the secret of the authorship of 'Tinsel'.

ALL: (*interested, except* ROV) Ah!

ROV: 'Tinsel'! What's that?

BIT: The last novel, by somebody who calls himself 'Marius', haven't you read it?

ROV: I never read novels. Real life is bore enough.

MAR: Just my view. I'd like to go through the excitement of a novel, but to read one, never!

AN: (*warmly*) But his is an exception.

QUAT: I believe you – ten editions in four weeks.

BIT: We gave it a column – all gush, too.

MAR: (*sarcastically*) It has wrought one miracle they tell me. People buy instead of borrowing it. It haunts every parlor, obtrudes in every conversation! And you never even heard of it. (*to* ROV) What have you missed by going round the globe!

SYD: I think it greatly overestimated.

MAR: (*pointedly*) Really! you and I seldom agree, but we do in this case. (*He bows coldly.*)

AN: (*to* SYD, *excitedly*) Its very easy to criticise a work which we have not the heart nor the brains to understand.

SYD: (*smiling*) So you belong to the Tinsel worshippers.

AN: I acknowledge it with pride. The author's modesty, as well as his work, prove him to be a man in advance of his age.

MAR: (*aside to* AN) You'll betray yourself! (AN *starts violently, pauses, and comes down stage in confusion.* MAR *returns to* ROV.)

SYD: (*aside*) Hem! she's not quite a block. She *is* capable of animation. (*Crosses to her.*) I had no idea that you took such an interest in – in literature.

AN: (*coldly polite*) Of course not. When did you ever trouble yourself to discover what interests me?

SYD: (*seriously*) I admit I was in the wrong.

AN: It does not signify. We have merely another proof that our tastes and inclinations do not harmonize. (*Goes up.*)

SYD: (*aside. Shrugs his shoulders.*) I see. Her enthusiasm was merely to spite me. She defended the novel because I attacked it.

BIT: (*group with* MR. *and* MRS. QUAT) At all events, I'm on the track of the author now.

ALL: (*except* ROV, *in different tones*) Indeed! Really!

BIT: I have discovered a breach in his defences. (*to* QUAT *suddenly*) *You* are the breach.

QUAT: (*Coughs.*) I'm the breach, am I?

BIT: I learn from the publishers that he's a particular friend of yours.

QUAT: Well, sir!

BIT: Well, sir, I shall haunt you day and night; wake your midnight slumbers, pursue your walks and pepper your meals with the ceaseless demand – who is Marius?

QUAT: Oh, lord! (*Rises.*)

BIT: (*Follows* QUAT.) Henceforth, I'm your bottle-imp. Your ink-bottle imp! From your trembling lips I'll drag forth the secret, and blazon it forth to the world in double-leaded small pica – 'Found at last! Marius is' – ! for instance, our friend Austin! (ROV *and* AN *turn up stage, laughing.* BIT *claps his hand on* SYD*'s shoulder.* SYD *starts; all look at him.* QUAT *takes advantage of the silence to slip* SYD*'s letter into* MAR*'s hand, and to say to her aside: –*)

QUAT: Here's a letter for Diana! Hide it! (*He goes up laughing, as if at* BIT, MAR *follows, concealing the letter.*)

SYD: (*recovering*) Why select me?

BIT: Well, you *might* have written it. Anybody could. Poor trash! (*to* QUAT) So you brave me!

QUAT: I defy you! (AN *drops down stage.*)

BIT: Now, by St. Guttenberg [*sic*], the *Press* shall squeeze it out of you.

QUAT: Spare me your puns.

BIT: Wait till I bring my heavy wit to bear on you.

QUAT: Heavy wet and beer! Let me get away from this. My dear Mrs. Austin, you won't accuse me of cowardice in flying from such a shower? (*Kisses her hand.*)

BIT: Where's my hat? I start in pursuit.

MRS. Q: (*meeting* QUAT, *who drops* AN*'s hand*) That kiss was altogether too long.

QUAT: I'll make that all right. The next I give *you*, shall be shorter. (*Tucks her arm under his and going.*)

MRS. Q: You see how my tyrant bears me off! If you ever miss me, search Blue-beard's closet. (*They go up and confront* BIT *with his umbrella.*)

BIT: Stand and deliver.

QUAT: (*placing* MRS. Q *before him*) Take all my dross, but spare my life.

BIT: (*Moves out of the way.*) Place to the ladies. (QUAT *darts to door on the other side of his wife.*) Coward!

MRS. Q: Fly, I'll protect you.

QUAT: Keep him till I get down stairs. (*Exit. Ladies laugh.*)

BIT: We shall meet again. (*confidentially to* MRS. Q, *and gallantly offering his arm*) I don't wish to violate matrimonial confidences, but would you mind telling me – who is Marius?

MRS. Q: I will, on one condition.

BIT: Yes, yes.

MRS. Q: That you find out first and let me know. (*Exits.*)

BIT: Ha, ha, ha! – he, he, he! But no matter. (*Exits, is heard outside, calling out –*) Who is Marius? Who is he?

MAR: (*calling off after them*) Remember, I expect you all to tea this afternoon.

SYD: (*at door*) If the ladies will excuse me, I should like to show Mr. Roverly my collection. (*to* ROV) You can give me some valuable information. (*Opens door and waits.*)

MAR: Tell me one thing first, Mr. Roverly. How do the ladies of the Congo dance?

ROV: The ladies of the Congo do not dance. All laborious duties are performed by their servants. (*Bows and exits with* SYD.)

MAR: (*Puts her hat on table.*) Did you ever see such a lazy fellow? I believe he would class kissing among the laborious duties.

AN: And you would like to convince him of the contrary?

MAR: I would like to see him in love.

AN: With you? (*taking her arm*)

MAR: With anybody, to rouse him from his insufferable apathy. It's a thousand pities.

AN: Hem! Let me feel your pulse.

MAR: (*withdrawing her arm*) Nonsense! you know he was my first love, when I was in frocks, and we always retain a certain interest in such people. Ah, me! I thought then his indifference was adorable.

AN: Set about his cure.

MAR: Such cures are always fatal to the physician.

AN: *Love*, fatal?

MAR: I know one case. The lady dotes on a shadow. (*Shows slyly* SYD's *letter which she had received from* QUATTLES.)

AN: (*with a cry*) From Pascal!

MAR: And screams with joy at the very sight of her lover's writing.

AN: You must not call him my *lover*! you profane the ideal!

MAR: (*withdrawing letter*) Then you don't love him?

AN: There has not been a syllable of love between us.

MAR: Then it doesn't matter whether you get the letter or not. (*Pockets it.*)

AN: (*coaxing*) Please!

MAR: (*Shows half the letter.*) Do you love him?

AN: (*doubtfully*) N–No!

MAR: Very well then. (*Pockets it again.*)

AN: Margery – Don't torment me so.

MAR: (*holding the letter aloft*) Do you love him?

AN: (*after trying to catch the letter*) Well, then – I love him as one loves a being of another world, a character in a novel, or a play. It is a pure love, free from earthly dross.

MAR: I see – the ore freed from what the miners call the 'slag'.

AN: Yes.

MAR: Take it, on that assurance. (AN *takes letter, and turns away.*) But as for your unknown correspondent, I venture the belief that he wouldn't object to a little slag. Men don't understand ideal love.

AN: (*Crosses to table.*) Ah, you don't comprehend *him*.

MAR: No, I confess I don't understand how a sensible man can waste time on such stuff as *that*. (*Points to letter.* AN *kisses the letter, and sits to read it.*) Is that your pure love without *slag*?

AN: You don't know how full my heart is.

MAR: Pour some into mine, it's empty.

AN: (*Looks at letter, hesitates, then folds it.*) No. You shan't hear it. You would only laugh.

MAR: Is it as funny as all that?

AN: Now you *shall* hear it. (*Opens letter.*)

MAR: (*Sits and sighs.*) Good gracious.

AN: (*Reads.*) 'My dear one –'

MAR: (*negligently*) Oh, he calls you his dear one.

AN: Of course.

MAR: I don't see why 'of course'.

AN: In the realms of ideal love, there are no cold formalities.

MAR: Pardon my ignorance.

AN: (*Reads.*) 'In my barren life, alone amid a throng in which not one soul comprehends me – linked to a wife to whom my thoughts are as a sealed book' – (*Speaks with deep earnestness.*) Oh, that woman! (*Reads.*) 'I had despaired of sunlight and happiness, when you, my star, my sun, arose. How different seems the world! How full of life and splendor! Thy spirit only has illumined my path! What must be the joy, the ineffable joy of beholding that spirit wedded to its form!'

MAR: I'm afraid the earthly slag is coming in.

AN: (*annoyed*) Well, wait. (*Reads.*) 'The more enchanting your letters, the more my regret that I can only gather these glorious thoughts from the cold surface of the paper, not drink them in from your beauteous lips, nor – (*hesitates*) nor – press my glowing gratitude upon them.'

MAR: Is *that* the usual custom in the realms of the ideal?

AN: (*Rises.*) No, no. *I* never write to him in that way, but men are so immoderate in their – their –

MAR: In their pure love free from earthly dross.

AN: (*looking at letter, hesitating*) I hardly dare finish.

MAR: Oh, a little slag more or less doesn't matter.

AN: (*hesitatingly*) Well then – (*Reads.*) 'Let the last barrier fall that separates us. Let me gaze into your eyes, and whisper the words that ever vibrate through my being, the words –' (*Stops and puts letter behind her.*)

MAR: The words: 'I love you.' (AN *starts up.*) Why not say it! Of course, it's purely ideal. He only loves you as one loves a character in a novel, or a play. (*Laughs.*)

AN: (*who has walked nervously about*) I may as well confess – this letter displeases me excessively.

MAR: Are you sure?

AN: It destroys the charm, the purity of my feelings. (*Throws letter down on table.*) Why does he drag in all that is so commonplace, so base!

MAR: (*as AN crosses up stage*) Because, you see, my dear, in our commonplace world the ideal love you dreamed of is impossible. (AN *sighs.*) And now, you perceive, it's high time to end this farce.

AN: (*beside her*) To end this farce? Madge, if you knew that this dream is all the charm that life has for me! Before I had read his book, what was I? A thing that had been bought and sold. My husband did not marry me for love, he did not even woo me! I was an item in his calculation, an encumbrance with his inheritance. He hates me: I condemn him! I would long ago have shrivelled up into a soulless clod, but that these letters have kept my heart green. (*Sinks on sofa.*)

MAR: (*approaching*) Very flattering to your husband.

AN: My husband is a creature of the world. Pascal is a man of genius.

MAR: Ah, he signs himself Pascal?

AN: After the hero of his novel. (*thoughtfully*) I have confessed in my letters to him, that perhaps I was most to blame for my wedded misery, but he refuses to believe it; he says, my husband neglects me, because he won me too easily.

MAR: (*Sits by her.*) I wonder your Pascal doesn't propose a divorce, so you can marry *him*.

AN: Haven't I explained that he too is married, chained to a petty, frivolous creature, whose sole idea of marriage is the dream of a school-girl, not the strong common sense affection capable of those sacrifices, which the rough reality of everyday life demands? (*Moves away.*)

MAR: As you seem to understand the duties of married life so well, (*Rises.*) why don't you practice them with your husband?

AN: (*Stops.*) Am I married to such a man as Pascal? If I were, I would know how to appreciate him. No, I am speaking of his wife. I only hope some day to meet that woman face to face. (*At this instant she finds herself in front of the mirror, and stops to change the roses in her hair.*)

MAR: And if you did chance to meet her face to face?

AN: (*looking into the glass*) I should say to her: 'Madam! A woman who sits beside a clear spring, perishing with thirst, and refuses to drink, unless from a golden goblet – a woman possessed of the noblest of husbands, and who makes herself wretched for the want of a few petty attentions, is – more of a fool than most of her sex. That is all I have to say to you, madam!' (*Bows to glass and comes down.*)

MAR: (*half aside*) I wonder if she's pretty?

AN: (*pauses a moment at mirror*) What if she is? What is mere beauty of face in a woman whose eyes are cold with disdain, and whose voice is harsh with peevish complaint?

MAR: (*Sits at table.*) You seem to have drawn quite a portrait of her for your own satisfaction.

AN: (*beside sofa*) I can see her at this moment, sitting there, stiff and rigid, staring into vacancy. Pascal enters. He approaches her with all gentleness and kindness. 'My love,' he says, 'I have something to propose!' – 'What is it?' cold as an iceberg. The mercury in his disposition settles to zero. 'Why, only, that they give Lohengrin tonight at the new Opera House, shall we go?' – And she: 'You forget, sir, how little my present state of mind harmonizes with music.' – 'Well, my love, I confess I bought the tickets, thinking –' 'Bought the tickets!' and she starts up, 'Without consulting my convenience! But you never consult my convenience! I'm your slave, to be ordered wherever you choose to go. You may keep your tickets. You may enjoy yourself alone. As for me, I'm too – too – wretched!' (*She puts her handkerchief to her eyes, and sinks in chair with pretended sobs.*)

MAR: Ha! ha! ha! There's a good actress lost in you, my dear, or a –

AN: (*Throws away handkerchief and laughs.*) Ha, ha! Or a capital shrew! Is that what you mean? (*Goes up a little.*)

>   (SYDNEY and ROVERLY *enter. At sight of* SYD, AN *stops laughing and assumes in reality the hard and icy expression she has been mimicking.*)

Opera House: The Metropolitan Opera House was built in 1883 on the west side of Broadway filling the entire block between 39th and 40th Streets.

MAR: What a pity, you came a moment too late to enjoy a delicious bit of acting. (*to* ROV) Well, how did you like the collection? (*They go up.* SYD *comes down beside* AN.)

SYD: (*with a kindly air*) Apropos of acting, my love, I have something to propose.

AN: (*frigidly*) What is it?

SYD: There's a new piece tonight at the theatre. Suppose we take Roverly –

AN: *You* may go, but you will have to dispense with my company. (MAR *glances at* AN.)

SYD: Why?

AN: Because – what do my reasons matter! I don't feel like it, that is all.

SYD: Your customary answer to everything I suggest. (*Goes up stage a little.*)

AN: Who asked you to suggest anything? Why don't you avoid the refusal (MAR *advances a little.*), if you can't receive it with equanimity, or at least with politeness. (*She turns and meets* MAR.)

SYD: (*About to reply hotly, checks himself, and throws himself in a chair, and stretching his arm upon the table, feels unconsciously the crumpled letter which* AN *has cast aside and toys with it.*)

AN: (*to* MAR) That is just like him! If I don't comply with his wishes instantly, he grows petulant; instead of trying what a little coaxing would accomplish.

MAR: My dear Annis, I am afraid that your capital acting just now is due to frequent rehearsals at home!

AN: (*Turns to her.*) Margery, you wish to insinuate –

MAR: That the two scenes are as like each other as two eggs. Don't you see it yourself? (*Goes to* ROV.)

AN: (*thoughtfully*) Have I really been playing the part I despised? (*Turns toward* SYD, *irresolutely, but at that instant she perceives that he has taken her letter up from the table, in an absent manner.*) Good heavens! Oh! (*She rushes forward, with a cry, and tears the letter from him, and hides it in her bosom, then stands trembling. All look at her. Slight pause.*)

MAR: (*aside, a step down, alarmed*) What imprudence!

ROV: (*aside*) A domestic scene. What a bore! (*Goes up to a plant and examines it.*)

SYD: (*rising slowly*) What is the meaning of this, Annis?

AN: I – I don't know. What do you wish?

SYD: An explanation of your conduct.

AN: The – letter?

SYD: Yes, the letter.

MAR: (*advancing, cheerfully*) It belongs to me.

SYD: (*Pauses, looks at each.*) Indeed! Then why need my wife conceal it so carefully?

MAR: She knows its contents are not for the curious, and she watches over it with a jealousy that does honor to her friendship, if not to her judgment. (*severely to* AN) Give it to me, my dear. It seems you are not to be trusted with a secret. You innocent baby, do you know you are compromising me? (AN *hands her the letter.* MAR *pockets it.* AN *goes up.*)

ROV: (*Comes forward abruptly, having listened jealously to the foregoing.*) So you receive compromising letters? (SYD *drops in chair.*)

MAR: (*at first haughtily, then with secret exultation*) And pray, how does it concern you?

ROV: (*resuming his apathy*) True, true! I beg your pardon sincerely. It was the heat. I am not accustomed to the close atmosphere of civilization. (*Takes his hat.*) I have the honor to take my leave.

SYD: (*Who has conquered his emotion, crosses to* ROV.) I'll accompany you. I believe I require a little air myself. We will leave the ladies to continue their dramatic efforts. (*Exits, with* ROV. MAR *goes quickly to* AN, *who reels, as if overcome with emotion.*)

AN: You have saved me.

MAR: Not a bit of it. Your husband don't believe a word I said.

AN: You think so?

MAR: (*Throws herself into seat, in despair.*) But Roverly does!

AN: (*going aside, petulantly*) Who cares about him?

MAR: (*At table, sighs.*) You're right, who cares about *him*!

AN: But Sydney! If he should really – Heavens! and yet, what could he suspect?

MAR: What does a man suspect when his wife receives a letter in secret?

AN: (*indignant*) Not a love affair!

MAR: What else?

AN: (*look of indignation*) What! could he believe me capable of a thing so low – so vulgar? (*calming down and smiling*) No, no! he can't think so meanly of me as that.

MAR: (*Rises.*) Are you sure, after your coldness to him?

AN: Then I'll shame him! I'll *prove* to him that my relation to Pascal –

MAR: Is wholly free from slag? (*Draws letter from her pocket and gives it.*) Unfortunately, this letter, with its glowing language, is hardly the thing for the purpose.

AN: Am I to blame for its glowing language?

MAR: Sydney will think you encouraged it.

AN: Encouraged it?

MAR: How will you convince him of the contrary?

AN: (*angrily*) True. (*in alarm*) But what am I to do? Advise me. You have such good sense, and I'm afraid I'm not overstocked in that way.

MAR: No! or you wouldn't have to appeal to me now.

AN: I beg of you, give me your advice.

MAR: Well, in the first place, are you sure that in your letters to Pascal you never gave the least approval of his passion?

AN: You really insult me, Margery.

MAR: Then demand your letters back. Lay them before your husband. That will clear you.

AN: (*embracing her, with joy*) Yes, and he'll be humiliated. Oh, how I revel in the thought of that. He'll confront me with the sternness of a judge; 'You say you can justify yourself! Where are your proofs?' 'Here!' – and I spread them all out like a pack of cards before him. At first, he's amazed, then staggered, then he devours them with increasing confusion, and occasional penitent glances at me. At last he hangs his head, not daring even to look up. Then I generously approach and release him from his embarrassment: 'I forgive you; but never – never – never again suspect your wife!'

MAR: (*laughing*) Don't be too hard on the poor sinner! (*Arranges her hat at mirror.*) The first thing is to write to Pascal. Good-bye!

AN: You are going?

MAR: I'll not disturb your communing with your ideal by my profane presence.

AN: You tease! Good-bye. (*Kisses her.*) In an hour I'll bring you the letter.

MAR: Good-bye. (*Exits.*)

AN: (*Hurries to writing-table near the lounge.*) Yes, I'll crush him. He, so haughty, yet so contemptible as to harbor suspicions of his wife. (*Sits and takes up pen.*) Ah, my poor unknown friend! there must be an end of these letters, which you say you prize so much. I begin to hate the man who compels me to give you pain. (*Writes.*)

> (SYDNEY *re-enters. He comes in quietly, and comes down hurriedly. She utters a low cry, and tries to conceal the letter.*)

SYD: Ah! you are no doubt about to answer your friend's letter.

AN: (*Rises calmly.*) No, not hers, my own letter.

SYD: So, you confess. (*Puts down his hat.*)

AN: I have nothing to conceal.

SYD: Then let me see it.

AN: No; at least not now.

SYD: Why not now?

AN: Because – I cannot explain – I only want a little time.

SYD: So as to concoct another story with Mrs. Gwynn. (*pause*) That woman is your evil genius.

AN: (*getting angry*) Of course, because she is the only person in the world who loves me.

SYD: (*with suppressed agitation*) Will you show me that letter?

AN: Not now.

SYD: Instantly!

AN: No!

SYD: I demand it!

AN: No! *No!* NO!

SYD: I command you to give it to me!

AN: (*sarcastically*) You command? At last you show your true colors: a master – a tyrant! And I am your slave – your property? Without rights – without soul or sense? No, sir. You can never bend me – never! *Never!* NEVER!

SYD: Then you drive me to adopt a course I would have spared you. (*Takes his hat up.*)

AN: Spared me! (*Laughs bitterly.*) As if you would spare me a single torture you could possibly inflict. Well, then, what is it? What course have I driven you to adopt?

SYD: (*Lays hat down again.*) I have not asked you for your love.

AN: (*bitter laugh*) I appreciate your generosity to the utmost.

SYD: But I do demand that you keep my name and my honor untarnished.

AN: Your name! Your honor untarnished! (*Bursts out into genuine laughter.*) Oh, really! This is too good. (*Sinks into chair at table.*)

SYD: So you are lost to every sense of shame; if my honor is your sport, I will take means to protect it. (*Seizes his hat and going.* AN *laughs in mockery.*) There is but one way. (*She stops her laughter suddenly to hear what he says.*) A separation!

AN: (*Starts up.*) A separation!

SYD: Yes, madam, a separation!

AN: Very well, a separation.

SYD: A separation!

AN: By all means. A separation! (*They exeunt right and left as the –*)

CURTAIN FALLS

ACT II

A drawing-room at MRS. GWYNN's. *An arch at right leads to another parlor.*
Another opens upon a conservatory; one up stage left leads by a spacious hall to the
exterior. A mantle, with fire, at center. Window with recess, left. Two doors lead
off from left, down stage. All the openings are closed with curtains. Those at left
are half drawn. The furniture is very rich. A chandelier hangs center, unlighted.
Time: afternoon of the same day. MARGERY *is discovered at piano, center, with*
a tête-à-tête seat below it. Table right; sofa left. Easy chairs near table. The curtain
rises to music, which MAR *is playing. She starts up abruptly, and throws herself on*
seat.

MAR: I never saw Roverly show so much interest. He was positively excited when
    I claimed that letter. Was it jealousy? (*Starts up.*) If so, then it was love, too.
        (ANNIS *rapidly enters in street costume.*)

AN: Oh, I'm so glad to find you!

MAR: I'm so happy you came! What do *you* think? Was it jealousy? Is he in love?

AN: (*surprised*) He? Who?

MAR: (*recovering*) Oh, no one! (*Kisses her.*) You surprised me in some timid
    attempts at sentimentals.

AN: You sentimental?

MAR: Strange, isn't it? I'm really afraid there is something wrong with me here,
    (*hand to head*) or, perhaps, here! (*hand to heart*) But I'll wait for further
    symptoms, before I become alarmed.

AN: (*absently, and nervously looking around*) Yes.

MAR: Why, you are all in a flutter. What's the matter?

AN: I've had an awful scene with Sydney. (*Both sit.*)

MAR: You frighten me.

AN: That is, he was nearly awful – awe-inspiring, I mean. He evolved a degree of
    passion that was really dramatic in its intensity. I was never so much im-
    pressed in my life.

MAR: (*Laughs.*) Beware, or you'll wrong – Pascal!

AN: (*petulantly*) Pascal!

MAR: Well, what was the upshot of the scene?

AN: He threatened – separation divorce!

MAR: No! Divorce? Then his dramatics took the French emotional phase?

AN: (*Quite enjoying the subject, almost childish, goes to table.*) Yes, we are going
    to separate. But first he shall realize how much he has wronged me. (*Sits.*)
    And so I *must* have my letters back from Pascal. I must have them back at
    once, at any cost.

MAR: Have you written to him?

AN: No. I came here to do it. Sydney might surprise me at any moment at home. He has become a perfect Othello. (*Rises.*)

        (BERTA *enters, with a card.*)

BER: A gentleman to see Madam.

MAR: (*Takes card.*) Mr. Roverly. (*delighted*) I will see him at once.

BER: Yes, Madam. (*Exits.*)

MAR: I wonder what brings him *here*!

AN: Perhaps he wishes to assist in your timid attempt to sentimentals.

        (ROVERLY *enters.*)

ROV: (*eagerly*) My dear Mar – (*Stops short on seeing* AN.) I did not expect the pleasure of seeing you again so soon.

AN: (*laughing*) Restrain your happiness. I shall shorten the pleasure as much as possible.

ROV: Oh, Mrs. Austin –

AN: I presume, I can use your room. (*aside to her*) To write. (MAR *nods.*) Au revoir, Mr. Roverly. (*Exits.*)

ROV: (*Drops glass, and goes eagerly to* MAR, *as soon as he sees* AN *off.*) Margery, I have come to ask your forgiveness.

MAR: For what?

ROV: For the display of temper this morning at Austin's.

MAR: Oh, that! I had forgotten all about it.

ROV: (*piqued, glass up*) If you consider the incident of so little importance, I suppose you regard me in the same light.

MAR: Now, what answer am I to make to that! (*Sits on sofa.*)

ROV: None, until you have heard my explanation. (*She motions him to a chair. He sits.*)

MAR: Well, explain away, but not too exhaustively, please, so that we may get to more agreeable topics.

ROV: (*drawing his chair closer*) How shall I describe to you what passed in my mind. (*agitated*)

MAR: (*aside*) He is really in earnest.

ROV: I am not clear about my own feelings: jealousy, anger, love. It might be one, or all of these. I only know that I was moved as I had never been in my life.

MAR: (*secretly delighted*) And you wish me to assist in clearing up this chaos of jealousy, anger, love and – doubt?

ROV: I thought the person who inspired these feelings might help to define them.

MAR: (*deliberately*) Hm! Possibly! At all events, we can try. Perhaps, if we institute a short examination – let us see! Did your agitation begin at the instant that the fatal letter was discovered?

ROV: No, decidedly.

MAR: So, if the letter really belonged to Mrs. Austin, your equanimity would not have been disturbed?

ROV: Not in the least.

MAR: That establishes your complete indifference as to her.

ROV: Certainly.

MAR: On the other hand, your agitation on discovering that the letter belonged to me – ?

ROV: (*Drops eye-glass, and draws closer.*) Establishes the reverse of indifference as to you. Doesn't it?

MAR: Gently, gently! We had better not get on quite so fast. Now, suppose I were to prove that the letter was of the most harmless character?

ROV: (*Glass up, takes her hand.*) If you would only do that!

MAR: And, if I did, you would resume your customary blasé indifference, I suppose. (*pause*) Well, unfortunately, you will have to postpone your relapse a little longer.

ROV: (*Glass up, draws back.*) What do you mean by that?

MAR: The letter is *not* harmless! (ROV *drops glass.*)

ROV: What does it contain?

MAR: A declaration of love. (*Rises.*)

ROV: (*Drops glass, excitedly.*) Which you return?

MAR: And what if I do?

ROV: (*moving away*) I should go mad.

MAR: (*secretly delighted*) Mad! Are you sure? (*Sits.*)

ROV: (*Sits again beside her.*) You are only trying me, playing with me.

MAR: (*aside*) He loves me.

ROV: (*earnestly*) Speak one word, Margery, I implore you!

MAR: (*restraining him*) There, there. Answer me calmly. If the writer of that letter stood before you, what would you do?

ROV: I believe I should kill him. (*Rises.*)

MAR: Kill him! What, really? (*Rises.*) It's too lovely. My poor boy, I've learned all I wished to know. You are suffering from a high degree of – (ROV *close to her, they meet face to face.*) conflagration of the heart.

ROV: Which you might extinguish, Madge, or it will kill me. (*Drops glass.*)

MAR: Ah, but if it proves a false alarm! These sudden flares are suspicious. (*Sits.*)

ROV: (*Sits.*) Madge, believe me, I loved you long ago, without suspecting it. When I left home to wander about the world, I carried with me the image of that lovely being, who had once betrayed to me the first feeling of her youthful heart.

MAR: It is not quite generous to remind me of my girlish follies.

ROV: It was a charming folly, only I was not man enough then to value it as it deserved. I went abroad to seek the happiness that was then so close at hand. But wherever I went, I was home-sick with the craving for familiar sights, and sounds, and faces. Camping in the wilds of forests, I dreamt of a home, of a loving wife, but, when I tried to clasp the vision in my arms, and look into that woman's face – for it seemed to be one I knew – it would vanish into empty air. Madge, that woman was you! Tell me, is that dream of home and happiness never to be realized?

MAR: (*softly*) Why should it not be?

ROV: Because, that letter –

MAR: Oh, that needn't stand in the way.

ROV: Then let me see it.

MAR: You won't trust me? (*drawing away*)

ROV: (*rising*) Yes, but you must acknowledge –

MAR: (*rising*) That you are the most suspicious, unreasonable, persistent and altogether horrid man in the universe, and I shall abominate you, if you don't change! (*going*) Now, you repeat that sentence to yourself twenty-five times while I'm gone. Perhaps it will reform you. I must look after Annis. (*Exits.*)

ROV: (*Drops glass.*) I am the most suspicious, unreasonable, persistent – (*Bell rings and* BERTA *enters right and exits left. He looks after her and then recommences.*) The most abominable, unreasonable, suspicious – (*Repeats this three times.*) Well, I am. But that letter – that letter! (BERTA *re-enters with a letter and is going out.*) What have you got there?

BER: A letter, M'sieu.

ROV: (*Goes to her.*) From your mistress? Let me see it.

BER: (*retreating*) Oh, M'sieu.

ROV: I won't hurt you. Come here! (*Brings her down and gives her money.*) I must see it.

BER: But, I do not know –

ROV: I only wish to read the address. (*Takes the letter and looks at it.*) For Pascal. Pascal who? Pascal where? What Pascal?

BER: (*They turn away and then to each other.*) How should I know – moi? (*wicked smile*) I should think it was quite, quite e-nough!

ROV: Yes, it's quite enough. Have you taken many letters like that?

BER: Oh, all ze time, M'sieu.

ROV: All the time! The devil! and where do you take them?

BER: To ze old gentleman, Dr. – Dr. – Quattell!

ROV: You don't mean to tell me they are written to *him*.

BER: (*Laughs.*) To ze Dr. Quattles! Ha, ha, ha! What sort of taste do you zink we have here? Oh, no! M'sieu, ze old doctaire, is only ze – ze – postman! He brings ze letters and takes avay ze responze, voila! (*Turns away, laughing.*)

ROV: A regular go-between. (*Scrutinizes the address.*) Are you sure your mistress writes these letters?

BER: (*Shrugs her shoulders.*) Who else could write them? You see ze handwriting is changee – deesguised, eh! – zat proves it.

ROV: (*Gives letter.*) Thank you.

BER: Oh, it was a pleasure to oblige such a nice gentleman. (*aside, going*) How madame will laugh when I tell her. Ha, ha, ha! (*Laughs slyly at* ROV *as she exits.*)

ROV: (*angrily*) Ahem! (*Sits.*) For Pascal! That is the way a woman addresses her lover and no one else. And yet she accuses me of being suspicious, unreasonable, persistent! Oh, woman! woman! (*Rises and crosses.*) What wild beast is so dangerous to man! (*Throws himself in seat.*)

        (SYDNEY *enters, speaking off.*)

SYD: (*as he enters*) Very well. I shall have a little quiet talk with Mrs. Gwynn – she shall tell me the truth about that letter. (*Sits.*) If Annis were innocent, after all! How handsome she looked in her anger! and how confoundedly anxious she seemed at the prospect of a separation! I almost fancied I felt a pang. (*hand to heart*) No, she is not innocent.

ROV: (*watching* SYD *from his seat*) He may know who Pascal is! I'll ask him. (*Rises.*)

SYD: (*Rises, as if with a sudden inspiration, and starts back upon seeing* ROV.) I was not aware you were here.

ROV: Mrs. Austin is in the next room.

SYD: (*taken aback*) My wife! – here?

ROV: (*suspicious*) Oh, you didn't call for her?

SYD: Not at all – that is – (*Takes up his hat and turns up to go.*)

ROV: (*distrustfully*) Then you did not know she was here, and you came to –

SYD: (*Gets mixed up in speech.*) Oh, yes, that is, I didn't come for her. I only came to inquire – to – very naturally you know, just to – to – I say that I dropped in merely to – casually you understand to – to – to find out if she got here – *safely.*

ROV: (*growing suspicious*) Is the journey of a few blocks from your house so hazardous? Permit me to remark, Mr. Austin, that your behavior is extremely singular.

SYD: (*haughtily*) Sir!

ROV: You call upon Mrs. Gwynn, but as soon as you learn that your wife is with her you beat a retreat.

SYD: Do I owe you an explanation?

ROV: You compromise the lady I have named, and I shall not permit you to do so with impunity.

SYD: By what right do you constitute yourself her champion?

ROV: By what right! (*Approaches* SYD, *and in a low tone.*) By the right of a man who *loves* her. (SYD *steps down a step.*) Do you admit my authority now?

SYD: (*coldly*) Not unless the lady reciprocates the affection.

ROV: (*Steps towards him.*) So you refuse an explanation?

SYD: While you ask it in that tone, I do.

ROV: (*going*) Then I shall force it from you.

SYD: (*coolly*) Indeed, and how, pray?

ROV: I shall call the ladies.

SYD: (*aside*) That won't do at all. (*aloud*) Mr. Roverly (*aside*), I shall learn nothing. (*aloud*) Mr. Roverly, I have reasons for keeping my visit here secret from my wife for the present; but I give you my word of honor that my motive does not concern Mrs. Gwynn in any direct manner whatever. (*Starts.*) By Jove, they're coming. (*Turns to go up.*)

ROV: (*barring his way*) First explain to me.

SYD: Another time, another place! Man alive, my wife is coming!

ROV: (*Crosses to conservatory.*) In here we shall be undisturbed.

SYD: But I tell you –

ROV: Come along with me, or I'll –

SYD: Oh, have it your own way, so I get away. (*Hurries out.*)

ROV: (*following him*) Now I shall know if that letter was meant for him. (*Exits.*)
        (MARGERY *enters gaily.*)

MAR: Well, Mr. Roverly, how many times – (*Looks around, surprised.*) Gone, I declare!
        (ANNIS *enters.*)
So, he is really taking a tragic view of the situation. (*to* AN) It's a nice mess you've got me into.

AN: (*changing from gay to serious*) What do you mean?

MAR: (*bringing her down*) Roverly loves me.

AN: (*close to her*) Is it possible. Poor dear! (*mock sympathy*)

MAR: (*resenting*) Why, poor dear?

AN: To be loved by an iceberg.

MAR: Let me tell you that this iceberg has got into the gulf stream.

AN: Melted so soon? This morning he was at the North Pole.

MAR: He may congeal again.

AN: Impossible.

MAR: Yes, that letter – (*suddenly and seriously*) I tell you, Annis, it won't do.

AN: What won't do?

MAR: I can't suffer suspicion to rest on me any longer. You must tell Roverly the truth.

AN: (*consternation*) Madge!

MAR: He'll keep your secret, as a matter of course.

AN: But consider my humiliation.

MAR: You must have known that this romantic affair would cause you trouble, sooner or later.

AN: It would be very well, of course, if a woman could weigh everything at the outset; but, even then, wouldn't heart *tip* reason up just a little, every time? And who would stop to reason if they knew that one step off the beaten path gave such a glimpse of the glorious land of romance! Oh, Madge, it's pleasant to jump the fence sometimes. (*Sits.*)

MAR: Possibly, only you must be ready to jump back again at short notice. For my part, I prefer a well-drilled heart that trots me steadily along, and never risks my neck.

AN: (*with a sigh, rising*) Well, if it must be, it must be. You may tell Mr. Roverly.

MAR: Excuse me, my dear. *You* must tell him.

AN: Don't ask that of me! Impart the dearest secret of my heart to a stranger!

MAR: (*Follows.*) If I tell him the letter was yours, his jealousy will prevent his believing me. (AN *tries to coax her; they sit on sofa.*)

        (ROVERLY *enters, followed by* SYDNEY.)

SYD: (*perceiving* AN) My wife! (*Bolts back.*)

ROV: The letter was not for him. He has given me his word of honor. (*aside*)

MAR: (*Turning from* AN, *perceives him.*) Ah! (*quizzically*) I began to think the penance I imposed had put you to flight.

ROV: (*calmly*) Only as far as the next room, where I could perform it undisturbed.

MAR: Did it do you good?

ROV: No.

MAR: (*Takes* AN*'s hand and brings her forward.*) Then I recommend a physician who will cure your malady with a single prescription.

ROV: Mrs. Austin?

AN: (*Rises. Frightened, and aside to* MAR) You don't want me to – to – right away?

MAR: A good doctor attacks the disease at the first manifestation, before it seizes the whole organism.

AN: But I must have time to think.

MAR: You are her first patient, Mr. Roverly, and she is naturally nervous. Don't be too obstinate, make the cure as easy as you can. (*Attempts to cross.*)

AN: (*following*) Don't go away.

ROV: (*alarmed at seeing her go*) No! no! don't go! (*aside*) If she should see Austin.

AN: You must stand by me.

ROV: You certainly must stand by her.

MAR: (*to* ROV) What's the matter with you?

ROV: Well, I'm naturally nervous, too; she's my first doctor.

MAR: (*Laughs.*) In that case, I'll assist. (*Turns to* AN, *and then speaks deliberately to* ROV *and at* AN.) Mrs. Austin will prove to you that you are under a delusion with regard to a certain matter, – a delusion which must be removed, if you expect to reach the summit of earthly happiness, as depicted in your dreams. (*to* AN) Now, go on.

AN: (*very nervous*) First of all, Mr. Roverly, I must beg of you to keep it a secret from everybody. Especially my husband.

ROV: (*surprised*) Your husband? (*glass up*)

AN: (*Nods*) Will you promise?

ROV: He shall never know. (*glancing at door and aside*) Unless he is listening now.

AN: I have, or rather, I am – perhaps I should have said, I was – indeed, you know, I never – oh, how shall I begin. (*to* MAR)

MAR: I suppose I must begin for you. Mr. Roverly, the letter which you inquired about –

ROV: (*eagerly*) The letter, yes!

MAR: Which I pretended was mine –

ROV: You pretended?

MAR: Yes, sir, pretended! Well, it was written to – (*Looks at* AN.)

AN: To me, Mr. Roverly!

ROV: (*pause, incredulous*) To *you*?

AN: Margery claimed it to save me from embarrassment. (*Turns away.* MAR *going to piano, turns back to* ROV.)

ROV: Indeed! (*pause. He looks from* AN *to* MAR.) And the other letter which your maid has just taken?

MAR: (*sweetly*) Oh, you saw that, too?

ROV: Yes, I saw that, too.

AN: (*low, serious tone*) That, also, was mine. (MAR *turns to her.*)

ROV: (*Looks at her, then aside, resolutely.*) It's a conspiracy. But I'll tear it to rags. (*to* MAR) Madam, you are to be envied the possession of such friends!

MAR: What do you mean by *that*?

ROV: That I admire Mrs. Austin's generosity; but, unfortunately, I cannot meet it in a spirit of trust and confidence.

MAR: (*angrily*) You doubt her word?

ROV: I couldn't pay her a handsomer compliment. It is simply impossible for a virtuous wife to engage in a correspondence which she is compelled to keep secret from her husband. (AN *looks away, abashed; he watches her keenly.*)

MAR: (*to* AN, *impatiently*) You hear, Annis, speak out.

AN: (*in low, sad tones*) But if it be the truth, Mr. Roverly.

ROV: (*first with joy*) If it be the truth – (*Stops, doubts, then aside, while the ladies*

exchange glances of appeal.) No, they are playing with me! (*aloud*) My dear
Mrs. Austin don't attempt to assume a guilt of which you are simply incapable.
(AN *turns up stage, offended.*)

MAR: (*angrily*) You seem to think *me* capable of it.

ROV: You are different. There is no guilt in your case. You are free. You can
bestow your love where you please, and it injures no one (*sadly*), no one but
me and I lost years ago the right to your constancy. (*to* AN) But you, your
very thoughts and feelings belong to the man to whom you pledged your
faith at the altar. (*to* MAR, *as if reasoning with her*) Don't ask your friend to
make this sacrifice, for she does not realize the vileness of which she accuses
herself.

AN: (*flaring up*) This is too much.

ROV: (*aside*) Can it be true?

AN: Vileness! (MAR *throws herself into seat.*) Now I'll tell you everything, from
the beginning to the end.

ROV: (*aside*) This is not assumed! (*Smiles gladly, but suddenly remembers that* SYD
is in the next room.) Good heavens! her husband is in there! (*aloud, and
trying to calm her*) Don't say another word. I believe you, I do indeed.

AN: No, I will speak now. I distinctly avow myself guilty of the action you call by
that horrible name. (MAR *turns to look at her.*)

ROV: Yes, yes, it's all right! I implore you –

AN: You say that my thoughts and feelings belong to the man to whom I pledged
my faith at the altar! Do you know how that pledge was obtained? What
pretence, what constraint was used! I tell you a woman has rights which sur-
vive the injury thus done her, and one of these –
                              (SYDNEY *enters and* ROV *sees him.*)

ROV: Mrs. Austin, your husband –

AN: (*exultant, and not heeding*) Ah, that he were here, I would tell him to his face
that letter was mine!

ROV: Stop! for your own sake –

AN: It was written by a man of soul and genius.

ROV: For heaven's sake –

AN: In it he avows his love.

ROV: (*as* SYD *comes forward*) Oh!

SYD: He does!

AN: (*Screams.*) Ah!

SYD: Does he?

MAR: Good heavens!

ROV: I felt it coming.

SYD: A man of soul and genius, is he? Thank you, I will find him, and when I do,
as sure as there is justice on earth, I will kill him. (*Exits.* AN *sinks on sofa.*)

MAR: (*Crosses and looks at* ROV.) This is all your fault. I hate you.

ROV: It was a mere accident.

MAR: Accident? It was your horrible suspicions.

ROV: Let me explain.

MAR: Explanations of any kind are now at an end between us. (*Turns her back on
him and goes to* AN.)

ROV: I will return when you are calmer, Madge! I may then have a chance to justify myself. (*Exits.*)

AN: Did you hear what he said? He will kill him.

MAR: Kill him! How can he kill him, when he doesn't know his name?

AN: That's true! how foolish I was! (*Laughs, nervously.*) I shall never tell his name,
   for I don't know it myself. (*thoughtfully*) I never thought Sydney capable of
   such passion. I never saw him look better than when he felt worst. Oh, dear!
   Margery, I am treading a very dangerous path. (*Sinks on seat.*)

MAR: I thought you were fond of straying off. You see how hard it is to jump
   back. You were caught on the fence this time!

AN: (*Rises, gaily.*) No, I'm over without a scratch. If this is the worst that happens,
   it's not so dreadful after all. (*Sits at piano.*) What have you got new? (*Touches
   a note.*)

               (SYD *re-enters.*)

SYD: I must intrude again, Mrs. Gwynn.

AN: (*Her back is to him. She stops playing.*) It is he! (*agitated*)

SYD: I beg you, first of all, to pardon my abrupt leave-taking. Feeling, emotion,
   surprise mastered me. (AN *touches the keys softly.*) It was very foolish. My
   wife shows me how to take such matters coolly. (AN *plays louder. He goes to
   her.*) Annis! (*She plays, unheeding.*) Annis, I would like to speak with you.

MAR: I'll retire.

SYD: (*pointedly*) No; you have always had the kindness to act as my wife's *confi-
   dante* –

MAR: (*pointedly*) Of course! poor thing, she had nobody else to look to for sympathy. (*Sits.*)

SYD: (*Bows, with a cynical smile.*) I merely wished to ask you – (*to* AN, *who
   suddenly plays louder*) I fear my business will make some discord in your
   music.

AN: (*Stops.*) We've been rather used to it since we married.

SYD: Then we had better arrive at once at a harmonious understanding. I beg you
   will notify your family of our resolution as soon as possible.

AN: (*Half turns.*) What resolution?

SYD: To separate! (*Goes up, turns.*) Well?

AN: (*pauses, then*) I'll do so with pleasure. (*Resumes her playing.*)

SYD: You are at liberty to lay all the blame on me. The world, in these matters, is
   apt to judge the husband more leniently than the wife.

AN: How generous! (*Plays.*) Have you anything more to tell me?

SYD: (*angrily*) No! (*Turns to go.*)

AN: (*looking after him*) Can he really feel this?

SYD: (*Stops and turns.*) I forgot, there is one thing more. Will you remain in my
   house and keep up appearances, as usual, until the divorce is procured? It can
   hardly be your wish to furnish our friends with this little delicacy in the way
   of social scandal until it is quite unavoidable.

AN: (*restraining herself*) Very good. Will it be for long?

SYD: I hope not! (AN *starts, convulsively.*) I shall see my lawyer at once.

AN: (*rising, and speaking excitedly and trembling*) And let him make all haste, will
   you? – all possible haste.

SYD: I shall urge it. (AN *reseats herself at piano and hammers it.*) You will stay here to tea, I presume. (*to* MAR) If you permit me, I shall call for my wife! (*ironically*) It is so pleasant to afford the world a picture of conjugal happiness!

MAR: You know how welcome you always are, Mr. Austin.

SYD: You are very good. Allow me. (*Bows and exits.*)

> (AN *has looked after him intently, and playing mechanically, slower and slower, until he goes. Then she stops.*)

AN: He is gone! Really gone! and in that temper.

MAR: Thank goodness!

AN: (*Bounds up and clenches her hands.*) Oh, oh, oh! I could – (*Takes stage.*) He's not human. He's a block – a stock!

MAR: You ingrate! Hasn't he met all your wishes half way, with the most touching eagerness. (*Advances to her.*)

AN: (*passionately*) Am I so worthless that he won't make a single effort to retain me?

MAR: (*sitting, watching her closely*) He saw how useless that would be!

AN: (*eagerly, sitting beside her in the tête-à-tête*) Do you think so? Do you believe that is why he was so cold? (*thoughtfully*) Well, if he had only admitted he was in the wrong, and begged me fervently to forgive him, perhaps I – ! I'm not made of marble. (*rising angrily*) But he wants no forgiveness from *me*. He's only too glad to get rid of me. (*Half breaking into tears, goes to back of piano.*)

MAR: Shall I tell you something, Annis?

AN: (*Raises her head, but does not turn.*) Well? (*Wipes her eyes with her handkerchief, and blows her nose.*)

MAR: Come and sit down. (AN *comes down.*) Sit, dear, you may faint at what I'm about to say.

AN: (*Sits, wiping her eyes.*) What do you want?

MAR: Now listen to me.

AN: I am listening.

MAR: You love your husband.

AN: (*Bounds up.*) What!

MAR: I say you are in love with your husband. (AN *laughs hysterically, and moves away.*) Or, if you are not, you are on the road to it.

AN: (*struggling with herself*) You are too funny! Love *him*! the man I detest – I despise! (*Breaks into tears, and hurries up stage.*)

MAR: Don't cry. All will be well. When Sydney sees your letters, he will acknowledge that you are not so *greatly* to blame, and forgive you.

AN: (*passionately and coming down*) Haven't I told you I don't want his forgiveness? But I will justify myself. He shall not harbor one low thought of me, not he, of all the world.

> (BERTA *enters, with a letter.*)

BER: From Dr. Quattles, madame. (*Gives letter to* MAR *and exits.*)

AN: From him! Let me see it. (*Takes if from* MAR, *opens and reads it rapidly.*) Oh, good heavens!

MAR: What is it?

AN: Pascal will only part with my letters on one condition.

MAR: And that –

AN: He is to be allowed to place them in my hands himself.

MAR: Earthly slag.

AN: What shall I do?

MAR: Hold out your hand and take them.

AN: That is impossible. If Sydney should discover, he would kill him.

MAR: But he shan't discover! What! are there two daughters of Eve possessed of so little brains that they can't circumvent one Adam? You write boldly to Pascal, and appoint an interview. Dr. Quattles is coming to tea. I'll hand him the letter.

AN: (*after a pause, to think*) But what place shall I name? The park?

MAR: In the park! – where everybody will see you. Twenty-four hours afterwards your husband will know everything, and twenty-four hours after that – Bang! – bang! Pascal dead! Sydney arrested! and Annis raving mad!

AN: (*Goes up, stopping her ears.*) Stop! stop! for heaven's sake.

MAR: Fix your rendezvous here! tomorrow night. It's my charity bazaar, – my bubble party, you know. The house will be full of people; a stranger speaking to you won't be noticed.

AN: True.

MAR: I'll engage your husband, show him how to blow bubbles, while you explode yours with Pascal. Very appropriate, eh?

AN: I'll write to Pascal at once, and enclose one of your invitations. (*going*)

MAR: Don't forget to mention some mark by which he will know you – say a tea-rose in your belt.

AN: How clever you are! I quite forgot he never saw me, and doesn't know my name.

MAR: And let him wear a primrose in his buttonhole, or his hair.

AN: (*delighted*) Oh, I'll fix all that! (*Returns and hugs her violently.*) Oh, Margery! (*Exits.*)

> (MAR *rings.* BERTA *enters with lamp. A man-servant enters with tea service. Both are placed on table. Another lamp is placed on piano.*)

MAR: (*sitting on sofa*) I hope this meeting will lead to no fresh complications. That must be prevented. If I only knew who this Pascal – or his inventor and author – 'Marius', is! (*suddenly, rising*) Dr. Quattles must tell me. I am going to ask Pascal to my house, and I ought to know him.

> (QUATTLES *enters.*)

QUAT: Here I am, promptly, you see!

MAR: Speak of the –

QUAT: The rest is understood. (*They shake hands, and sit beside each other.*)

MAR: Where's your wife?

QUAT: Circumnavigating the globe, with Roverly.

MAR: How?

QUAT: In spirit only; she is tearing his travels from him, piece by piece. I left her at it, for Bitteredge made his appearance, and I fled.

MAR: To rush into another danger.

QUAT: How so?

MAR: I also demand to know who Marius is.

QUAT: You're joking.

MAR: I never was more serious. You know that, like yourself, I am acting as courier between your great unknown and one of my lady friends.

QUAT: Whom I strongly suspect to be none other than yourself.

MAR: Now *you* are joking! Have I ever suspected you of being Pascal? though, I believe, you'd jump at the chance of playing the sighing Romeo!

QUAT: The sighing Romeo, perhaps; but not the dying Romeo. I understand that your cruel Diana intends to cast him off.

MAR: Let's be serious. Diana's husband knows all.

QUAT: Does he?

MAR: And is going to get a divorce.

QUAT: Sensible!

MAR: And subsequently kill Pascal.

QUAT: Better still. It will prevent his writing a second novel. (*Rises.*)

MAR: (*Rises.*) Diana asks the return of her letters. Pascal retorts, by demanding an interview.

QUAT: Will she grant it?

MAR: Yes, unless you permit me to try to coax him myself.

QUAT: He'll never relinquish the hour of Paradise he proposes to spend with his ideal.

MAR: Let me try him. Who is he?

QUAT: My word is given to keep the secret. But *I* can talk to him; perhaps my arguments –

MAR: Arguments to a man in love!

QUAT: Why not?

MAR: You never were in love, that's clear!

QUAT: I never was, over head and ears! I kept my cranium above water to think with!

>   (MRS. QUATTLES, ROVERLY, *and* BITTEREDGE *enter, she carries a curious antique vase in her arms.*)

MRS. Q: (*Stops.*) Of course! Tête-à-tête with a pretty woman, as usual!

MAR: Oh, Mrs. Quattles!

MRS. Q: (*to* QUAT) So that's why you flew on ahead of us.

QUAT: My dear, I left you frozen up with Roverly, in Alaska, and concluded to take advantage of it to – to – warm up here.

MRS. Q: (*annoyed*) Well, I –

BIT: Leave his punishment to me! (*Squares himself over the piano.*) Can you tell me who Marius is!

QUAT: Give me one moment's peace. (*Crosses to* MRS. Q. BIT *seizes his arm.*)

BIT: Not until I get an answer. Children cry for Marius! – who is he?

QUAT: Reptile! (*Sits at piano, and commences to drum violently.* BIT *moves away, hands to ears.* MRS. Q *follows him with her vase.* ROV *goes to* MAR.)

MRS. Q. (*to* BIT) Oh, Mr. Bitteredge, let him alone, and look at my pretty vase! A souvenir, from Mr. Roverly, of his travels in Japan.

BIT: Very fine! (*looking at it*) The bottom's out!

MRS. Q: That makes it more valuable.

BIT: Yes, you can use it as a telescope. (*pointing it at audience, so they can see the bottom is out*)

MRS. Q: (*retaking it*) Scoffer! (*Calls* QUAT. *He comes down. She shows him the vase. He does not look at the bottom, but, as she places it on table, he stoops down to examine it. The three admire it.*)

ROV: (*to* MAR) You are still angry with me? (*He has approached her slowly, and she has received him stiffly.*)

MAR: Angry! not at all.

ROV: You must admit I had cause. That letter –

MAR: (*pointedly*) That letter, Mr. Roverly, belonged to me!

ROV: No, Madge, it did not. Mrs. Austin's conduct has convinced me.

MAR: (*Laughs.*) Convinced you! (*Laughs.*) How easily men can be gulled by a little play-acting! (*He starts. She observes him, and aside.*) Take that!

ROV: (*excitedly*) So it was deception after all?

MAR: (*maliciously*) No, sir! It was the simple truth. (*Curtseys and goes over to* MRS. Q, *who shows her the vase.*)

ROV: (*nonplussed*) Which am I to believe? If she should really correspond with this Pascal, or Marius or whatever his devilish name may be! (*to* QUAT, *whom he meets as he leaves his wife's side*) I say, doctor, who is Marius?

QUAT: Oh, lord! here's another.

BIT: Hurrah! here's an ally! (*Crosses to* ROV, *taking his hand.*) Between us (*Crosses to* QUAT), we'll pump him dry. (*to* QUAT) Who is he?

MRS. Q: (*coming to* QUAT) You expect to make that man speak? Why, he hasn't even told *me*! and yet he declares that he loves me.

QUAT: I? – I never made such a sweeping assertion.

MRS. Q: Listen to the monster! But I'll get it out of him yet. (*Seizes him by the arm and confonts him.*) Tell me, this instant – who is Marius?

QUAT: You may tear me limb from limb –

MRS. Q: Ugh! you little wretch! (*Releases him, and he goes to* MAR.)

MAR: Who is he? Who is Marius?

QUAT: Heavens and earth! Am I a bulletin board on election night? (*Crosses, aside.*) Wait a bit.

ROV and BIT: Come! Who is he?

MAR and MRS. Q: The name! – the name!

QIAT: I surrender! (*They have all made a step towards him; now step back, with an exclamation.*)

ALL: Ah! (BIT *gets out his note-book.*)

QUAT: I answer on one condition – that you ask me nothing more!

MRS. Q and ROV: Very well! ⎫
BIT: So be it! ⎬ Together
MAR: We promise! ⎭

QUAT: And yet my conscience –

ALL: Oh!

MRS. Q: Never mind your conscience. That's been a hard pillow for you to sleep on, this many a year.

ROV, BIT, MAR: Come, come! who is Marius?

(SYDNEY *enters.*)

SYD: Marius! – what's this? (*aside*)

QUAT: You wish to know who Marius is?

(ANNIS *enters, and stops.*)

AN: Is he going to tell?

BIT: Out with it! I've got an introductory paragraph written already.

QUAT: (*Strikes an attitude.*) My friends, look at me!

BIT: What for?

QUAT: Don't you observe anything?

MRS. Q: Nothing that amounts to anything.

QUAT: Oh, you! – you never did comprehend my greatness.

MRS. Q: True. I never examined you under a microscope.

QUAT: (*Resumes attitude.*) Peace! Well, then, I *am* Marius. (*All look at each other and separate in disgust. He crosses and chuckles.*) That's a settler! (*to BIT, who is sharpening his pencil*) If you want a few points about me, in addition, say that I was born on the first of April, and always give myself away, in the most unselfish manner. (*Sits, and takes up a magazine.*) How happy they all look.

AN: (*Comes to MAR and gives her a letter secretly.*) Here! (MAR *takes it.*) It's for Pascal, making the appointment. (*Sees SYD.*) Sydney! (*startled*)

MAR: (*Pockets letter and bows to SYD, who is watching AN.*) You see, Mr. Austin, with what a start of joy your wife receives you. (*Gives her hand, and in an ironical tone.*) You are ever so welcome.

ROV: She receives him with a smile – while to me – (*Goes up stage.* BIT *and* MRS. Q *follow him up.*)

MAR: (*half aside, to SYD*) One word of advice. In giving to the world your picture of conjugal happiness, don't make your picture too bright; I mean don't lay on the colors too thickly. (*Crosses to QUAT.*)

SYD: No fear. My wife will supply all the shadows.

(AN *goes to sofa.* SYD *overacts affectionate conversation.* AN *is reserved and sits.* ROV *has turned away annoyed from* MRS. Q.)

MAR: (*aside to QUAT*) Since you will not reveal his name, nothing remains but the rendezvous. (*He nods and rises.*)

ROV: (*who has observed them, aside*) What is she whispering to him?

MAR: (*aside to QUAT*) When I hand you your teacup, I will give you Diana's letter, making the appointment. (*She goes to the tea-table, which should be near center.*)

ROV: I'm convinced he's her go-between, in that correspondence.

SYD: (*to AN*) I bring you the glad tidings that the lawyers will be able to arrange our divorce in twenty days.

AN: Really! (*trembling*) What happiness! (*Crosses to MAR.*) May I help you?

(MRS. Q *and* BIT *come down to table at right.* QUAT *retreats across front to SYD.*)

MAR: Certainly! (*aside to her*) Don't break the cups, you are trembling so! (*Goes to back of sofa, and hands a cup to* MRS. Q *and to* BIT.) Fortify yourself (*to BIT*) for another attack. I'm with you.

BIT: With an ally so accustomed to victory, I'm certain we'll succeed.

MAR: So we shall, tomorrow evening. (QUAT *goes up.*)

AN: (*Who has controlled herself, brings a cup smilingly to* SYD.) Allow me to add a stroke of the brush to your picture of married tenderness.

SYD: (*Takes cup.*) I hardly thought the subject was in your line.

AN: (*bitterly*) I have made such rapid progress under your direction!

> (SYD *goes up to mantel.* BIT *joins him.* AN *takes a cup, and sits.* MAR *has offered a cup to* ROV, *who has declined.* MAR *brings a cup forward to* QUAT.)

MAR: You don't deserve it, my lord Marius, but I intend to heap coals of fire on your head. (*She has placed the letter under the saucer, and hands all to* QUAT.)

QUAT: You are very good. (*Takes the cup and saucer, but drops the letter on floor.* MAR *picks it up quickly, and pushes it under the saucer into his hands.*)

MAR: How awkward. (*Goes up and pours herself a cup.*)

QUAT: It was so warm, it burnt my hand.

MRS. Q: (*aside: having seen the letter fall*) What was that?

ROV: (*who has also seen it*) A letter.

MRS. Q: (*Crosses to* QUAT.) What was that billet?

QUAT: What billy? Billy what?

MRS. Q: Billet doux. The one you just took with your tea.

QUAT: I take a billy with my tea! – take tea with Billy doo! – It was an optical delusion.

MRS. Q: And are you an optical deluder. (QUAT *retreats up.*) A pretty Don Giovanni you make. (*Follows him.*)

MAR: (*Crosses to* AN.) Your letter is mailed.

AN: (*anxious, watching* SYD) I hope it's safe.

MRS. Q: So you won't explain! Very well, sir. (*Crosses and exchanges a word with* ROV, *who is annoyed, and continues watching* QUAT, *at the same time getting down stage.*)

QUAT: Gad! she really has got it bad this time. (*Lays down cup and saucer, and conceals letter in music-book on piano.*) There! It's out of her reach anyhow.

AN: (*Has observed* QUAT.) What does this mean?

> (SYD, *parting from* BIT, *meets* QUAT. MRS. Q *joins* BIT.)

QUAT: (*aside to* SYD) In the music-book!

ROV: (*aside*) What's he saying to Austin?

QUAT: (*same*) Letter for you.

SYD: From Diana! (QUAT *nods, and leaves him.*)

ROV: Can Austin be the man, after all?

MAR: What imprudence. (*Crosses to table to get sugar for her tea.*)

AN: If it should fall into Sydney's hands!

SYD: If Annis should find it! I must take it out of there. (*Looks around for a place to place his tea cup, and finally puts it on mantel.*)

ROV: (*aside*) He's fishing for the letter. (*Goes up.*)

AN: I must get it away from there.

> (AN, ROV *and* SYD *now slowly approach the piano unobserved by each other.*)

MAR: (*crossing to* QUAT) Wretched man, what have you done? (*Sits.*)

QUAT: (*finishing his tea*) Drank one cup all up. (*aside to her*) You don't suppose
      I'm going to let my wife find such a letter on my person!
                (SYD, ROV and AN *now reach the piano. She sits on stool and*
                touches the book just as he is about to lift it from its rest. All start
                up.)
SYD: (*going right*) Can she suspect?
AN: Has he any idea?
MRS. Q: (*has come down to* QUAT) Now, then, confess!
QUAT: My love, your distrust lacerates my heart.
MRS. Q: (*Looks over him.*) Where have you concealed it?
QUAT: My heart?
MRS. Q: (*sternly*) The billet-doux!
QUAT: (*Turns his pockets, coat and pants, inside out.*) Convince yourself. (*She*
      inspects all narrowly, and they go up to window, continuing this business.
      ROV *has reached the piano by this time, and as* AN *is about to turn and*
      resume her seat there, she sees ROV.)
ROV: I'll have a look at it. (*as he sits*)
AN: (*Calls to him, before he touches the book.*) Are you going to play something,
      Mr. Roverly?
ROV: (*aside*) Confound it! (*aloud*) Ah! if I can find the piece I'm looking for, I
      shall certainly give you a little music! (*Takes up the book and rises.* SYD *and*
      AN *drop down each side of him, quickly.*)
MAR: (*Who has been sitting at the tête-à-tête, rises.*) What is it – an Indian war-
      whoop, or a German operetta? I'll find you something we can both play.
      (*Takes the book out of his hand, and goes to piano.*) Will you accompany
      me?
ROV: With pleasure. I hope my fingers can pick out the notes.
MAR: We'll see who has the deftest fingers!
SYD: May I assist in turning the leaves? (*Is about to take book.* AN *snatches it*
      from him.)
AN: For heaven's sake!
SYD: (*Starts.*) What's the matter?
AN: (*confused*) I – I – have an awful headache, suddenly, and music sends me dis-
      tracted.
MAR: (*to* ROV, *maliciously*) It seems we are to be deprived of the pleasure of
      admiring your legerdemain.
ROV: We may console each other. (*They go to sofa.*)
SYD: (*to* AN) Shall I take you home?
AN: No, no, thank you! I'm better now. (*going*)
SYD: Hadn't you better leave the book here?
AN: Oh, – oh, to be sure! I'm so absent-minded.
SYD: How she watches me! She *must* suspect something. (*Replaces book on piano.*)
AN: How he looks at me. He mistrusts. (*Sits.*)
SYD: (*going up stage and picking up another book*) I must wait another oppor-
      tunity.
                (QUAT *and* MRS. Q *have come down and sit with* BIT.)
AN: I may have a better chance later on. (*Rises, and goes to sofa.*) Pardon an

intruder. (ROV *and* MAR *make room for her.*) Do let us talk; it's better than music.

ALL: Yes, yes, yes! I, – I, oh, um! (*Several attempts are made by each member of the different groups to begin the conversation. All fail. There is then a pause.*)

AN: Everybody is so quiet!

QUAT: Yes, somebody say something.

(*Another dismal pause ensues. Each group looks at the other.*)

BIT: (*after a pause, not looking up*) Hush! – an angel is passing!

MRS. Q: Well! (*Has observed* SYD *stepping softly towards the piano.*) It requires the imagination of a journalist to take Mr. Austin for an angel. (*All laugh, looking at* SYD.)

SYD: (*aside*) Confound it. (*Goes up, laughing to hide his confusion.* MAR *slowly goes toward piano.*)

BIT: (*Rises.*) Something going on here. (*aloud*) Ladies and gentlemen, I want your assistance. I am in search of a plot for a comedy.

QUAT: What, another American dramatist?

BIT: I'm going to write this one all by myself.

ROV: (MAR *moves towards piano.*) In real life we have only tragedies, unless they degenerate into farce. Do they not, Mrs. Gwynn?

MAR: (*detected, and coming abruptly from piano*) What of that? If we must shed tears, I'd rather shed them laughing than crying. (*Sits.*)

AN: (*sitting beside* MAR) Mr. Bitteredge, write a comedy about the misunderstood wife! There's plenty of material for that. (ROV *is now moving to the piano.*)

QUAT: (*rising and coming forward*) Yes, my wife will take the leading part, at a moment's notice.

MRS. Q: If I may kill you off in the fifth act, with pleasure.

ROV: (*Having got to the piano, now pulls the letter from the book.*) At last! (*In suppressed tone, moves away.*)

SYD: (*seeing the action, bounds up.*) The deuce! (*Goes to* ROV.)

AN: My letter in Mr. Roverly's hand! (*Stands irresolute, with* MAR *beside her.*)

SYD: (*low tone to* ROV) I'll trouble you to give me that letter.

ROV: (*same*) And why?

SYD: It belongs to me!

ROV: To you? (*Looks at envelope.*) It is addressed to Pascal.

SYD: I am Pascal.

ROV: So you are unmasked at last. (*Drops glass.*)

SYD: The letter!

ROV: You shall have it – but one question, first. What do you call a man who asserts an untruth upon his word of honor?

SYD: (*pauses, as if remembering the conversation he had earlier with* ROV) What do you mean?

ROV: Do you hesitate to answer?

SYD: The man is a liar, of course.

ROV: A liar, of course! (*Hands him the letter.*)

AN: (*aside to* MAR) Madge see! Oh, heavens!

ROV: You have pronounced your own sentence, Mr. Austin. (*Turns, then goes up stage.*)

SYD: My own sentence!

QUAT: (*Who has seen the whole action above, comes quickly to* SYD.) Your wife has seen the letter. Get rid of it.

SYD: Here, take it! Send it after me.

QUAT: I can't take it, my wife's looking! Stop! drop it in the vase at your side. It belongs to us. I'll take it home.

SYD: Good! (*Affecting indifference, looks at letter and tosses it into the vase. He then goes to piano.*)

AN: (*Turns to* MAR.) You saw that?

MAR: I'll send the vase to my room. (*Rings bell at her side.*)

QUAT: Well, my dear! time for us to start. (*Buttons up his coat, and comes to the vase.*)

MRS. Q: Yes, dear. Just let me get my vase.

QUAT: Don't trouble yourself, dear, I'll carry it.

MAR: (*to* AN) Good!

MRS. Q: No trouble at all, dear. I brought it, I'll take it away. (*Seizes the vase.*)

QUAT: I couldn't think of it, darling. (*Grasps vase.*)

MRS. Q: I insist.

MAR: Don't give it up, doctor!

QUAT: I won't! (*Seizes vase and lifts it up.*) I've got it!
> (*tableau of laughter and gladness, on the part of* SYD, AN *and* MAR, *changing instantly to consternation, as* -)

MRS. Q: (*darting on the letter, which has fallen through the vase and upon the table*) No, sir! I've got it.
> (*tableau of alternate consternation and triumph as the* -)

CURTAIN FALLS

ACT III

The same scene, lighted up for a fête. All the lights are ablaze. The curtains open, showing the rooms right and left lighted and filled with guests. Servants are passing bowls and pipes around. The conservatory is flooded with a cool blue light. The apartment left is glowing red from the fire. A large pot or vase of tropical flowers surmounts a divan, center. A cluster of flowers near the conversation seat at left. And the piano is moved to the right and covered with flowers. MARGERY *enters, meeting a* SERVANT, *who has been serving guests in the conservatory and who is crossing to exit.*

MAR: Take those away now, and let every one know that supper is served below.

SERV: Yes, madam. (*Crossing and up.*)

MAR: You know Dr. Quattles?

SER: Oh, yes, madam.

MAR: As soon as he comes, let me know instantly.

SERV: Yes, madam. (*Exits.*)
> (ANNIS *enters.*)

AN: Have you seen Sydney?

MAR: No. Did you leave him at home?

VIII *Love on Crutches*. Tableau photo by Sarony from Act II. Left to right: Edith Kingdon, Otis Skinner, Ada Rehan, James Lewis, Mrs. Gilbert, John Drew

AN: He dressed and said he was going to the club. If he should come!

MAR: If he does, I'll keep him away. Remember this is the spot for your rendezvous with Pascal. Have you got your tea-rose? Yes. (*Sees it in her girdle, re-
adjusts it.*)

AN: What's the use? He never got my letter.

MAR: I trust to the wit of the Doctor. I'm sure it's all right. We'll know very soon.
(AN *sits*.) But I must leave you a few moments, dear. My guests demand it.
(*Kisses her.*) Don't be disheartened. I shall send Berta to tell you the instant
the Doctor comes. (*She goes up among the guests, and gradually off through
apartment; some follow.*)

AN: (*sitting*) Yes. This is the spot. How my heart goes. It thumps so hard it actually
shakes me. I fancy everyone can hear it. It's not because I'm afraid! I'm not
afraid. What have I to fear? (*Rises.*) If Sydney should find me here! But I'm
not doing anything wicked. Pascal would not betray me. (*Goes up.*)
(SYDNEY *enters, evening-dress, primrose in his buttonhole. He
takes a bowl and pipes from servant as he enters and later on places
them on divan. Comes down.*)

SYD: I wonder what she'll be like. Hideous, perhaps? All sorts of old stories come
up at such moments. Who's that? (*Sees AN.*) By Jove, what a delicious figure.
(AN *turns.*) My wife! The devil! (*Plucks the flower from his buttonhole and
stuffs it in his tail pocket.*)

AN: (*exclaiming with him*) Sydney! (*Tears the rose from her girdle and casts it
behind her.*)

SYD: (*aside*) What can she be doing here? She can't know of my rendezvous.

AN: (*going toward left*) Good evening!

SYD: Where are you going?

AN: Do you suppose I could remain here – alone – with a strange man?

SYD: A strange man! My love – allow me to introduce myself. I'm your husband.
(*Bows.*)

AN: For only three weeks more!

SYD: But meanwhile –

AN: Meanwhile we ought to observe the proprieties which befit the relations we are
so soon to occupy towards each other.

SYD: If you were not in such an ill-tempered mood, I should like to speak with you.

AN: (*coming forward*) You can't resist the temptation to give me a last scolding!
Why take the trouble?

SYD: I'm not going to find fault. Let us sit down. (*She sits extreme left.*) There is
no need to let the people in the next room hear what we have to say. (*She
comes and sits center; he sits beside her; she moves to the edge of the divan.*)
Annis, tell me the truth, do I inspire you with such repugnance?

AN: I beg you'll come to the point.

SYD: (*Glances at the edge of sofa.*) I believe I am at the point now. (*pause*) Why do
you hate me?

AN: (*Rises.*) Why do I hate you? You ask that! Have you not taken from me everything that gives to life its value and its charm?

SYD: Now, my dear –

AN: I tell you, life was beautiful to me before I saw you. Not a bird in the air was freer – not a bird that sings was happier. I felt that I could love, and I knew I would strive to make one that loved me happy. Then *you* came – you married me. (*Crosses.*)

SYD: And clipped your wings, eh? I married you – was that so dreadful? Come now! You married me under no false pretences. (*Rises.*) Remember that I assumed nothing.

AN: Did you stop to think what I assumed? (*He turns and looks at her.*) Had I no right to expect that a man who asked me to be his wife meant to make me happy if he could?

SYD: It's rather late in the day to discuss that. We didn't speak of it when we married.

AN: Was it necessary to speak of it? Had I not the right to take it for granted? When you men make a contract do you strive to fulfil it?

SYD: We pay if we can.

AN: How do you pay? Do you fling the money in your creditor's face? That is what you have done to me. (*He turns abruptly at her.*) Politeness – good breeding – ordinary attention? Oh, yes – I got them all – and with them the keenest reminder that I must look for nothing more. As for love! – (*Laughs.*) That was out of the question.

SYD: On both sides.

AN: (*Sits suddenly and earnestly.*) I loved you on the day you asked me to be your wife. (SYD *looks at her surprised.*) There is not a girl living who does not feel tenderness towards the man who puts that question, and to whom she answers 'Yes.' But after! – you are right! You clipped my wings and stopped my song. My cage was a prison, and you became my jailor.

SYD: Why, Annis! (*Sits.*) I never saw you so animated – nor so handsome! And you say you loved me at the first! By Jove – (*Suddenly seizes her hand and passes his arm about her waist. She bounds away from him in genuine anger.*) What have I done now? I thought I was making up for lost time.

AN: It was an insult! An insult!

SYD: From your husband?

AN: From the man who has cast me off. Yes.

SYD: Well – we are married yet –

AN: And so I'm still your slave – for three weeks longer.

SYD: Come – come – let us talk this over before we part.

AN: It is too late. I welcome the separation.

SYD: (*bitterly*) You expect to find some one to console you?

AN: (*Turns away sadly.*) No. That dream is over now.

SYD: Then there *is* some one else! Have you no shame?

AN: None! (*instantly and proudly. They face each other.*)

SYD: (*after a pause*) I beg your pardon. But I may give you one word of warning. When we live apart we shall not be more free than we are now. People will judge you the same. And if you meet this some one openly –

AN: (*sadly – sitting on tête-à-tête*) I shall not meet him.

SYD: You will not see him again?

AN: I have never seen him.

SYD: (*Sits by her, after a pause of surprise.*) But he writes to you – and you to him. These matters do not end in that way.

AN: With some, perhaps – not with us. If I can look you in the face and tell you
that all the love stored in my heart was given to this man, because no one else
had asked it; if I can tell *you* this, it is because that man is to me a being of
another world – not to be seen, to be touched, to be spoken with – for a
glance – a word – a touch is guilt.

SYD: I wish I were the man! (*Sighs and takes her hand, smoothing it.*) I never knew
till now what a pretty hand you had. (*Raises her hand. She attempts to withdraw it.*) No – don't take it away – I won't do it again. (*deliberately*) I think,
Annis – I've been an idiot! But I fancied I had something to complain of in
you. (*She is about to speak.*) Don't speak – let me finish. There were
times – several times – when I felt hurt by the way you took my advances.

AN: (*quickly*) That was after –

SYD: Yes, after! – What do you understand was before?

AN: Before? You mean at first –

SYD: Certainly at first. Before the after.

AN: Well, there was your indifference – your coldness, that kept me at a distance.

SYD: I *was* an idiot.

AN: Let *me* finish.

SYD: Certainly, dear! But just let me fix your ear-ring! It's got crooked. (*Toys with
her ear.*) Just bend down a little – curious how these things get twisted. Now
it's all right.

AN: (*wholly unconscious of his growing tenderness, but not vindictive any longer*)
What was I saying?

SYD: That I was an idiot.

AN: No. I didn't call you that. When we part, we part without reproaches.

SYD: I wish we could do that. But we can't. (*She looks at him.*) I reproach myself
for having been so blind. The blame is mine – and I ask you to forgive me all
the unhappiness I have knowingly or unknowingly caused you in the course
of our short married life. (*He has spoken the last part looking down and
away, but without any taint of whine. She looks at him amazed.*)

AN: You ask me to forgive you?

SYD: Things are bad enough now between us – but we can part friends.

AN: I should be sorry to know I had misjudged you – when it was too late.

SYD: Then we are not compelled to part enemies.

AN: No. We are not enemies.

SYD: Then, of course, we are friends – and, if we are friends, we can help each
other to be happy. Of course you have been very much prejudiced against
(*She is about to speak.*), and very justly. I admit that. But if things hadn't
gone so far, I might have been able to prove that – that – I was not utterly –
detestable.

AN: (*aside*) I never saw him like this.

SYD: Will you, Annis – shall we be friends? (*Offers his hand.*)

AN: (*frankly*) Gladly, Sydney! –

SYD: (*Looks at her, then at her hand.*) It weighs on my heart to think – (*Kisses her
hand.*) It's a beautiful hand.

AN: You found that out rather late. (*Crosses.*)

SYD: Yes. I realize my folly. (*taking her hand again*) It never entered my head to
read the lines of this fair hand, and learn my life's fortune from them. I can't

ask the question now – what use would there be? You have found the ideal
of your dreams in some one else! (*dropping hand*)

AN: (*turning away*) Perhaps you will, too.

SYD: Well, I confess – I thought I had found her already.

AN: (*Turns quickly*.) What's that? (*He does not answer.*) Ah, well! (*shyly*) I suppose
I made myself perfectly hateful. (*Sits.*)

SYD: It was simply retaliation for my abominable conduct. (*Sits beside her.*)

AN: (*quickly*) But that was because I drove you to it.

SYD: Yes – only I drove you to driving me to it.

AN: (*warmly*) No, no – you are unjust to yourself.

SYD: (*same*) No – *you* are to yourself.

AN: But I –

SYD: No – no – I know! (*slight laugh*)

AN: Don't let us begin to quarrel again. (*laughing*) Better go halves in the blame –
and exchange forgiveness. (*Offers both hands.*)

SYD: (*Draws her gently to him.*) With all my heart. (*Kisses her brow.*)

AN: Why, what are you doing – (*looking up into his eyes*)

SYD: I – I think I kissed you.

AN: Did you? I never felt anything like it before.

SYD: (*suddenly*) Annis! (*She draws back at arm's length – he still holding her
hands.*)

AN: What will people say?

SYD: What will they say? I'm your husband.

AN: To be sure – but only for the present.

SYD: (*sadly*) For the present only! (*Attempts to draw her to him.*)

AN: What has come over you? Do you want my eyes scratched out by my rival?

SYD: (*look of wonder*) Your rival?

AN: Yes, my rival – your ideal. (*He draws her to him and kisses her warmly.*)
There – there – there is somebody in the next room.

SYD: It seems as if I were kissing you for the first time.

AN: (*softly and gently trying to break away*) Hark! There is some one coming, I
tell you. (*Releases herself and moves away.*)

SYD: Annis! (*Holds his arms open. She stops irresolutely; looks around, then runs
to his arms for an instant – and breaks away and runs out.*) It was like a
dream! And I have lost that woman forever! (*Puts his hand in his pocket to
get handkerchief, pulls out the flower signal; looks at it; then dashes it down;
takes out handkerchief to wipe his brow.*)

> (ROVERLY *enters. They look at each other.* SYD *crosses to exit.*
> ROV *comes down.* SYD *stops, as if changing his mind, and walks up
> to* ROV, *who receives him coldly.*)

SYD: I say, old fellow, instead of cutting each other's throats, at sight – let's ask
and answer one question. What induced you – an old friend – to insult me so
grossly yesterday?

ROV: Have you really the coolness to make that inquiry?

SYD: I know it seems ridiculous – but I can't think I'm dealing with a maniac.

ROV: Sydney Austin – am *I* dealing with a madman or a fool? Did you not assure
me on your word of honor, in that conservatory yonder, that there was
nothing between you and Margery Gwynn?

SYD: Well – what then?

ROV: What then? You are corresponding with her.

SYD: I? With Mrs. Gwynn?

ROV: You confessed to me that you were Pascal. You received a letter addressed
     to Pascal. That letter came from Mrs. Gwynn!

SYD: Ha, ha, ha! From Mrs. Gwynn! Ha, ha, ha! It's a joke!

ROV: It's not a joke – and your hilarity is out of place.

SYD: You assert seriously that Mrs. Gwynn wrote to me – to Pascal – this letter?
     (*Tears it from his pocket. It is folded.*)

ROV: (*Glances at it.*) Yes. That is the letter.

SYD: (*seriously, and becoming agitated*) Impossible. You are mistaken. You must
     be mistaken. (*Crosses.*)

ROV: I saw it in the hands of her maid.

SYD: (*aside*) Margery Gwynn – Diana! It cannot be.

ROV: And the note you got at tea, yesterday afternoon, was also from her.

SYD: (*Catches his arm.*) How do you know?

ROV: I saw her give it to Quattles, who placed it in the music book.

SYD: (*sinking into seat, crushed*) That shallow, fashionable doll my ideal! What a
     fool I have been! She, frivolous – vain –

ROV: Take care!

SYD: I beg your pardon. (*Takes his arm.*) Come, I'll tell you the whole story. (*as
     they go off into conservatory*) It's a regular romance.

ROV: Never mind the romance. Let us have the facts. (*Exits.*)

          (*Bright dance music is heard off left. MARGERY enters, watches the
          two men off, then crosses to right and calls ANNIS, who enters
          timidly.*)

MAR: Come! There goes your husband! (AN *sinks on chair.*) What! Your wings
     drooping so soon, my little butterfly! Are you trembling to meet your Pascal –
     your ideal?

AN: For heaven's sake, spare me your wit. I'm almost beside myself.

MAR: (*Sits.*) Why – what's the matter with you?

AN: I wish I'd never met Pascal! I mean, never knew him – that is, never written to
    him – or that Sydney had! – Oh, dear! (*petulantly*) I don't know what I wish.

MAR: My dear! You are in the position of the donkey between the two bundles of
     hay. You starve to death because you can't make up your mind which to
     choose.

          (QUATTLES *hurries in.*)

QUAT: Ah, ladies! There you are. (AN *gives a shriek.*)

MAR: (*Rises.*) It's only the doctor! (*to* QUAT) You dare to face me again?

QUAT: Why not? What have I done?

MAR: It was your fault my note went astray, and fell into your wife's hands.

QUAT: What of it?

MAR: Of course she read it – didn't she?

QUAT: What of that? She couldn't tell whom it was from, and ha! ha! ha! she
      thought it was intended for me!

MAR: And you *had* to deny it?

QUAT: Of course I had to deny it, or I couldn't have got the letter back and posted
      it to its proper owner.

AN: And she questioned you?

QUAT: Oh, yes, She questioned me. That goes without saying. Questioned me? Oh, yes!

MAR: And what did you tell her?

QUAT: The truth! I always tell my wife the truth.

AN: (*aside*) Good heavens! (MAR *suppresses her.*)

QUAT: I know it's not usual to tell your wife the truth. Well, I told her exactly what the letter told her. That an unknown lady had opened a correspondence with an unknown author. That they had never met – and that they arranged this interview to exchange letters and break off the correspondence.

AN: (*relieved*) There's nothing to be alarmed at in that.

MAR: But what did she say? What did she do? Since she knows of this rendezvous – we are in her power –

QUAT: As to what she *said* – she said nothing, but she kept up a deuce of a thinking! As to what she did – she sat down and wrote an account of the whole matter to that rascal Bitteredge – to give him an item for his paper. He'll be eternally grateful.

MAR: She's a treasure.

QUAT: She is. She has ordered a brand new costume for tonight, and a whole bunch of tea-roses. Something's in the wind, I'm sure. But your letter is in Pascal's hands – and he'll be here to the minute, on the wings of Love! (*Goes up.*)

MAR: (*aside to* AN) You hear! Quick! Get your tea-rose. Hold your head up. Come. (*Drags her left.*) Kindle the brightest fires in your eyes – the reddest roses in your cheeks – for your ideal! (*Exeunt.*)

QUAT: (*who has not seen them go off*) Here's your ideal! Hallo! Flown! And the ideal's got another man with him? What's up! Well, I'll get an ice and prepare for Eudoxia's game, with her bunch of tea-roses.

> (*He is offered a bowl by servant as he goes off. Takes it and exits with servant, left, as* SYDNEY *and* ROVERLY *enter, right.*)

SYD: Now you know everything.

ROV: And nothing remains but to apologize with all my heart for yesterday's insult.

SYD: (*shaking hands*) We were both deceived, and you shall avenge us both (*slapping him on the shoulder*), on your faithless mistress.

ROV: How can I?

SYD: Nothing easier! Take my place! Take her letters. (*Gives him a package of letters.*) And take my primrose. I threw it down somewhere – Oh, here it is. (*Crosses and picks it up.*) It looks a little wilted. Type of a lost passion.

ROV: By Jove – I'll do it.

SYD: Of course you'll do it. You know how the matter stands! This is the place of rendezvous (*Fastens the flower in* ROV*'s coat.*) And you are Pascal – as large as life!

ROV: I shall be anxious to see how she looks when I disclose myself as her ideal.

SYD: So shall I.

ROV: And confront her with her rapturous effusions. (*Looks at packet.*)

SYD: I say – may I listen?

ROV: With all my heart! Get behind the shrubs. (SYD *conceals himself behind the shrubs.*) I'll first study my part a little. (*Opens one of the letters and sits.*)
          (ANNIS *enters,* MARGERY *gently pushing her on.*)

MAR: (*aside to* AN) Be bold!

AN: Stay near us! (*Sees* ROV, *and in alarm.*) Good heavens!

MAR: What's the matter?

AN: The primrose.

MAR: Why that's only Roverly!

AN: Look at his buttonhole.

MAR: The primrose! So it is!

AN: That lump of ice – my ideal!

MAR: It's an outrage! The traitor! The hypocrite!

AN: I don't want to meet that creature. (*going*)

MAR: (*suddenly*) Give me the flower! Give me the letters!

AN: What are you going to do? (*Takes flower from belt and gives it, and gives letters.*)

MAR: (*fastening flower in her belt*) He has deceived us both! We'll be revenged, and you shall see how well I'll do it. Get behind there! (*Pushes her behind screen, then advances and attracts* ROV's *attention, by opening and shutting her fan. He turns.*)

ROV: Madge! (*His apparent surprise gives place to a sarcastic smile.*) Have I the pleasure of addressing the fair Diana? (*Bows.*)

AN: (*aside*) It is he, the wretch!

SYD: (*aside*) It was she – after all!

MAR: (*to* ROV) The fair Diana is anxious to hear what the noble Pascal has to say.

ROV: (*sarcastic*) Permit me to lay my homage at your feet.

MAR: (*indignantly*) I never knew you were such a hypocrite. Protesting love for me and at the very same time –

ROV: (*laughing*) Corresponding in secret with – yourself! Where's the treachery?

MAR: (*Laughs bitterly.*) Ha! ha! ha! and your imprudence. (*showing her bundle of letters*) Describing yourself as an unfortunate married poet, with an unsympathetic wife!

AN: (*aside*) So he did! Why did he do that?

ROV: (*showing his bundle of letters*) And you pretending to be a crushed wife, with a brute of a husband!

SYD: (*aside*) So she did. There's something wrong there.

MAR: Exciting my sympathy on false pretences! And I dreaming how I could make you happy.

ROV: I'm inconsolable at having frustrated your kind intentions.

MAR: Spare your sympathy. I shall never marry such a goose as wrote those letters.

ROV: (*tapping pocket*) Oh, come! You never thought you were writing these to a fool!

MAR: No? Suppose I only amused myself by leading the creature by the nose a bit!

SYD: (*aside*) Led by the nose! And by her!

ROV: (*joyfully*) What! You were only playing with Pascal?

MAR: Yes – and *you* were the stake I played for.

ROV: (*ecstasy*) Is it possible!

MAR: And having won the game –

ROV: Yes –

MAR: (*Curtseys.*) I now decline the prize. (*Exits excitedly, followed by* AN. ROV *pulls the flower from his coat, flings it down and stamps on it.*)

>(QUATTLES *runs on, excitedly, bringing his bowl and pipe and puts them down.*)

QUAT: Here! Sydney! Where – (*Stops on seeing* ROV.) I beg your pardon – I was looking for – some one else.

SYD: (*coming forward*) I thought I heard my name called. What's the matter?

QUAT: Oh, nothing. (*Glances at* ROV, *and then aside to* SYD.) Something's up!

SYD: Well, be open, old man! Roverly's in our secret.

QUAT: Well! (*Laughs.*) My wife! (*Laughs.*) My wife is coming here with a tea-rose in her waist. I had my misgivings all along. She's coming to trap Pascal. (*Laughs.*)

ROV: Then I'm off. (SYD *holds him.*)

QUAT: We had all better be off – but not far off. (*Laughs.*) We'll catch her. Oh! Eudoxia! Eudoxia! – if I can only catch you this once! Here she is! (*All separate and conceal themselves:* SYD *and* ROV *in conservatory;* QUAT *behind center shrubs.*)

>(*Several guests stroll on, among them* MRS. QUATTLES – *she wears a veil over her head, partly to conceal her face when necessary, and a tea-rose (very large) in her girdle.*)

MRS. Q: This is the place of rendezvous. No one about wearing a primrose in his coat. I'm determined to see who Pascal is – and whom he is after! I feel in my bones that it is Epenetus. The traitor! Guilty after all! Ah! There's a man with a flower! (*Some other guests have strolled in with whom she converses, as they cross the scene.*)

>(*Later,* BITTEREDGE *enters, with a large primrose in his button-hole, evening dress, two fob-chains, crush hat, etc.*)

BIT: (*Consults a note which he pulls from his coat pocket.*) Here's that letter from Mrs. Quattles. (*Puts on glasses – reads:*) 'Pascal is to wear a primrose. Diana is to wear a tea-rose.' I've got the biggest primrose I could find – and if the lady comes! (*Slaps his breast.*) Brace up Bitteredge – this is your opportunity! Either for a sensation – or for life! An unknown creature in love with the author of 'Tinsel'! If she's romantic – susceptible – and rich! my fortune's made! (*Looks round slyly.*) The tea-rose! It's she!

>(*The stage is now empty of guests, as* MRS. Q *comes forward. The guests fill the other apartments presently.*)

MRS. Q: (*peeping around*) The primrose! (*with a start*) My goodness! (QUAT *and* SYD *meet at back.*) It's Bitteredge after all! How could that donkey have written such a book? (*She comes forward.*)

SYD: (*aside, to* QUAT) What's this?

QUAT: (*same*) Don't say a word.

BIT: Hem! Di–Di–ana!

MRS. Q: (*affected voice*) Pascal!

BIT: Your – Pascal!

MRS. Q: And you – you are really he!

BIT: (*Takes her hand. She half turns her head away.*) I am your prim-rose, and you are my tea-rose.

SYD: (*to* QUAT) I say – can you stand that?

QUAT: I wouldn't miss it for the world. (*Puts up a large opera-glass to look at them.*)

BIT: I wish she'd lift that veil. I can't tell whether she's fifteen or fifty! (*Rapturously, tries to put his arm around her.*) Oh, how I have waited for this minute!

SYD: Come away, Quattles.

QUAT: Oh, I can stand it if she can!

MRS. Q: You must keep your distance. It's not right. (*Sits.*)

BIT: (*Sits by her – aside.*) That sounds like fifteen. If I could only see her face! (*aloud*) Let me swear to you that my love –

MRS. Q: Oh, if you talk of love – I fly.

BIT: But it's Platonic – purely Platonic – you know what Platonic affection is?

MRS. Q: Is – is Platonic affection *quite* proper?

BIT: Quite proper! (*aside*) That sounds like fifty at least. (*aloud*) I will explain. Let us suppose two beings – two abstractions – they love each other – (*She starts.*) – psychologically – they are drawn together! (*He draws her nearer.*)

MRS. Q: No – no!

BIT: I can't explain if you fidget. Now, then – one draws the other. The masculine abstraction draws the feminine – or the feminine draws the masculine, so that the two entities – you comprehend?

MRS. Q: No.

BIT: I'll be explicit. The two entities or abstractions, by a series of unconscious, uninterrupted progressions – pass into one concrete self! You follow me?

MRS. Q: Yes, I follow you, but I can't keep up with you! (*aside*) This man's an impostor.

BIT: There's a shade of difference, in the psychological – the heart –

MRS. Q: Let us leave out the heart.

BIT: I was going to. The heart is eliminated. The sensation experienced is not the throbbing of the bosom – it is the palpitation of the thoughts.

SYD: (*aside*) That's good.

ROV: (*aside*) Very good! Original, too.

QUAT: Sh! Sh!

BIT: By a process congeneric to the attractions of passion, the abstract entities proceed to the terminus and *summum.*

MRS. Q: That'll do. I think I'd better go. (*Rises and starts to leave.*)

BIT: (*detaining her*) Impossible! We have arrived at the summum! When we get to the summum – all is subjective.

SYD: (*aside*) He's going to kiss your wife, Quattles.

QUAT: Then I guess we'd better all arrive at the terminus. (QUAT, SYD *and* ROV *advance.*)

BIT: Angel of my dreams! One glance – only one! (*about to kneel*)

QUAT: (*advancing*) With pleasure. (MRS. Q *gives a shriek and tries to fly.*) Sydney, give the lady your arm! (SYD *takes her arm and holds her tightly.*) Don't run, my dear. (*Unveils her.*)

MRS. Q: (*to* SYD) Please don't keep me!

BIT: The deuce! (*about to retreat when* ROV *locks arms with him*)

ROV: Don't give it up so.

QUAT: I think we have arrived at the summum, my love, just in time. (BIT *laughs.*)

ROV: By a process congeneric –

SYD: To the psychological. (*All laugh.*)

QUAT: (*to* BIT) Can you tell me who Marius is?

(MARGERY and ANNIS enter.)

BIT: He! he! He! he! Very good joke! I saw through it all along. Was only hunting up a sensation for tomorrow's issue. If they don't turn up, we must make 'em ourselves! See! I'm not Marius, of course – but who is?

MAR: (*with gesture of contempt towards* ROV) Allow me to present him! (*All stare.*)

MRS: Q: Is it possible?

BIT: No, it's not possible! How could he write a novel while he was in Africa?

AN: (*to* MAR) That's true!

MAR: (*to* ROV, *with joy*) To be sure! You were not here!

ROV: (*firmly, at a nudge from* SYD) Nevertheless – I persist –

AN: No – no – you never wrote those letters from Africa! But you know who Pascal is?

MRS. Q: And I insist upon his telling. I think I'm entitled to know, after all I've gone through.

BIT: Gone through –

MRS. Q: And escaped from!

SYD: (*advancing*) My friends – further mystery seems useless. I am Marius!

BIT: Another fraud!

SYD: (*looking at him*) Perhaps more of a fool than a fraud. I accept the ridicule of my disclosure as a punishment for my blindness. I had the best wife ever bestowed on man, and I neglected her to chase a shadowy ideal (*Crosses to* MAR.), who now exults in leading her captive by the nose. (*Holds out his hand to* ROV, *who places the packet of letters in it.*) Madam – here are your letters! (*About to cross,* AN *seizes the letters from his hand.*)

AN: They are my letters.

SYD: (*Advances to her.*) Yours! Then you are Di–Diana! (*Looks at* QUAT.) I say, Quattles –

QUAT: We are floored, my boy!

AN: Are you angry with me? Do my letters prove that I love Pascal too much?

SYD: (*Clasps her in his arms.*) We'll read them together. (*They go up a step.*)

QUAT: Well, those two lovers had to swim through a sea of ink to get to each other.

MRS. Q: Epenetus! You are responsible for everything!

QUAT: Not for your psychological congenerics.

MRS. Q: (*Flings the tea-rose down.*) The next time – you'll lose me.

QUAT: I'm afraid not. We'll never find such another ass as Bitteredge. (*She pursues him to corner, as* SYD *and* AN *come down.*)

EPILOGUE

SYD: (*Takes pipe and bowl.*) But come! We forget our bubble party.
QUAT: (*Takes pipe and bowl.*) Come, shepherds! take your pipes and play.
Like bubbles blow your cares away.
MAR: (*to* ROV, *as she blows a bubble:*) Now watch, my dear, and you will see –
The figure of your jealousy;
First like a drop suspicion glows,
Then swells by fancy till it grows!
MRS. Q: I wish to goodness all my troubles
Could end in nothing – like these bubbles.
QUAT: Oh! all you women blow your bubbles,
Until your trouble swells and doubles.
AN: (*advancing*) In every marble block, 'tis said,
A perfect statue there is hid –
And need but Art to chip away
The crust that hides it from the day.
Are you in love? And is the one
Your fate is linked to – seeming stone?
Have you in vain essayed to find
A heart within – a soul or mind?
Then try with patience, art and skill,
With steadfast love and earnest will,
To pierce the husk of human clay,
And bring the soul to light of day.
But go not roughly. Cut too deep
And all is marr'd. The art's to keep
The middle course of gentleness –
Know when to yield, and when to press.
SYD: Yes – don't go at him with an axe!
BIT: No – scrape him gently – men are wax!
MRS. Q: Bah! men are flint, as you are, Quattles!
QUAT: Yes – *you* strike fire in all *our* battles.
AN: In this – each woman, if she loves,
Is master of the needed art
To find within the coldest block
A gentle, loving, manly heart –
That heart to ease of ev'ry trouble,
And make its care an airy bubble.

CURTAIN

A LIST OF THE FIRST PUBLICATIONS OF AUGUSTIN DALY'S PLAYS AND SELECTED MODERN EDITIONS

Augustin Daly produced a vast number of plays during his long career. Of the many that he wrote or adapted, over fifty have been printed. Daly himself privately printed a considerable number of his plays; the more popular were reprinted by commercial publishers, such as Samuel French or Dick and Fitzgerald.

After Business Hours. A comedy in four acts (from the German of Dr. Oscar Blumenthal) by Augustin Daly. (As produced at Daly's Theatre for the first time Tuesday, October 5, 1886) New York: Privately printed for the author – as manuscript only, 1886.

An Arabian Night in the Nineteenth Century. A comedy in four acts, from the German of von Moser. By Augustin Daly. As acted at Daly's theatre for the first time, November 29th, 1879. New York: Printed as manuscript only, for the author, 1884.

As You Like It. A comedy in five acts. From the play by William Shakespeare. Arranged by Augustin Daly; with an introduction by William Winter. New York: Privately printed, 1890.

The Belle's Stratagem. Condensed from Mrs. Cowley's comedy and arranged in three acts by Augustin Daly. As first produced at Daly's Theatre New York, April, 1892. [New York]: Printed from the prompt book of Daly's Theatre, 1892.

The Big Bonanza. A comedy of our time in five acts. (From the German of Von Moser.) By Augustin Daly. As acted at Daly's New Fifth Avenue Theatre for the first time, February 17th, 1875. New York: Printed as manuscript only, for the author, 1884.

'The Countess Gucki'. A comedy in three acts by Franz von Schoenthan written expressly for Miss Ada Rehan. Adapted by Augustin Daly. [New York]: Privately printed for Augustin Daly, c. 1894.

The Country Girl. A comedy in three acts. Altered and adapted by David Garrick, from 'The Country Wife' by William Wycherley, and arranged for representation to-day by Augustin Daly. [New York]: Printed as played at Daly's Theatre, New York, February 16, 1884, 1884.

The Critic. A conceit in one act. A condensed version of Sheridan's play. Privately printed, 1889.

Divorce. A play of the period, in five acts. By Augustin Daly. As acted at the Fifth Avenue Theatre for the first time, September 5th, 1871. New York: Printed as manuscript only, for the author, 1884.

Dollars and Sense; or, the Heedless Ones. A comedy of to-day in three acts. By Augustin Daly. As produced at Daly's theatre, New York, for the first time

October 2d, 1883. New York: Printed, as manuscript only, for the author,
1885. (Adaptation of A. L'Arronge's *Die Sorglosen.*)

A Flash of Lightning. A drama of life in our day, in five acts. By Augustin Daly.
First produced at the Broadway Theatre (late Wallack's), under the management of Mr. Barney Williams, June, 1868. New York: Printed, as manuscript
only, for the author, 1885.

Foresters, a pastoral comedy in four acts. New York: 1892. Prompt book no. 12,
printed for rehearsal purposes.

'Frou-Frou'; A comedy of powerful human interest, in five acts, by Augustin Daly,
esq . . . New York: Samuel French & Son; London: Samuel French, [*c.*
1870]. (French's standard drama. No. CCCLIX.)

The Great Unknown. A comedy in three acts (From the German of Schoenthan and
Kadelburg) by Augustin Daly. As acted at Daly's Theatre for the first time,
October 22, 1889. New York: Privately printed for the author as manuscript
only, 1890.

Griffith Gaunt; or, Jealousy. A drama, in five acts. By Augustin Daly. Author's ed.
New York: S. French & Son; London: S. French, *c.* 1867. (Wemyss' acting
drama, no. III.)

Hazardous Ground. An original adaptation in four acts, from Victoria Sardou's
'Nos Bono Villegeios', by Augustin Daly . . . Author's edition. New York:
W. C. Wemyss, Publisher, 1868. (Wemyss' acting drama. No. IV.)

Horizon. An original drama of contemporaneous society and of American frontier
perils. In five acts and seven tableaux. By Augustin Daly. As acted at the
Olympic Theatre, New York City, for the first time, March 21st, 1871. New
York: Printed, as manuscript only, for the author, 1885.

'Horizon'. In: *American Plays*, ed. by Allan Gates Halline. New York: American
Book Co., 1935.

The Hunchback. A comedy in five acts by Sheridan Knowles, as first produced at
Daly's Theatre, New York, 29 November 1892, and here printed from the
prompt-book as then used. [New York]: Privately printed for Augustin Daly,
1893.

The Inconstant or the Way to Win Him. A comedy by George Farquhar arranged in
4 acts by Augustin Daly with a few prefatory comments and an original
epilogue by William Winter, Esq. Acted for the first time at Daly's Theatre,
January 8, 1889. [New York]: Privately printed for Mr. Daly, 1889.

An International Match. A comedy in four acts (From the German of Franz
Schoenthan) By Augustin Daly. As produced at Daly's Theatre for the first
time, February 5, 1889. New York: Privately printed for the author, 1890.

The Last Word. A comedy in four acts (From the German of Franz von Schoenthan) By Augustin Daly. As originally produced at Daly's Theatre, New York
October 28, 1890. [New York]: Privately printed for Augustin Daly, 1891.

Leah, the Forsaken. Arranged from the 'Deborah' of Mosenthal. Expressly for Miss
Bateman, and originally produced at the Howard Atheneum, Boston, December 8th, 1862 [New York]: Printed for the author, 1863.

A Legend of 'Norwood'; or Village Life in New England. An original dramatic
comedy of American life, in four acts. Founded on a novel by Rev. Henry
Ward Beecher. By Augustin Daly . . . New York: The author, 1867.

Lemons. A comedy in three acts. (From the German of Julius Rosen) By Augustin Daly. As acted at the Fifth Avenue Theatre January, 1877. [New York]: Privately printed for Augustin Daly, [c. 1877].

Little Miss Million. A comedy in four acts. (From the German of Blumenthal) By Augustin Daly. Here printed from the prompt book as produced at Daly's Theatre, October 3, 1892. [New York]: Printed as manuscript for the author only, 1893.

The Lottery of Love. An eccentric comedy in three acts. (From the French of Bisson and Mars) By Augustin Daly. As acted at Daly's Theatre for the first time, October 9, 1888. [New York]: Privately printed for the author, 1889.

Love in Harness. A comedy in three acts. (From the French of Albin Valabregue) By Augustin Daly. Originally produced at Daly's Theatre, November 16, 1886. [New York]: Privately printed (as manuscript only) for the author, 1887.

Love in Tandem. A comedy in three acts from the French of Bocage and De Courcy. By Augustin Daly. As produced at Daly's Theatre, New York, for the first time, Tuesday, February 9, 1892. New York: Printed as manuscript only, for the author, 1892.

Love on Crutches. A comedy in three acts. (From the German of Stobitzer) By Augustin Daly. As acted for the first time, at Daly's Theatre, New York, Tuesday, Nov. 25th, 1884. New York: Printed, as manuscript only, for the author, [1885].

Love's Labour's Lost. A comedy written by William Shakspere. Arranged in 4 acts for the present stage by Augustin Daly. Produced at Daly's Theatre, March 28, 1891, and here printed from the prompter's copy with a few prefatory thoughts upon the comedy by William Winter, esq. [New York]: Privately printed for Mr. Daly, 1891.

Madelaine Morel. A play in four acts. (From the German on Mosenthal.) By Augustin Daly. As acted by Daly's Fifth Avenue company at their temporary theatre (Late the 'Globe'), for the first time May 20th, 1873. New York: Printed as manuscript only, for the author, 1884.

Man and Wife. A play in five acts (based on a novel by Wilkie Collins) by Augustin Daly. As acted at the Fifth Avenue Theatre, for the first time, September 13th, 1870. New York: Printed, as manuscript only, for the author, 1885.

Man and Wife & Other Plays by Augustin Daly. Edited with introductory note and play list by Catherine Sturtevant. Princeton, New Jersey: Princeton University Press 1942. (America's lost plays, vol. XX)
Contents: *Man and Wife; Divorce; The Big Bonanza; Pique; Needles and Pins.*

The Merchant of Venice by William Shakespeare. A comedy in five acts as arranged for representation at Daly's Theatre, by Augustin Daly, and there produced for the first time on Saturday, November 19th, 1898. With a few prefatory words by William Winter. Souvenir edition. [New York]: Privately printed, 1898.

The Merry Wives of Windsor. A comedy by William Shakespeare. As arranged in four acts, by Mr. Augustin Daly, for production at Daly's Theatre, January, 1886. [New York]: 1886.

The Comedy of a Midsummer Night's Dream. Written by William Shakespeare and

arranged for representation at Daly's Theatre, by Augustin Daly. Produced
there for the first time, January 31, 1888. [New York]: Privately printed for
Mr. Daly, 1888.

Monsieur Alphonse. A play in three acts. By Alexandre Dumas, Fils. Adapted and
augmented by Augustin Daly. As acted at the Fifth Avenue Theatre, for the
first time, April 25th, 1874. New York: Printed as manuscript only, for the
author, 1886.

Much Ado About Nothing; a comedy in five acts, by William Shakespeare, as
arranged for production at Daly's Theatre by Augustin Daly. With an introductory chapter by William Winter. [New York]: Privately printed for Mr.
Daly, 1897.

Nancy and Company. An eccentric piece in four acts. (From the German of Rosen)
By Augustin Daly. As first acted at Daly's Theatre, Wednesday, February 24,
1886. New York: Printed as manuscript for the author, 1884.

Needles and Pins. A comedy of the present, in four acts. (From the German of
Rosen.) By Augustin Daly. As acted at Daly's Theatre for the first time,
November 9th, 1880. New York: Printed as manuscript only, for the author,
1884.

A Night Off; or, A page from Balzac. A comedy in four acts. (From the German of
Schönthan brothers.) By Augustin Daly. As produced at Daly's Theatre for
the first time, Wednesday, March 4th, 1885. New York: Printed, as manuscript only, for the author, 1885.

Our English Friend. A comedy in 4 acts. By Augustin Daly. As acted at Daly's
Theatre, for the first time, November 25th, 1882. New York: Printed, as
manuscript only, for the author, 1884.

The Passing Regiment, a comedy of the day, in five acts. (From the German of G.
von Moser and Franze von Schonthan). By Augustin Daly. As acted at Daly's
Theatre for the first time, November 10, 1880. New York: Printed for the
author, 1884.

Pique. A play of to-day, in five acts. By Augustin Daly. As acted at Daly's New
Fifth Avenue Theatre for the first time, December 14th, 1875. New York:
Printed as manuscript only, for the author, 1884.

The Railroad of Love. A comedy in four acts (From the German of Schoenthan and
Kadelburg) By Augustin Daly. Acted for the first time at Daly's Theatre, New
York, Tuesday, November 1, 1887. [New York]: Privately printed for the
author as manuscript only, [c. 1887].

The Recruiting Officer. A comedy by George Farquhar, esq. Re-arranged and adapted for modern purposes, by Mr. Augustin Daly. As produced at Daly's
Theatre, N.Y. [New York]: 1885.

The School for Scandal. A comedy in five acts. By Richard Brinsley Sheridan. As
re-modeled and arranged for the Fifth Avenue Theatre, by Augustin Daly.
Souvenir edition. [New York]: Printed for Mr. Daly, 1891.

7-20-8: or, Casting the Boomerang. A comedy of to-day, in 4 acts. (From the German of Von Schoenthan.) By Augustin Daly. As acted at Daly's Theatre for
the first time, February 24th, 1883 . . . New York: Printed as manuscript
only, for the author, 1884.

She Wou'd and She Wou'd Not. A comedy by Colley Cibber. Re-arranged and adapted into four acts by Augustin Daly. As produced at Daly's Theatre, January 13, 1883. [New York]: (Printed for Daly's Theatre), 1886.

'A Sister's Sacrifice'. In: *Werner's Readings and Recitations No. 4.* Compiled and arranged by Elsie M. Wilbor. New York: Edgar S. Werner & Company, [c. 1891].

Taming a Butterfly. An original adaptation, in three acts. By Augustin Daly and Frank Wood. First produced at the Olympia Theatre, in New York, Thursday evening, February 25th, 1864. [New York?]: Printed for the authors, 1864.

The Tempest; arranged for four acts by Augustin Daly. Here printed from the prompt book, as acted at Daly's Theatre, New York, April 6th, 1897. With a preface by William Winter. [New York]: Privately printed for Mr. Daly, 1897.

A Test Case; or, Grass Versus Granite. A comedy in four acts. (From the German of Blumenthal and Kadelburg) By Augustin Daly. As produced at Daly's Theatre, New York, for the first time November 10, 1892. New York: Printed as manuscript only for the author, 1893.

Three Preludes to the Play, by Augustin Daly: 1. 'Love's young dream' (from the French); 2. 'A wet blanket' (adapted from the French); 3. 'A sudden shower' (adapted from the French). As acted at Daly's theatre. [New York: Douglas Taylor & co., 187-?]

Twelfth Night, or What You Will. By William Shakspere. Arranged to be played in four acts, by Augustin Daly. Printed from the prompt book, and as produced at Daly's Theatre, February 21st, 1893. With an introductory word by William Winter, esq. [New York]: Privately printed for Augustin Daly, 1893.

Two Gentlemen of Verona; a comedy in four acts, by W. Shakspere. Re-arranged by Augustin Daly and here printed from the prompt book of Daly's Theatre; as represented there for the first time on February 25th, 1895. With a few prefatory words by William Winter. New York: Privately printed for Augustin Daly, 1895.

Two Old Comedies. The Belle's Stratagem and *The Wonder.* Reduced and re-arranged by Augustin Daly for production at Daly's Theatre during the season 1893–94. [New York]: Privately printed from the prompt books of Daly's Theatre, 1893.

Under the Gaslight: A totally original and picturesque drama of life and love in these times, in five acts. By Augustin Daly . . . As originally played at the New York Theater in the months of August, Sept. and Oct., 1867. New York: Printed for the author, 1867.

Under the Gaslight; or, Life and love in these times, an original drama, of American life. In four acts. By Augustin Daly . . . London: T. H. Lacy, [1868]. (Lacy's acting edition, no. 1201).

'Under the Gaslight'. In: *Hiss the Villain: Six English and American Melodramas,* ed. by Michael Booth. New York: Benjamin Blom, Inc., 1964; London: Eyre & Spottiswoode, 1964.

BIBLIOGRAPHY

Major sources on Daly and his work include materials in several collections. The Folger Shakespeare Library in Washington, D.C., has by far the largest collection, with 12,000 items, of which 9,000 are correspondence. A second major collection is in the Billy Rose Theatre Collection, Lincoln Center for the Performing Arts, New York, which includes the Augustin and Joseph F. Daly correspondence, plays in typescript, and 43 volumes of scrapbooks. Columbia University Library, New York, holds the records of Daly's Theatre, including production floorplans, property plots, accounts and business records, and correspondence. Harvard University Library has a sizeable collection of clippings of reviews of Daly's plays, and the University of Pennsylvania Library, in its Ada Rehan Collection, owns typescripts of plays and correspondence. Additional papers and correspondence are to be found in the Robert Frost Library of Amherst College, Amherst, Massachusetts, The University of Rochester, the University of Virginia, and the Library of Congress.

DALY ON DRAMA:

'American Playwrights on the American Drama'. *Harper's Weekly*, 2 February 1889, pp. 97–99.

Daly, Augustin. 'The American Dramatist'. *The North American Review*, 142 (May 1886), 485–92.

'The American Drama'. *New York Herald*, 24 October 1874.

DALY'S CAREER:

Asermely, Albert A. 'Daly's Initial Decade in the American Theatre, 1860–1869'. Unpublished Ph.D. dissertation, The City University of New York, 1973.

Daly, Joseph Francis. *The Life of Augustin Daly*. New York: Macmillan, 1917.

Dithmar, Edward A. *Memories of Daly's Theatres*. New York: Privately printed, 1896.

Felheim, Marvin. *The Theater of Augustin Daly*. Cambridge, Mass.: Harvard University Press, 1956.

Hall, Margaret. 'Personal Recollections of Augustin Daly'. *The Theatre* (New York), 5 (June to September 1905), 150–53, 174–78, 188–91, 213–15.

Kobbe, Gustav. 'Augustin Daly and His Life-Work'. *Cosmopolitan*, 27 August 1899), 405–18.

Wayne, Palma. 'Mr Daly'. *Theatre Arts*, 38 (1954), 67–69, 93–96.

Welch, Deshler. 'Augustin Daly, Dramatic Dictator'. *The Booklover's Magazine*, 3 (April 1904), 491–504.

White, Matthew. 'Landmarks of Mr. Daly's Career, and His Work for the American Stage'. *Munsey's Magazine*, 21 (August 1899), 740–44.

Winter, William. 'Augustin Daly'. *The Theatre* (New York), 3 (Christmas 1888), 436–37.
'Memories of the Players – Augustin Daly'. *Colliers*, 26 April 1913, pp. 19–20, 26.

DALY ACTORS AND MANAGEMENT:

Andrew, Richard Harlan. 'Augustin Daly's Big Four'. Unpublished Ph.D. dissertation, University of Illinois, 1971.
Ayres, Alfred. 'The Stagecraft of Augustin Daly'. *The Theatre* (New York), 2 (December 1902), 26–27.
Cutler, Jean Valjean. 'Realism in Augustin Daly's Productions of Contemporary Plays'. Unpublished Ph.D dissertation, University of Illinois, 1962.
Dexter, A. 'Plays and Play-Acting'. *Atlantic Monthly*, 10 (September 1862), 288–91.
Dithmar, Edward A. *John Drew*. New York: Frederick A. Stokes, 1910.
Drew, John. *My Years on the Stage*. New York: E. P. Dutton, 1922.
Eytinge, Rose. *The Memories of Rose Eytinge*. New York: Frederick A. Stokes, 1905.
Forbes-Winslow, C. *Daly's, The Biography of a Theatre*. London: W. H. Allen, 1944.
Henderson, Mary C. *The City & The Theatre*. Clifton, New Jersey: James T. White, 1973.
Hutton, Laurence. *Plays and Players*. New York: Hurd and Houghton, 1875.
Izard, Forrest. *Heroines of the Modern Stage*. New York: Sturgis and Walton, 1915.
Lathrop, George Parsons. 'An American School of Dramatic Art: II. The Inside Working of the Theatre'. *Century*, 56 (June 1898), 265–75.
McKay, Frederick E. and Charles E. L. Wingate, eds. *Famous American Actors of Today*. New York: Crowell, 1896.
Mander, Raymond and Joe Mitchenson. *The Lost Theatres of London*. New York: Taplinger, 1968.
Martin, Charlotte M., ed. *The Stage Reminiscences of Mrs. Gilbert*. New York: Charles Scribner's Sons, 1901.
Michalak, Marion Victor. 'The Management of Augustin Daly's Stock Company, 1869–1899'. Unpublished Ph.D. dissertation, Indiana University, 1961.
Morris, Clara. *Life on the Stage*. New York: McClure, Phillips, 1901.
Stage Confidences. Boston: Lathrop, 1902.
Ranous, Dora Knowlton. *Diary of a Daly Debutante*. New York: Duffield, 1910.
Reed, Ronald Michael. 'The Nature of the Scenic Practices in Augustin Daly's New York Productions: 1869–1899'. Unpublished Ph.D. dissertation, University of Oregon, 1968.
Schaal, David. 'The Rehearsal Situation at Daly's Theatre'. *Educational Theatre Journal*, 14 (March 1962), 1–14.
Skinner, Otis. *Footlights and Spotlights*. Indianapolis: Bobbs-Merrill, 1924.
Strang, Lewis C. *Players and Plays of the Last Quarter Century*. 2 vols. Boston: L. C. Page, 1902–3 (II, 124–28, 204–7).
Towse, J. Ranken. 'An American School of Dramatic Art: I. A Critical Review of Daly's Theatre'. *Century*, 56 (1898), 261–64.

Ventimiglia, Peter James. 'The William Winter correspondence and the Augustin Daly Shakespearean Productions of 1885–1898'. *Theatre Journal*, 30 (May 1978), 220–28.
Winter, William. *Ada Rehan; A Study*. New York: Privately printed, 1898.
   The Wallet of Time. 2 vols. New York: Moffat, Yard, 1913.
   Vagrant Memories. New York: George H. Doran, 1915.

BACKGROUND AND CRITICISM:

Bogard, Travis, Richard Moody, and Walter J. Meserve. *The Revels History of Drama in English. Vol. VIII: American Drama.* London: Methuen, 1977.
Booth, Michael. *Hiss the Villain: Six English and American Melodramas.* London: Eyre & Spottiswoode, 1964.
Brown, T. Allston. *A History of the New York Stage . . . To 1901.* 3 vols. New York: Dodd, Mead, 1903.
Crawford, Mary Caroline. *The Romance of the American Theatre.* Rev. ed. Boston: Little, Brown, 1927.
Dimmick, Ruth Crosby. *Our Theatres Today and Yesterday.* New York: H. K. Fly, 1913.
Eaton, Walter Prichard. *American Stage of Today.* New York: Small, Maynard, 1908.
Hapgood, Norman. *The Stage in America, 1897–1900.* New York: Macmillan, 1901.
Hartman, John Geoffrey. *The Development of American Society Comedy from 1787 to 1936.* Philadelphia: University of Pennsylvania, 1939.
Herron, Ima Honaker. *The Small Town in American Drama.* Dallas: Southern Methodist University Press, 1969.
Hewitt, Barnard. *Theatre U.S.A. 1668–1957.* New York: McGraw-Hill, 1959.
Hornblow, Arthur. *A History of the Theatre in America.* 2 vols. Philadelphia: J. B. Lippincott, 1919.
Hutton, Laurence. *Curiosities of the American Stage.* New York: Harper & Bros., 1891.
Leverton, Garrett H. *The Production of Later Nineteenth Century American Drama.* New York: Columbia University Teacher's College, 1936.
Meserve, Walter J. *An Outline History of American Drama.* Totowa, New Jersey: Littlefield, Adams, 1965.
Moody, Richard. *America Takes the Stage: Romanticism in American Drama and Theatre, 1750–1900.* Bloomington. Indiana University Press, 1955.
Moses, Montrose J. *The American Dramatist.* 2d ed. Boston; Little, Brown, 1917.
Odell, George C. D. *Annals of the New York Stage.* 15 vols. New York: Columbia University Press, 1927–49.
Quinn, Arthur Hobson. *A History of the American Drama, from the Civil War to the Present Day.* New York: Appleton-Century-Crofts, 1936.
Rahill, Frank. *The World of Melodrama.* University Park: Pennsylvania State University Press, 1967.
Scott, Clement. *The Drama of Yesterday & To-Day.* 2 vols. London: Macmillan, 1899.

Shaw, George Bernard. *Our Theatres in the Nineties.* 3 vols. London: Constable, 1932.

Towse, John Rankin. *Sixty Years of the Theatre.* New York: Funk & Wagnalls, 1916.

Wilson, Garff B. *Three Hundred Years of American Drama and Theatre.* 1st ed. Englewood Cliffs, New Jersey: Prentice-Hall, 1973.